ROMULUS

SEVENTEEN S

BIOGRAPHY

Romulus Linney

Romulus Linney is the author of three novels, thirteen long and twenty-two short plays, which have been seen, over the past twenty-five years, in resident theatres across the United States, as well as in New York, Los Angeles, London and Vienna. They include *THE SORROWS OF FREDERICK, HOLY GHOSTS, CHILDE BYRON, APRIL SNOW* and *THREE POETS*. Six of his one act plays have appeared in *Best Short Plays*. *Time Magazine* picked *LAUGHING STOCK* as one of the ten best plays of 1984, his adaptation and direction of his 1962 novel *HEATHEN VALLEY* won the National Critics Award and appears in *Best Plays of the Year 1987-88*, and his play "2" won the same award for the season of 1989-90 in its Humana Festival production at the Actors Theatre of Louisville, and appears in *Best Plays of the Year, 1989-90*. He has received two Fellowships from NEA, as well as Guggenheim, Rockefeller, and National Foundation for the Arts grants, a 1980 Obie Award, three Hollywood Drama-Logue Awards, the Mishima Prize for Fiction, the 1984 Award in Literature from the American Academy and Institute of Arts and Letters, and a 1992 Obie Award for Sustained Excellence in Playwriting. He has directed his plays for the Milwaukee Repertory, the Alley Theatre, the Philadelphia Festival for New Plays, the Whole Theatre Company, the San Francisco Bay Area Festival, the Actors Studio, the Theater for the New City, and the Signature Theatre Company. Work for film and television includes CBS: *THE THIRTY-FOURTH STAR*, PBS: *FEELING GOOD*, and a film version of his play *HOLY GHOSTS*. He is a member of the Ensemble Studio Theatre, the Fellowship of Southern Writers, and a Director of the Corporation of Yaddo. A graduate of Oberlin College and the Yale School of Drama, he is Professor of the Arts at Columbia University and Adjunct Professor of English at the University of Pennsylvania. He lives in New York City.

Other Books for Actors from Smith and Kraus

MONOLOGUES

The Best Men's Stage Monologues of 1992
The Best Men's Stage Monologues of 1991
The Best Men's Stage Monologues of 1990
The Best Women's Stage Monologues of 1992
The Best Women's Stage Monologues of 1991
The Best Women's Stage Monologues of 1990
Street Talk: Character Monologues for Actors
Uptown: Character Monologues for Actors
One Hundred Men's Stage Monologues from the 1980's
One Hundred Women's Stage Monologues from the 1980's
The Great Monologues from the Humana Festival
The Great Monologues from the EST Marathon
Monologues from Contemporary Literature: Volume I
Monologues from Classic Plays

YOUNG ACTORS

Great Scenes for Young Actors from the Stage
Great Monologues for Young Actors
5 Original Plays from A.C.T.'s Young Conservatory
The Mini Scene: A New Technique for Training Young Actors
Scenes and Monologues for Very Young Actors

ADVANCED ACTORS

The Best Stage Scenes for Women from the 1980's
The Best Stage Scenes for Men from the 1980's
The Best Stage Scenes of 1992
The Actor's Chekhov

PLAYS FOR ACTORS

The Best Plays of 1992 by Women Playwrights

If you require pre-publication information about upcoming Smith and Kraus monologue collections, scene collections, play anthologies, advanced acting books, and books for young actors, you may receive our semi-annual catalogue, free of charge, by sending your name and address to Smith and Kraus Catalogue, P.O. Box 10, Newbury, VT 05051.

ROMULUS LINNEY

SEVENTEEN SHORT PLAYS

by
Romulus Linney

Plays For Actors Series

SK
A Smith and Kraus Book

A Smith and Kraus Book
Published by Smith and Kraus, Inc.

Manufactured in the United States of America

First Edition: October 1992
10 9 8 7 6 5 4 3 2 1

Cataloging in Publication

Linney, Romulus, 1930-
[Plays, Selections]
Romulus Linney, seventeen short plays / by Romulus Linney. -- 1st ed.
p. cm. -- (Plays for actors)
Includes bibliographical references.
ISBN 1-880399-21-0 : $14.95
I. Title. II. Series
PS3562.I55A6 1992b
812'.54--dc20 92-27781
CIP

Smith and Kraus, Inc.
Main Street, P.O. Box 10, Newbury, Vermont 05051
(802) 866-5423

DEDICATION

I was an actor before I became a writer, and I loved every minute of it. At Oberlin College, Yale Drama School, and six summers of stock, through Iago and Everyman and Vershinin to Leo Davis in *ROOM SERVICE*, I had a wonderful time with every character I played. Then a sea change occurred in my personality and I became a writer, first a novelist, then a playwright. I often wondered to what degree I remained an actor, acting the part of a writer.

In any case, I love to give actors good parts. I am always glad to hear from them when they enjoy playing my creations, and when I direct my plays, I relish working with them through their own creative process, for which I have the greatest respect.

So I am happy that Smith and Kraus is publishing this selection of my short plays, which can hold in one volume a great number of roles for actors. The plays included here run from ninety minutes in length to eight, with many speeches and monologues, as well as scenes, for auditions. I hope readers will enjoy reading these plays and actors will enjoy playing them.

Lord Byron wrote, "I am acquainted with no *immaterial* sensuality so delightful as good acting."

I agree. I dedicate this book to every actor in the world.

Romulus Linney

ACKNOWLEDGMENTS

The Playwright expresses his thanks to the theatres who first produced these plays:

AMBROSIO: *The Signature Theatre Company*

THE LOVE SUICIDE AT SCHOFIELD BARRACKS: *Herbert Berghof, HB Playwrights Foundation and Cheryl Crawford at the ANTA Theatre*

SAND MOUNTAIN MATCHMAKING: *The Whole Theatre Company*

WHY THE LORD COME TO SAND MOUNTAIN: *Philadelphia Festival for New Plays*

THREE POETS: *The Theatre for the New City*

JULIET: *The Ensemble Studio Theatre*

YANCEY: *The Actor's Theatre of Louisville Apprentice Program*

THE DEATH OF KING PHILIP: *The Actor's Theatre of Louisville*

EL HERMANO: *The Ensemble Studio Theatre*

THE CAPTIVITY OF PIXIE SHEDMAN: *The Phoenix Theatre*

GOODBYE, HOWARD: *HB Playwrights Foundation*

CAN, CAN, CLAIR DE LUNE, GOLD AND SILVER WALTZ, and SONGS OF LOVE: *The Whole Theatre Company*

CONTENTS

PREFACE

Grab your dinner napkins, theater lovers! Romulus Linney has just laid out a seventeen-course banquet for you to enjoy.

It would be wonderful if any volume of short plays could capture the incredible variety to be found within these covers. That they're all the work of one talented playwright is a testament to Linney's amazing gifts. From modern-day Appalachia to Spain to medieval Japan each of these seventeen plays transports us, in a few brief pages, to another place and time. And it's a tribute to Linney's talent that you'll find a unique world of style and language with each of these excursions.

Language. Linney prizes it and relishes in its expressiveness. For example, in some of the works set in his native Appalachia, the words are as thick and sweet as honey. They should almost be read aloud to capture the full nuance of their richness. Having once had the chance to sit on the front porch of Linney's boyhood home sipping lemonade with his aunt, I was able to understand first-hand how acute Linney's ear is to the rhythm and color of the dialect he heard as a child. The key is in Linney's ability to hone in on the lyrical quality to be found in the working language of ordinary people. That lyricism is what allows him to capture the full measure of their dignity and humor. Reading so many other modern writers for the stage, I find myself thirsty again for a playwright who really <u>loves</u> language and who knows how to bend it to his purpose. If Linney were a boastful man he might say, as Clink does to Rebecca in ***Sand Mountain Matchmaking***, "Rub yoreself agin other legs here, b'grannies, you'll commence thinking better about me."

Here's probably a good place to utter a word of caution to those about to act any of these Appalachian plays on stage. Linney gives you all you need to capture the quality of the accent. There's no need to throw on a heavy drawl. Just let Linney's phrasing and punctuation be your guide. (In fact, one of the joys of working on the plays of a fine writer is knowing you can relax, knowing you can trust his or her skill.)

In other parts of this book, on the other hand, you will find language used in completely different ways. The terse language in ***Ambrosio*** has been stripped down to its essence. Nothing is left but the harsh staccato drumbeat of evil itself, as if each work had a small knife attached. Meanwhile, in works like ***The Death of King Philip*** or ***Komachi*** Linney creates a poetic style deceptive in its simplicity.

PREFACE

And with gifts like these, you can bet that in contemporary urban pieces like ***Juliet*** or ***El Hermano*** Linney also knows how to make language do his bidding. The knowing reader or actor will see it and understand how craftily Linney has veiled his skills behind the seemingly everyday chatter to be found in a barroom or a rehearsal hall. The language is charged, but never self-conscious.

In dwelling on Linney's use of language I've yet to talk about one of the most delightful aspects of reading these plays. All seventeen are examples of the art of the one-act play at its best. Throughout his career, Linney has been one of our busiest practitioners of the one-act form and the results here are easy to see. There's tremendous dramatic compression to be found in the plays assembled here. Within seconds you're plunged into a distinct world and you'll quickly grasp the essence of the characters that people that world. Even at his most lyrical, Linney is never a man to waste time. A long-time resident of New York City, perhaps it's the Big Apple's feverish pace that's taught him how to "get on with the show," and stands, therefore, as the perfect counterpoint to his more leisurely southern side.

There's at least one more remarkable fact that should be mentioned about our playwright. The American theater seems to be a place where talented writers often burn themselves out quickly or abandon us to seek greater material gains in film and television. Romulus Linney is one of those exceptions that seem to prove the rule. The longer he's with us, the stronger his work grows and the more afield this man and his restless curiosity take us. As his numerous awards testify, he's one of the treasures of the contemporary theater. His lively imagination and gentle humanity will keep feeding us theater lovers lively fare for many, many years to come.

But enough from me already. Turn the page(s)! The banquet is about to begin...

John Dillion
Artistic Director
Milwaukee Repertory Theatre

INTRODUCTION

From rambunctious rural American comedy to intellectual contemplation of the roots of repression during the Spanish Inquisition, Romulus Linney is a playwright with many voices, all of them linked by his humanitarian regard for individualism and by his instinct for humor as an essence of character. Because of the diversity of his work, the plays have a particular appeal for actors, who can find in them a world of colors, emotions and characters.

On one level, the challenge can be to assume flavorful accents, as in the backwoods dialect in his Appalachian plays. Or the challenge can be to transport oneself in time and history, as in his three contrasting views of heroic female poets, each written in a different style. ***Komachi*** is a ninth century Noh play; ***Hrosvitha***, the 10th century tale of a cloistered nun who became Europe's first woman playwright, and ***Akhmatova***, a tribute to the martyred Russian poet suppressed by Stalin. From here it is a long leap to the American frontier and ***The Death of King Philip***, the story of an abduction and a love affair between a fearsome Indian chief and a minister's wife. ***The Love Suicide at Schofield Barracks*** is one of his morality plays, a contemporary investigation of what drives people to a suicidal defense of their beliefs.

Having seen the plays in this book before reading them, I was, of course, shadowed by memories of performances: Kathleen Chalfant as Akhamatova; Leon Russom as the confident suitor in ***Sand Mountain Matchmaking*** and in the title role of ***Why the Lord Come to Sand Mountain***, and the author himself in ***Gold and Silver Waltz***, an autobiographical reflection on his youth. Naturally other actors undertaking these plays will see themselves in the roles; the characters are constantly renewable, one reason why Linney has become so popular in our regional theater.

Even with 17 plays, this volume can offer only a sampling of a large body of work. The emphasis is necessarily on the shorter plays, the vignettes as well as the one-acts, although both ***Ambrosio*** and ***The Captivity of Pixie Shedman*** are full-length pieces. Actors interested in the playwright might also look at ***Holy Ghosts***, his uproarious view of religious cultism; ***Heathen Valley***, that remote "valley that God forgot," and "Tennessee", a mountain tale in which the actress playing the central role begins in old age and returns to adolescence. In that play, as in ***The Death of King Philip***, actresses have to trace an entire life in a brief span of stage time.

INTRODUCTION

Linney is a master of the self-revealing monologue and also of the confrontational dialogue, as in ***El Hermano***, a play about male bravado. Seemingly casual conversation can be dense with portent and imagery. As actors will discover, there are also opportunities for physicalized humor, as in those "Sand Mountain" comedies and the deceptively simple ***Songs of Love***. In that sketch, two aged residents of a nursing home strike a pose of silence in order to resist interference from meddling relatives.

One of the choicest plays in this collection is ***Goodbye, Howard*** a vintage Linney comedy in which three elderly sisters keep a death watch over their celebrated brother. As Howard lays dying, the women unveil their envies and their eccentricities. Which of the roles would an actress choose? - the argumentative sister or the sweet-tempered one or the woman who is always blissfully confused. Or for an audition piece, perhaps she should try all three. Each is equally amusing as the play spins and turns to its double-twist ending.

The fact that the playwright is also a director (and has worked as an actor) enhances his knowledge of the practicalities of performance: of what works and does not work on stage. ***Juliet*** is a rare instance in which he looks to the stage itself for inspiration; in most of his plays he finds an intuitive theatricality in life.

Mel Gussow
August 27, 1992
New York Times

ROMULUS LINNEY

SEVENTEEN SHORT PLAYS

AMBROSIO

for James Houghton
and the Signature Theatre Company

AMBROSIO, 30, a charismatic and very handsome monk.
ROSARIO, 18, a very young novice.
DON PEDRO, his uncle, 30's, a pleasant looking Spanish gentleman.
ELVIRA, a Spanish Lady in her 50's.
ANTONIA, her beautiful daughter, 17.
THE INQUISITOR GENERAL, 70, dignified and judicious.
FRAY DIEGO LUCERO, 40, a friar, ascetic and dilligent.

Place: Cordoba, Spain.
Time: 1500

The play is freely adapted from characters and incidents in the 1797 novel, THE MONK, by Matthew G. Lewis, and from histories of the Spanish Inquisition by Juan Antonia Llorente, Henry Charles Lea, and others.

AMBROSIO was first presented in a joint premiere by Signature Theatre Company of New York, James Houghton, Artistic Director, and the Milwaukee Repertory Theatre, John Dillon, Artistic Director. It opened first in New York, on April 12, 1992, with the following cast:

AMBROSIO............................Peter Ashton Wise
ANTONIA..............................Marin Hinkle
ELVIRA................................Jacqueline Bertrand
ROSARIO..............................T. Ryder Smith
THE INQUISITOR GENERAL....Garrison Philips
LUCERO...............................Mark Alan Gordon

It was co-directed by Romulus Linney and James Houghton, set design by E. David Cosier, costume design by Teresa Snider-Stein, lighting design by Jeffrey S. Koger, production stage manager, Deborah Natoli.

AMBROSIO

White walls, a blood red floor, two Spanish chairs, a bench/table.

Icon of the Virgin Mary on the back wall. At times, projections.

Scene 1

Cathedral of the Capuchins.

Characters enter, stand waiting. Enter AMBROSIO, a handsome monk.

Ambrosio: God created us. God is good. Why is there so much evil in the world? *(Around him stands-DON PEDRO, a distinguished Spanish gentleman, and ROSARIO, a young novice monk. They listen.)* What do we seek? Love. What do we find? Envy, wrath, sloth, gluttony, avarice, pride and lust. "Through the center of the marriage bed runs a river deep and profound." Peasant folksong. Fortunate are they who find it. *(Around him stands ELVIRA, a Spanish Lady, leaning on a cane. Beside her, ANTONIA, her seventeen year old daughter. They listen.)* The rest of us live for work, family, power. We are condemned to a never ending thirst for our passions, until old age, sickness and death force upon us a virtue we could not achieve in life. Furies invade our houses, driving us to maim our children as our mothers and fathers maimed us. We become ashamed of our hopes. We ridicule our dreams. Love becomes lust. *(AMBROSIO sees ROSARIO and stares at him for a moment.)* Bound upon a wheel of need, we despise the world. Life is filth, as we suspected. Evil, violence and suffering everywhere, in deadly random profusion. You might just as well call it the Devil. Who escapes him? *(Around him stand THE INQUISITOR GENERAL, an Archbishop, with a white collar and hood and with him, DIEGO LUCERO, a friar, in a black robe. They listen.)* I escape. You escape. Cleansed by guilt, purged by self reproach. Penitent, humble, patient. Seeing life for what it is, one instant in time. *(AMBROSIO stares again, briefly, at ROSARIO.)* And when it is over, then for the faithful, great and legitimate pride: for we will love Almighty God forever, in eternal skies of everlasting light. We understand. We are safe. We defy Satan. God made evil so we can freely choose the good. *(Music. DON PEDRO nods to ROSARIO, who exits. AMBROSIO goes to the INQUISITOR. He kneels, kisses his ring. He rises and bows to LUCERO. They walk apart, talking.)*

Antonia: I must speak to him!

Elvira: Why?

Antonia: I want him for my confessor!

Elvira: We can't ask him here.

Antonia: We must.

Don Pedro: May I be of help to you? I am Don Pedro Juan de Lastanosa. *(DON PEDRO talks to them, smiling. AMBROSIO, LUCERO and the INQUISITOR come forward.)*

Inquisitor: We are now free from bigamists, adulterers, witches, thieves, murderers, and every sort of common criminal, who, whatever their guilt, were not in league with the Devil. The Holy Office never meant its Inquisition to become a source of injustice. It will be so no longer.

Ambrosio: Under your Grace, the Holy Office is as temperate as it is effective.

Lucero: Your eloquence is a great weapon in our struggle.

Inquisitor: With God, Ambrosio.

Ambrosio: With God, your Grace.

Lucero: With God.

Ambrosio: With God. *(THE INQUISITOR and LUCERO move away. They come face to face with DON PEDRO, who bows to them. Exit INQUISITOR and LUCERO.)*

Don Pedro: I enjoyed your sermon, Father.

Ambrosio: I am glad.

Don Pedro: I am a visitor to Cordoba, who admires your eloquence. I believe these ladies wish to speak to you. *(DON PEDRO steps back. ANTONIA rushes past him and speaks to AMBROSIO.)*

Antonia: Do you hear confessions?

Elvira: Bow! *(ANTONIA kneels before AMBROSIO.)*

Antonia: Do you?

Elvira: Forgive her. She should learn her catechism, and confess to any priest who will hear her.

Antonia: I want to confess to you.

Ambrosio: Why?

Antonia: I don't know. I must.

Elvira: Well, to some one!

Antonia: No, to you!

Elvira: Antonia!

Antonia: Father!

Ambrosio: Your names?

Elvira: Donna Elvira Dalfa, plaza San Iago, by the palace d'Albornos. My daughter Antonia.

Antonia: Confession, Father.
Ambrosio: It is heard here every day.
Antonia: Neither you nor my mother understand. As I love my God, I love His Church, and divine theology. It is hard to tolerate the harsh men who lecture me, and will not let me learn. I need the counsel of a gentle and intelligent priest. *(Pause.)*
Ambrosio: Wednesdays.
Antonia: Thank you, Father.
Elvira: Thank you, Father. *(ANTONIA and ELVIRA turn to go and face DON PEDRO.)*
Antonia: Thank you, sir. *(DON PEDRO bows to them. Exeunt ANTONIA and ELVIRA. DON PEDRO watches them go. Exit AMBROSIO. DON PEDRO stands looking after AMBROSIO. Music.)*

Scene 2

AMBROSIO'S cell in the Capuchin Monastery. AMBROSIO, praying. Light on the icon of the Virgin Mary.

Rosario: Father. *(AMBROSIO continues his prayer.)* Father. *(AMBROSIO ends his prayer, crosses himself.)*
Ambrosio: Yes?
Rosario: A novice.
Ambrosio: Yes? *(Enter ROSARIO, shyly, a small basket in his hand.)*
Rosario: You council novices at this hour?
Ambrosio: Not in my cell.
Rosario: Father Abbott sent me to you.
Ambrosio: What is your name?
Rosario: Rosario.
Ambrosio: Let us pray.
Rosario: My uncle, Don Pedro Juan de Lastanosa, sends you his good wishes, Father, and a gift.
Ambrosio: Thank him for me.
Rosario: You met him today, in the Cathedral.
Ambrosio: Where have I seen you before?
Rosario: I never miss your sermons.
Ambrosio: In the congregation?
Rosario: Yes.
Ambrosio: Did you approve?
Rosario: You never spoke better, except once.
Ambrosio: When was that?

Rosario: The day I came here. You preached about that painting of the Blessed Virgin.

Ambrosio: Let's look at her now, together. *(AMBROSIO and ROSARIO turn and sit together on the floor, backs to us. Light glows on the painting. A beautiful Virgin Mary stares down at them.)*

Ambrosio: What beauty in that face. How graceful the turn of the head. What sweetness in her eyes.

Rosario: You said that then.

Ambrosio: Someone unknown sent her to me, wrapped in old burlap. I adored her the minute I saw her.

Rosario: You said that, too. And I wondered what you were really thinking.

Ambrosio: What did you decide?

Rosario: "If she came to life what would I do?"

Ambrosio: Such ideas you have. *(They swing around, sitting on the floor, facing each other.)* Still, that is exactly what I was thinking.

Rosario: How could you not love a woman that beautiful?

Ambrosio: Rosario. What I adore is the painter's skill and the divinity it embodies.

Rosario: Other passions are gone forever?

Ambrosio: Yes. What's in the basket?

Rosario: The gift. Some flowers I know you like.

Ambrosio: How long have you been a novice here?

Rosario: Almost a year.

Ambrosio: I am sorry we have not met before.

Rosario: So am I.

Ambrosio: Now we will pray to the Blessed Virgin, for Don Pedro Juan de Lastanosa, and for you, and for me. But first, let me see the flowers. *(Music. ROSARIO hands the flowers to AMBROSIO who smells them, smiling. ROSARIO watches him closely. Then they kneel together before the portrait of the Virgin Mary, and pray.)*

Scene 3

Cathedral. Confession, before there were booths.
Two chairs. AMBROSIO and ANTONIA.
They are smiling.

Antonia: My last confessor slept and belched and smelled of garlic.

Ambrosio: It is not the business of confessors to be charming.

Antonia: I'm not sure he could read.

Ambrosio: Nor to be learned.

Antonia: What should he do then?
Ambrosio: His duty.
Antonia: And what is that?
Ambrosio: Love.
Antonia: And what is that?
Ambrosio: Love is something—by God's Grace—one is.
Antonia: To be near you means everything to me.
Ambrosio: I will hear your confession now.
Antonia: What happens in monasteries? Tell me!
Ambrosio: What happens in monasteries is prayer. Endless, selfless prayer.
Antonia: For what?
Ambrosio: You. Your mother. Criminal, beggar, old man dying, baby being born, the glory of God. A great abbey in prayer— *(He makes a fist, then opens it.)* —is as powerful as the sun.
Antonia: Does that make you happy?
Ambrosio: Not exactly. Happiness is too weak a word.
Antonia: So you aren't happy.
Ambrosio: Confession, now.
Antonia: Talk to me first.
Ambrosio: Are there no men in your life?
Antonia: Of course.
Ambrosio: Aren't you interested in them?
Antonia: You think it interesting, waiting to be bought? To lie down and open my legs? To get up and wash babies and linen? When I want to read and read and read. Instead, I must marry, at seventeen, and listen to a stupid husband. I dread the thought of it.
Ambrosio: Are you ready to make your confession?
Antonia: What are you thinking?
Ambrosio: *(Smiling.)* Of you.
Antonia: Oh.
Ambrosio: What's the matter?
Antonia: I'm crying. Bless me, Father, for I have sinned.
Ambrosio: How long has it been since your last confession? *(Music.)*

Scene 4

A bench in the garden of AMBROSIO'S monastery. A bush, growing roses. Branches projected. ROSARIO, seated. Enter AMBROSIO. ROSARIO rises.

Rosario: Father?

Ambrosio: Rosario.
Rosario: Do you like this garden, too?
Ambrosio: After confessions, it is very refreshing.
Rosario: I make up verses here.
Ambrosio: Are you a poet, Rosario?
Rosario: *(Reciting vigorously.)*

I saw mankind with vice encrusted,
I saw that Honor's sword was rusted!,
That few for aught but folly lusted!,
That he was still deceived, who trusted
In love or friend!
(AMBROSIO, listening, stands next to ROSARIO.)
Let me, Oh Lord! from life retire,
Let me in this belief expire,
To God I fly!

Ambrosio: *(Smiling.)* Retire?
Rosario: *(Violently.)* Yes, go! Be a hermit!
Ambrosio: Rosario, it is one thing to be disgusted by mankind, but another to completely forget it. Could you face total solitude?
Rosario: Could you?
Ambrosio: Never. I couldn't live anywhere else. I was put on the doorstep of this monastery, raised by peasants, then sent to school and spent all my life, here. This abbey is your asylum, too, where you are protected from one world but remain in another, a world of good friends.
Rosario: Would to God I'd never met these good friends! Or met you!
Ambrosio: Me?
Rosario: I should live in a sewer!
Ambrosio: Rosario!
Rosario: I wish I'd never seen this place!
Ambrosio: Or me?
Rosario: *Yes you!! (Exit ROSARIO, running. AMBROSIO, stunned, stands up and starts after him, then stops. He is shattered. He looks about blindly, shocked. He sits back on the bench, staring ahead at nothing. Pause. Re-enter ROSARIO, slowly. Pause.)*
Rosario: I am sorry.
Ambrosio: Are you in control of yourself?
Rosario: Oh, yes. Thanks no doubt to a perfect monk's perfect prayers.
Ambrosio: Rosario, what is the matter with you?
Rosario: What friends do I have? Cold brothers in a cold monastery!
Ambrosio: I will be your friend.
Rosario: You will be my judge.

Ambrosio: I set aside the judge. The monk and the priest. Think of me as your father and your friend.

Rosario: You will hate me!

Ambrosio: Never!

Rosario: Whatever I tell you, you will tell no one else?

Ambrosio: I promise.

Rosario: By the blood of Jesus Christ?

Ambrosio: By the blood of Jesus Christ. What is this mystery?

Rosario: Love is love, Father. Man or woman, it is the same! *(AMBROSIO tries to leave. ROSARIO jumps at him, seizes him. Struggle. ROSARIO throws AMBROSIO backward, so he can't get away. Both men stand facing each other, gasping for breath.)*

Rosario: Do not think, Ambrosio, that I would ever steal you from the Church. You were left on the doorstep of this monastery and it must always be your home. God forbid my love should harm you!

Ambrosio: But it would!

Rosario: Never! I heard you preach. I begged my uncle to bring me here as a novice. I have been so happy, just to be near you. Let us spend our lives together, celibate brothers. When we die, our bodies will lie in the same grave. What could be more innocent than that?

Ambrosio: Impossible.

Rosario: The discipline of this monastery is not perfect. I can see you often.

Ambrosio: You would misunderstand my every word. Your feelings would overwhelm everything.

Rosario: Are you sure?

Ambrosio: You will leave this monastery or I will denounce you.

Rosario: You would do that?

Ambrosio: Yes. *(AMBROSIO tries again to go. ROSARIO jumps in his way. He takes a dagger from under his robe.)*

Rosario: No, you won't! *(He puts the blade to AMBROSIO'S throat. Then to his own.)* You won't have to! *(ROSARIO runs off. AMBROSIO stands shaking. He is stunned, disoriented. He slowly pulls himself together and kneels, his knuckles white in prayer.)*

Ambrosio: He waited a year. *(Pause.)* I can't stop thinking about him. *(Pause.)* Would he hurt himself? *(He bows his head and prays. Behind him, very slowly, enter ROSARIO. He watches AMBROSIO. AMBROSIO, sensing him there, stops praying.)* Rosario?

Rosario: Yes?

Ambrosio: You've come back?

Rosario: Yes.

Ambrosio: Why?

Rosario: I could not leave you in anger.
Ambrosio: Tell me you will not hurt yourself.
Rosario: If you don't want me to.
Ambrosio: Sit. *(ROSARIO sits on the bench next to AMBROSIO.)* I won't force you. But I will ask you to save me from myself. Take my love with you and leave me my immortal soul.
Rosario: That's cruel.
Ambrosio: Do that for me.
Rosario: I have no will but yours.
Ambrosio: Otherwise, you will send me to hell.
Rosario: Will I?
Ambrosio: Yes.
Rosario: I will leave the monastery today.
Ambrosio: Today?
Rosario: There is an abbey in Murcia. My uncle, Don Pedro, will find me a place there.
Ambrosio: So soon?
Rosario: If at all.
Ambrosio: I did not know love was so hard.
Rosario: It's like death.
Ambrosio: Goodbye.
Rosario: Give me something to take with me.
Ambrosio: What?
Rosario: A rose, from that bush. *(AMBROSIO bows, and goes to the rose bush. He reaches in it to break off a rose. He screams and steps back in horror.)*
Ambrosio: Ah!! *(He hold up one arm. A snake, mimed, hangs from it by its fangs.)* Viper!! *(ROSARIO seizes the serpent by the back of its head, pulls its fangs from AMBROSIO'S arm and flings it into the bushes. He forces AMBROSIO to the ground.)*
Rosario: GIVE ME YOUR ARM! *(ROSARIO slices into AMBROSIO'S arm with his knife, bites into the wound, fiercely sucks poison and blood from AMBROSIO'S arm. Lights out. Music.)*

Scene 5

The Dalfa home. Two high backed Spanish chairs. In them sit ELVIRA and ANTONIA. They are looking at a diamond on a black cloth.

Elvira: It is worth a fortune.
Antonia: Who is he?

Elvira: Don Pedro Juan de Lastanosa. From Murcia. Won't you see him?
Antonia: No.
Elvira: I can't be here forever! You are seventeen years old. You will be alone. With no money and no position! Speak to the gentleman.
Antonia: No.
Elvira: He's here now. *(A light, into which steps DON PEDRO, waiting.)* Behave yourself. *(ELVIRA goes to DON PEDRO. ANTONIA sighs. ELVIRA returns with DON PEDRO.)* Don Pedro. *(Exit ELVIRA. ANTONIA turns to him, politely.)*
Antonia: Good afternoon.
Don Pedro: I am happy to see you again. *(ANTONIA nods coolly.)* It was in the Cathedral of the Capuchins. You were thinking of the monk, not of me. He means a great deal to you.
Antonia: Yes, he does.
Don Pedro: I am a widower, looking for a wife to give me love and keep me from sin. Such a woman must be strong in her faith. A husband can do many things for a wife, but he can't give her faith or save her soul. For that, she must trust her confessor and deliver herself into his care.
Antonia: I agree.
Don Pedro: I can think of no one better.
Antonia: Thank you.
Don Pedro: Your mother wants you to marry.
Antonia: Yes.
Don Pedro: Do you?
Antonia: No.
Don Pedro: Then we'll say no more about it. A short visit, and I'll be gone.
Antonia: Thank you.
Don Pedro: Of course. *(Pause.)*
Antonia: I am glad you like Father Ambrosio.
Don Pedro: I rejoice that you have him, and he has you.
Antonia: I did not think anyone would ever understand that.
Don Pedro: I do. *(Pause.)*
Antonia: If we married, I would be away from Cordoba, from the Monastery of the Capuchins and from Father Ambrosio.
Don Pedro: I travel, often. I spend a great deal of time here. So would you. But never mind. *(Pause.)*
Antonia: Murcia is by the sea. Do you fish?
Don Pedro: Many ships. And farm. Both.
Antonia: House?
Don Pedro: Four wings, joined, with courtyards.

Antonia: A library?

Don Pedro: Three rooms, floor to ceiling.

Antonia: Books on theology?

Don Pedro: A thousand.

Antonia: Do you read them?

Don Pedro: I did once. But theology is about supernatural beings in other worlds. I am more interested now in human beings on earth.

Antonia: Erasmus?

Don Pedro: In Spanish, as well as Latin. All the Fathers of the Church. And Luther.

Antonia: Who?

Don Pedro: A young monk, in Saxony. I like what he's doing.

Antonia: Practical men?

Don Pedro: Oh, yes.

Antonia: Why?

Don Pedro: Mankind has suffered more violence in our century than in all others combined. Agreed?

Antonia: Agreed.

Don Pedro: But we hear less and less about violence and more and more about the devil. Bad theology. Impractical. Heresy is the sin of the day, not violence. Do you think the devil exists?

Antonia: I have heard that question answered no.

Don Pedro: You are wise not to commit yourself. I might be an Inquisitor in disguise.

Antonia: Not if you read Erasmus. *(Pause.)* But isn't the devil responsible for all evil?

Don Pedro: I have heard that question answered no.

Antonia: Ambrosio says he is. Ambrosio says God made the devil so we can choose God instead.

Don Pedro: I know he says that.

Antonia: What do you say?

Don Pedro: I am a practical man. I agree. Do you play at theology?

Antonia: Passionately.

Don Pedro: All right. 1. God is all good and all powerful. Agreed?

Antonia: Agreed.

Don Pedro: 2. God must want a good world in which the devil does not exist.

Antonia: Agreed, and furthermore, God gets what he wants.

Don Pedro: That's 3. Therefore:

Antonia: It's a good world. The devil doesn't exist.

Don Pedro: All right. But 4.—4.—come now—

Antonia: We observe that evil does exist: therefore:
Don Pedro: God does not exist, or:
Antonia: God is evil?
Don Pedro: Or God and the Devil were the same thing once and may be again.
Antonia: In which case:
Don Pedro: Good will be Evil and Evil will be Good all at once, as once perhaps it was.
Antonia: And the Devil will think he is doing good?
Don Pedro: Yes!
Antonia: That's impossible!
Don Pedro: I love the impossible! *(They smile together.)*
Antonia: All right. Love for me, then, an impossibility.
Don Pedro: "Fools desire the ordinary. The wise have impossible loves." *(Pause. ANTONIA laughs.)*
Antonia: That's not theology. You are so peculiar! Where did you hear that?
Don Pedro: Drinking song.
Antonia: Do you drink?
Don Pedro: Sometimes.
Antonia: Do you get drunk and talk and talk and talk?
Don Pedro: Sometimes.
Antonia: Do you stun women with torrents of verbal brilliance?
Don Pedro: I have been known to do that.
Antonia: And you admit it!
Don Pedro: Do you like to make fools out of men?
Antonia: Yes.
Both: And you admit it!
Antonia: Suppose I want an impossible love? No, maybe two or three?
Don Pedro: No one should suffer from poverty of experience, not even my wife.
Antonia: You take my breath away.
Don Pedro: I have brought you a present. Here. *(He hands her a small silver locket.)* Open it. *(She does.)*
Antonia: Oh!
Don Pedro: I collect paintings. Those are miniatures. The Abbey of the Capuchins on one side, and a portrait of its famous monk Ambrosio on the other. The inlays are emerald. I hope you like them.
Antonia: I do! *(Music.)*

Scene 6

Music. AMBROSIO'S cell. In his bed, ROSARIO, sleeping. AMBROSIO kneeling by the bed, praying. Above them the painting of the Virgin Mary.)

Ambrosio: In manas tuas, commendo spiritum meum. Amen. *(ROSARIO opens his eyes, sees AMBROSIO praying. He smiles, then closes his eyes again, and wakes himself up, moaning.)*
Rosario: Where am I?
Ambrosio: In my bed.
Rosario: How can that be?
Ambrosio: You have been unconscious for two days.
Rosario: Where have you slept?
Ambrosio: On the floor of the chapel, praying for you.
Rosario: Oh.
Ambrosio: You saved my life. But you swallowed much of the venom. No man poisoned by that viper has ever lived.
Rosario: Oh.
Ambrosio: We will pray for a miracle.
Rosario: How long will it be before another monk comes and takes your place?
Ambrosio: As long as you like.
Rosario: What did you think, when I lay dying?
Ambrosio: Please.
Rosario: Tell me!
Ambrosio: I understood what love is. I begged the Blessed Virgin to save you.
Rosario: Ah!
Ambrosio: What is it?
Rosario: The venom! My blood is on fire!
Ambrosio: Hold my hands!
Rosario: Ahh!!
Ambrosio: Rosario!! *(Pause. ROSARIO's spasm relents. He lies back on the bed.)*
Rosario: Ambrosio, look at my face. Closely. Have you never seen this face before?
Ambrosio: I think I have.
Rosario: You loved this face before you ever saw me.
Ambrosio: What?
Rosario: Feel the beating of this heart. Now. *(He puts AMBROSIO'S hand on his heart. He points to the portrait of the Virgin Mary. The light on her face brightens.)* Your Madonna. Look at her. Go. *(ROSARIO points to her. AMBROSIO goes and looks at her.)* Her face is mine. She was

painted for me. I sent her to the monastery. You put her in this cell to adore. When you loved the Virgin Mary, you loved me! *(The light is very bright on the painting. The face of the Madonna is clearly ROSARIO'S.)* Do you want me to live, Ambrosio?

Ambrosio: Yes!

Rosario: What would you give for me?

Ambrosio: Anything!

Rosario: Then I know what to do.

Ambrosio: Do?

Rosario: Help me up. *(AMBROSIO helps ROSARIO to stand. They move away as lights go out on them, then on the face of the virgin. Music.)*

Scene 7

(The underground burial vaults of the Capuchin Monastery. An open space. Projections on the side walls. A dim light at center. Enter ABROSIO, ROSARIO leaning against him.)

Ambrosio: But where? There's nothing down here but vaults and coffins.

Rosario: And the bones of holy men. *(Pointing at the dark walls.)* There! Three skeletons, in monk's robes! Ugh! They are nailed there, upright.

Ambrosio: Yes.

Rosario: And there, against that wall! A curve of skulls, with a robed skeleton lying beneath it, clutching a cross.

Ambrosio: Yes.

Rosario: And there! On the ceiling! Patterns, like flowerbeds, or sewing! But made of bone!

Ambrosio: Yes. *(A light glows in a doorway at one end of the vault.)* What's that?

Rosario: Stay here. Whatever happens, wait for me.

Ambrosio: All right.

Rosario: Swear.

Ambrosio: I swear. *(ROSARIO goes toward the light. He disappears.)* Where are you! What are you doing? *(Pause.)* Rosario? *(Enter DON PEDRO, quickly, toward AMBROSIO. He seizes him by the front of his cassock.)*

Don Pedro: Saved, from the serpent's poison!

Ambrosio: How?

Don Pedro: By me!

Ambrosio: Who are you?

Don Pedro: I am Satan! *(DON PEDRO throws AMBROSIO to the center of the vault, and moves around him, pointing at the walls.)* And now it is you who are in danger! Look about you, Ambrosio, at the bones of holy men.

Dead monks who lived in celibate scorn of life. How hideous their tomb and pathetic their remains! They did not serve God. They defied him! For the will of God is pleasure, body and soul. To deny it leads to the desolation you see around you and the death you feel within yourself. A garden of dead monks, grandly posed as if in triumph, their souls singing in heaven. But do you believe that, Ambrosio? Do you? I don't think so. This is not the will of God. I will show you the will of God. *(From where DON PEDRO entered, now comes ROSARIO. He carries his robe on one arm. He is naked.)* Love, body and soul, is the will of God. Refuse it, and you anger God, who created you. I know, for I was God's beloved, and I lived with, him, in bliss. We quarreled, as lovers do, and he threw me burning from heaven. Do you love this boy?

Ambrosio: Yes!

Don Pedro: Body and soul!

Ambrosio: Body and soul!

Don Pedro: You love God?

Ambrosio: Yes!

Don Pedro: And God won't let you have him?

Ambrosio: No!

Don Pedro: Can you give him up?

Ambrosio: No!

Don Pedro: Then take him.

Ambrosio: Sin!

Don Pedro: Who told you so? They did! Those bones against the wall! Monks! Fathers of a Church so proud they leave their corpses posed behind them! Sin is spurning love, not satisfying it! Killing the spirit, crucifying the body. Treachery, war, destruction. This is only a beautiful boy, who loves you. Take him. *(AMBROSIO turns away from DON PEDRO.)*

Ambrosio: I felt the snake bite me! *(AMBROSIO punches his arm with two fingers.)* Its fangs went in *here!* *(He rubs his skin, now smooth.)*

Don Pedro: I cured that, too. Are you afraid you are insane?

Ambrosio: Yes. A madman sees things that aren't there as real as life itself.

Don Pedro: That is because insanity, Ambrosio, is the denial of reality. Set yourself above the reality of your body and its desires, and you set yourself above God, who created you. You make God angry and he turns you over to me. *(DON PEDRO brings ROSARIO to AMBROSIO, joining their hands.)* Love, monk, and be silent. *(Exit DON PEDRO.)*

Rosario: Come. Great joys are waiting for us. *(AMBROSIO is led into darkness. Music.)*

Scene 8

(HOLY OFFICE OF THE INQUISITION. LUCERO and DON PEDRO.)

Lucero: Make your visit short.

Don Pedro: I have some doubts about the monk Ambrosio.

Lucero: Doubts?

Don Pedro: Since he is the confessor to the woman I hope to marry, I may be over-concerned, but I do not think so.

Lucero: Speak plainly.

Don Pedro: In the Cathedral, when you yourself were there, Ambrosio spoke of human violence and human suffering, and he said, "You might as well call it the Devil." Whose proper name, of course, is Satan.

Lucero: So?

Don Pedro: What troubles me is elusive. I see how I could be wrong.

Lucero: I am getting impatient with you.

Don Pedro: He said, and I quote him precisely, "Violence and suffering everywhere, in deadly random profusion." Then, "You might as well call it the Devil." He used the word "it," you see.

Lucero: It? No, I do not see!

Don Pedro: "It" diminishes Satan, surely! We read in Tertullian— "Against Marconian," Chapter 2, verse 10: "He was born the wisest of all the angels, before being the Devil."

Lucero: You read Tertullian?

Don Pedro: Only as a layman. I bring to the clergy what I cannot understand. That is what I am doing now. For, don't you see, "it" is such a paltry, dismissive word for Satan himself! Moreover, when Ambrosio said, "you might just as well call," and then said, "it!" Well, that's like a jest or a joke saying there really isn't a devil, just forces or random evils, not him, the Great Satan, Mephistopheles, Lucifer. Am I being foolish?

Lucero: You are being scrupulous about the confessor of the woman who may become your wife. I see that. But why come to me?

Don Pedro: Because all Cordoba knows Deigo Lucero is so fierce in his hatred of the Evil One, that Satan fears him as no other man.

Lucero: I see.

Don Pedro: Many say our Inquisitor General is confused by his age and burdens, which explains his continual moderation of the duties of the Inquisition. I know that Diego Lucero would look deeper into everything, including this monk. *(Pause.)* I understand I must report my suspicions of others, or sin myself. I also have concerns about a neighbor.

Lucero: Heretical concerns?

Don Pedro: If I ignore heresy, I am guilty of it myself. If true, his estate would be confiscated.

Lucero: Let the Holy Office know how you can be summoned, bring to me any further worries about the monk, and, if you wish, the names of anyone who may fall under your suspicions of heresy.

Don Pedro: I am deeply moved by your confidence in me.

Lucero: With God.

Don Pedro: With God. *(Exit DON PEDRO. Music.)*

Scene 9

(Confession. AMBROSIO and ANTONIA.)

Antonia: I was twelve years old. He was a servant. He brought me a little wooden ball and said we could play with it. He took me behind some thick hedges in the garden. He took off his shirt, and threw the ball at my feet. "Play dog," he said. "What?" I said. He got down on his hands and knees, seized the ball between his teeth and shook his head, and stuck his rump up into the air. I laughed at him. He wagged his head for me to get down on all fours with him. I did, playing. He passed the ball from his mouth to mine. "All fours," he said. Then he got up. I started to get up, too, but he grabbed my hands and put them to his waist. He opened his trousers and exposed himself.

Ambrosio: This was no sin of yours.

Antonia: But it was. The muscles in his stomach, his flesh so hard and rosy and full of strength and health. I wanted to touch him there. I tried to get up but he held both my wrists in one big hand. He tore the ball away and put himself to my lips. I couldn't help it. I opened my mouth.

Ambrosio: Lust is common to everyone.

Antonia: I screamed. That excited him more. He turned me around, pushed me down on my hands and knees, ripped my skirt and drawers away, like dogs, and—he—he—

Ambrosio: Did you want him to?

Antonia: I said yes, then no, and screamed again, as loud as I could. He got frightened. He ran away.

Ambrosio: Then why reproach yourself?

Antonia: Because I am beginning to dream about him. I know what he was doing to me wasn't my fault, but I can't stop thinking about him. If a man wanted to marry me, must I tell him?

Ambrosio: If you wish. You don't have to.

Antonia: And you? Father? My friend? What do you think of me now? *(Music. Lights fade on AMBROSIO.)*

Scene 10

(AMBROSIO'S cell. He is praying. Above him, the painting of the Virgin Mary is lit. ROSARIO appears. AMBROSIO is unable to continue praying.)

Rosario: *(Softly.)* Hello.

Ambrosio: Ah!

Rosario: I didn't mean to startle you. *(ROSARIO stands behind AMBROSIO, who leans back against him. The light on the Virgin dims.)*

Ambrosio: She seemed so close to me.

Rosario: She understood you.

Ambrosio: But then she didn't. Her face hardened. The Mother of God looked at me with contempt. I felt terrible. Then she backed away from me, in horror. And you appeared.

Rosario: I should have knocked.

Ambrosio: Who are you?

Rosario: You were going to ask about me.

Ambrosio: I went to Father Abbott. We talked about everything else. I said to myself: "Ambrosio! Ask! If he's what he says he is, you'll know! If—he—"

Rosario: Isn't? All you had to do was ask.

Ambrosio: And if Father Abbott said you don't exist—

Rosario: But he didn't.

Ambrosio: Because I couldn't ask.

Rosario: Ask me.

Ambrosio: Who are you?

Rosario: I am love, your reason to live.

Ambrosio: Yes!

Rosario: Now, who are *you?*

Ambrosio: When I was left at the monastery in the middle of the night, and the monks found me, they loved me. It was a few days before they could find a woman to nurse me, so they fed me milk and honey, and named me Ambrosio.

Rosario: For ambrosia, food for pagan gods?

Ambrosio: No. For the unknown monk Ambrosiaster, who wrote about Saint Paul in the fourth century, and for Ambrosius Autpertus, in the eighth century who wrote about the Apocalypse. And for Saint Ambrose, of course.

Rosario: What did he do?

Ambrosio: He brought the Church to the level of an Empire. When he was born, a huge cluster of bees swarmed around his face and body and left his skin forever smelling like honey. Ambrose comes from *ambra*, a spice precious to the early Church. Or, from *ambor*, father of light, and *sior*, tiny, since he was a father to all his spiritual children and small in his humility. Or, for *ambrosia*, the food of angels, which gives them their strength. I love these stories. *They* are who I am.

Rosario: They are who you were. But now?

Ambrosio: Now?

Rosario: You are love. And I am love. We are what you must have, or die.

Ambrosio: But are you really here?

Rosario: My hand! *(AMBROSIO grips it.)*

Ambrosio: Yes!

Rosario: I'm real! You're real!

Ambrosio: And Satan?

Rosario: Do you need Satan to love? Come now, Ambrosio, many priests and monks and bishops and archbishops and cardinals and even Popes had lovers. Everyone knows that. No doubt they had to, in order to be the wonderful men they were. Perhaps even Saints did, like Saint Ambrose. Can you understand that? Now?

Ambrosio: Yes.

Rosario: Then you must love?

Ambrosio: Yes.

Rosario: And you do!

Ambrosio: Yes!

Rosario: Then what is the matter? *(Pause.)*

Ambrosio: I want—more!

Rosario: Ah. *(ROSARIO smiles. Music.)*

Scene 11

(THE HOLY OFFICE OF THE INQUISITION. INQUISITOR. Enter LUCERO with AMBROSIO.)

Inquisitor: Good morning.

Ambrosio: Your Grace.

Lucero: We will do what we can for you.

Ambrosio: I thank you both. *(Pause.)*

Lucero: So!

Ambrosio: Heresy is traffic with Satan.

Lucero: Correct.

Ambrosio: Does the Holy Office consider heretical a man who, by mistake,

traffics with Satan out of—love.
Lucero: Love?
Ambrosio: Yes.
Lucero: What do you mean?
Ambrosio: A great love.
Lucero: I don't understand.
Ambrosio: The desire to live for someone else!
Lucero: I don't understand.
Ambrosio: Can love—truthful and strong and good—be heretical?
Lucero: If it's from the Devil, of course.
Inquisitor: Father Ambrosio, what is the matter here?
Ambrosio: A simple transgression.
Lucero: By who?
Ambrosio: No one important.
Lucero: Who?
Inquisitor: Let him alone. *(Pause.)* What else is troubling you?
Ambrosio: Are there those—who desire a man and a woman—at the same time? *(LUCERO and the INQUISITOR look at each other.)*
Lucero: I think so. Your Grace?
Inquisitor: I believe—yes.
Ambrosio: Why— *(Pause.)*
Lucero: Speak up!
Inquisitor: Let him think.
Ambrosio: Why would God do that to me? To punish me? What for? Pride? Arrogance? I see that, but where some are so good and others so—perhaps—I should have prepared my questions better.
Lucero: Let us go back to the transgression. By no one important. By who?
Ambrosio: A novice.
Lucero: In the monastery?
Ambrosio: Yes.
Lucero: A novice in the monastery has made heretical statements?
Ambrosio: No.
Lucero: There is a *WOMAN* in the monastery?
Ambrosio: No, of course not.
Lucero: Then why are you here?
Ambrosio: If a man, spoken to by Satan, speaks back, is that heresy?
Lucero: His name?
Ambrosio: Don't you understand my question?
Lucero: Give me a name. That is what I understand.
Ambrosio: I have wasted your time. *(AMBROSIO kneels quickly and kisses*

the INQUISITOR'S ring.)

Lucero: Just a moment.

Ambrosio: I have made a mistake.

Lucero: Yes, you have.

Ambrosio: With God. *(Exit AMBROSIO.)*

Lucero: Well?

Inquisitor: The life of a monk is constant prayer. It is hard. Many things come between him and his mind and God. You are too harsh.

Lucero: Your Grace, this man—

Inquisitor: You are too harsh. *(EXIT INQUISITOR. Lights out on LUCERO, humiliated and angry.)*

Scene 12

(AMBROSIO'S cell. ROSARIO in bed. AMBROSIO trying to pray. He can't. Above them, the portrait of the Virgin Mary, with ROSARIO'S face.)

Rosario: What's the matter?

Ambrosio: I gave up everything.

Rosario: So did I.

Ambrosio: I broke my vows. And worse!

Rosario: Worse?

Ambrosio: I am tormented by a thousand devils. Each one has either your face, or—hers.

Rosario: Hers?

Ambrosio: Yes.

Rosario: A woman?

Ambrosio: I mortified myself! I lashed myself! I washed my own blood from these floors and walls!

Rosario: And were proud of it!

Ambrosio: Stop.

Rosario: Then you went to your pulpit and preached your sermons. You came back to your cell walking on air.

Ambrosio: Please!

Rosario: And looked at the Virgin. A woman. And what did you think? Let me tell you.

Ambrosio: Stop!!

Rosario: Oh, if such a creature existed, only for me!

Ambrosio: For God's sake!

Rosario: If I could sink my hands into the beauty of that hair! If I could roll in my mouth the treasures of that breast!

Ambrosio: Blasphemy!
Rosario: If I could take her to bed! Well, *you did! Me!!*
Ambrosio: Demon!!
Rosario: Fool!!
Ambrosio: Whore!! *(AMBROSIO seizes the portrait, breaks it in two, throws the pieces down. Stares at them.)*
Rosario: Is she young?
Ambrosio: Yes!!!
Rosario: Beautiful?
Ambrosio: Yes!!!
Rosario: Trusting?
Ambrosio: Yes!!!
Rosario: You love her?
Ambrosio: Sometimes.
Rosario: And sometimes you don't?
Ambrosio: She—upsets me.
Rosario: When she upsets you, do you want to hurt her?
Ambrosio: Yes.
Rosario: Beat her?
Ambrosio: Ah!!
Rosario: Goodbye, Ambrosio. Have your slut.
Ambrosio: No!
Rosario: You expect me to share you with her?
Ambrosio: I want you, too!
Rosario: And you want God. And a slut. And me. *(Exit ROSARIO. AMBROSIO picks up the parts of the icon of the Virgin Mary and tries to put them together again.)*

Scene 13

(HOLY OFFICE OF THE INQUISITION. DON PEDRO and LUCERO, holding a fat packet of parchments.)

Lucero: He came to see us,
Don Pedro: Why?
Lucero: We never found out. He asked confused questions. If what a novice said was heretical, but wouldn't say what that was. Something about a woman. He got himself all tangled up and left quickly. You've been right.
Don Pedro: I'm sorry, for his sake.
Lucero: You've also done well with these. They would set in motion

interrogations, arrests and the confiscation of a great deal of property.

Don Pedro: I am glad to be of service.

Lucero: But they won't!

Don Pedro: Why not?

Lucero: Because the Inquisitor General is a fool. Because he won't DO anything. Because his procedures make arrests so difficult, the heretic is gone before he is caught, taking his sin and his gold with him!

Don Pedro: Given his age, couldn't the Inquisitor General be replaced?

Lucero: Only by their Majesties. Our Queen is very ill, and the King won't consider anything right now but her. I have submitted report after report! What happens? Not one reply. To me! Diego Lucero!! Who, if empowered here, would make my King bless my name a thousand times! Oh, I could tell you— *(Pause.)* But never mind.

Don Pedro: Diego Lucero, servant of God, let me try to reach them.

Lucero: What would that do?

Don Pedro: Their Majesties still tend to business. The waters of Murcia hold many fishing and trading rights, in which other countries are interested. While advising them about that, I could mention great difficulties here, caused by an incompetent Inquisitor.

Lucero: How incompetent?

Don Pedro: He refuses to prosecute a heretic.

Lucero: Oh.

Don Pedro: Yes.

Lucero: You would testify to that?

Don Pedro: Yes.

Lucero: With some proof?

Don Pedro: Yes.

Lucero: And present my position to their Majesties?

Don Pedro: I could try.

Lucero: As you please. *(Going.)* But you have never come to see me.

Don Pedro: *(Going.)* We have never met.

Lucero: I am completely ignorant of your existence.

Don Pedro: Completely.

Lucero: With God.

Don Pedro: With God. *(Exit DON PEDRO. Exit LUCERO. Music.)*

Scene 14

(Cathedral. AMBROSIO and ANTONIA. DON PEDRO behind them, listening.)

Antonia: I dream the same thing over and over. We are walking by a river and talking. I am naked, but you wrap me in a white gown of silk and we are climbing a huge mountain together. I run out of breath and choke. You breathe into my mouth and I am well again and so happy!
Ambrosio: Go and sin no more. Amen.
Antonia: Amen. Father. My mother is so sick and getting worse. She could die suddenly, without the blessing of the Church. I know you never leave the monastery except on Thursdays when you preach in the cathedral. But our carriage, covered, could bring you to us, and take you back.
Ambrosio: I am sequestered here. *(ANTONIA falls to her knees before AMBROSIO, her forehead on his leg.)*
Antonia: My mother needs you! I need you! Father!
Ambrosio: You're shaking.
Antonia: I depend on you! Bless my mother before she dies!
Ambrosio: Four o'clock. The western door of the Cathedral. *(Exit DON PEDRO.)*
Antonia: Thank you! *(Exit ANTONIA. Lights out on AMBROSIO. Music.)*

Scene 15

(THE HOLY OFFICE. A high backed chair. In it, the INQUISITOR. LUCERO stands beside him, with papers and pen. Enter DON PEDRO. He carries a portfolio.)

Don Pedro: I am grateful for this audience. *(THE INQUISITOR looks at the papers.)*
Lucero: Don Pedro Juan de Lastanosa.
Inquisitor: Where from?
Lucero: Murcia. What do you have to say?
Don Pedro: I hoped to marry a young woman named Antonia Dalfa. I engaged a painter, Martin Galuppi, to do miniature impressions of the Cathedral of the Capuchins and its famous monk since she admired it and him. The painter did the portraits. He became so interested in the Cathedral, he continued to make sketches of it. Last week, he came to me, shuddering. "You mustn't marry that woman," he said. "She is his."
Lucero: What?
Don Pedro: He overheard her confessing to him. She said she loved him. She was acting like she was his slave.
Inquisitor: Many young women become infatuated with priests.
Don Pedro: He said they were talking about the devil. I said I didn't believe him. "Go yourself," he said. "Wednesdays, early in the afternoon." I

went. I overheard them. Talking about being naked on a mountain, where they breathed into each others mouths. He is leaving his monastery on Wednesday, breaking his vows. He is going to her.

Lucero: To her house?

Don Pedro: Here is my deposition. The painter's deposition. That makes two. All that's necessary, I believe.

Lucero: Correct. *(DON PEDRO hands the INQUISITOR the depositions.)*

Don Pedro: My name, there. His, there.

Inquisitor: Do you fully understand what you are doing? *(DON PEDRO smiles at the INQUISITOR and at LUCERO.)*

Don Pedro: Oh, yes.

Inquisitor: Heresy is not about priests and love affairs.

Lucero: It is about traffic with the Devil.

Don Pedro: Otherwise I would not have bothered you.

Inquisitor: Where is the painter?

Don Pedro: He has returned to Italy.

Lucero: Where in Italy?

Don Pedro: I don't know. But his signature is verifiable. Martin Galuppi, the Venetian. Your procedure requires nothing else, I believe.

Lucero: He will be investigated.

Inquisitor: So will you.

Don Pedro: I am not afraid of the Inquisition.

Lucero: This will be seen to at once.

Don Pedro: Fine. Then arrest, if it pleases you, that heretic monk and his whore. Your Grace. *(Exit DON PEDRO.)*

Inquisitor: Ambrosio?

Lucero: Ambrosio.

Inquisitor: Heresy? Not Ambrosio.

Lucero: Reconsider this man. He has fallen. He is a sinner.

Inquisitor: That may be. But not a heretic.

Lucero: I *see* the difference. But for a monk this famous, the scandal is the same. You must take action.

Inquisitor: No, you don't see the difference. Scandals are only shocking. Heresy can shake the earth.

Lucero: Then let it!!

Inquisitor: Leave me! *(Exit LUCERO.)*

Inquisitor: Ambrosio? *(Blackout.)*

Scene 16

(Slow, somber music. Enter ANTONIA, then ELVIRA, very weak, in her

nightclothes, supported by AMBROSIO. ANTONIA sets two chairs facing each other. She and AMBROSIO help ELVIRA to sit, then AMBROSIO sits opposite ELVIRA and they quietly speak to each other while ANTONIA stands by, watching them with pleasure. AMBROSIO and ELVIRA cross themselves, and sit back, smiling at each other.)

Antonia: This is what I wanted. To have you here, with us. Thank you. *(ANTONIA helps ELIVRA up and supports her. They exit. AMBROSIO moves the chairs to a table and waits. ANTONIA re-enters. They sit at the table, facing each other. ANTONIA, content, smiles at AMBROSIO.)* "A river deep and profound." Do you remember that?

Ambrosio: Should I?

Antonia: You preached about it.

Ambrosio: I did?

Antonia: Rivers running through marriage beds. I found the words. It's Andalusian.

Ambrosio: Oh.

Antonia: Where did you hear it?

Ambrosio: I don't know. Maybe I read about it. What are the words?

Antonia: *(Reciting.)*

How shall I find my own true love?
How shall I live with my own true love?
How shall I sleep with my own true love?
To keep us close together?
Make me a bed with thick hard rope,
Make me a mattress strong,
Make me four oak posters tall,
To last our whole life long.
For down the middle of the marriage bed,
Flows a river deep and profound.
There let me find my own true love,
And live and sleep and drown.

(Pause.)

Ambrosio: Very nice.

Antonia: This is what I wanted. To have you here, with us. I can face life now as it is.

Ambrosio: And how is it—life?

Antonia: Better, thanks to you.

Ambrosio: I do very little.

Antonia: Until I confessed myself to you, I thought no one was really listening. God maybe, our Blessed Mother of God the Virgin Mary of course, but a human being—not one. You took me seriously, as I knew you would.

Ambrosio: How did you know I would?

Antonia: By looking at you. By seeing intelligence and kindness, put first. You have shown me what life is, and how I must live it.

Ambrosio: Have I?

Antonia: I can face marriage life now, as I know it will be. Just marriage with a man, who will be good to me, I hope. I believe in him because I believe in you.

Ambrosio: Marriage?

Antonia: I've had a proposal. From a man, to my surprise, I like very much.

Ambrosio: Have you slept with him?

Antonia: Of course not!

Ambrosio: Do you want to?

Antonia: Yes.

Ambrosio: With him or just a man?

Antonia: What's the matter with you? With him, my husband. My feelings for him are very strong.

Ambrosio: What are they, these feelings?

Antonia: I want to be a good wife, a good friend, and in time, a good mother.

Ambrosio: Do you want him to cut open your heart?

Antonia: What?

Ambrosio: To rip through your stomach like a knife?

Antonia: Well, no.

Ambrosio: Then your feelings are not as strong as you think.

Antonia: I think they are.

Ambrosio: For who? A *boy.*

Antonia: His name is Don Pedro Juan de Lastanosa. *(Pause.)* You met him once. *(Pause.)* Don't you remember? *(AMBROSIO stares at ANTONIA.)*

Ambrosio: Are you a demon, too?

Antonia: What?

Ambrosio: Could you be?

Antonia: What's wrong with you?

Ambrosio: If not, what are you? *(Pause.)*

Antonia: You're jealous!

Ambrosio: The man you are marrying is evil.

Antonia: I'm so sorry!

Ambrosio: He will destroy you.

Antonia: I've hurt you!

Ambrosio: Unless you've known him already!
Antonia: I wouldn't hurt you for anything in the world!
Ambrosio: That's what Rosario said!
Antonia: Who?
Ambrosio: Another demon. *(Pause.)* Suppose I am your husband?
Antonia: What?
Ambrosio: What else do you think we've been doing?
Antonia: I never meant for this to happen.
Ambrosio: TELL ME THE TRUTH!
Antonia: *(Shaken.)* All right!
Ambrosio: Do I cut open your heart?
Antonia: No.
Ambrosio: Rip through your stomach like a knife?
Antonia: No.
Ambrosio: Why can't I?
Antonia: I don't understand! *(They both get up.)*
Ambrosio: If you are only a woman, and nothing else—
Antonia: What else would I be?
Ambrosio: Then why not me, as well as him?
Antonia: I don't understand!
Ambrosio: Oh, please! *(AMBROSIO slams a small wooden ball down on the table.)*
Antonia: What's that?
Ambrosio: Something you told me about.
Antonia: What are you going to do?
Ambrosio: Open your mouth.
Antonia: No! *(AMBROSIO moves toward her with the ball. ANTONIA tries to run by him. He seizes and holds her from behind. They struggle.)* You're going to hurt me?
Ambrosio: Yes.
Antonia: But why? *(AMBROSIO tries to get ball into her mouth, but can't.)*
Ambrosio: You have to be one or the other!
Antonia: One or the other what?
Ambrosio: A slut or a demon!
Antonia: Slut? Demon?
Ambrosio: Or both!
Antonia: I gave you my love! *(AMBROSIO caresses her brutally.)*
Ambrosio: And your hair! And your mouth!
Antonia: Stop!
Ambrosio: And your breasts and your hips!
Antonia: You didn't mean any of it! *(AMBROSIO forces her to the table.)*

Ambrosio: All this time! Who talked about bodies and kissing?
Antonia: You've been playing with me!
Ambrosio: And you with me!
Antonia: You dreadful, terrible man!
Ambrosio: Over the table! *(AMBROSIO bends ANTONIA face forward over the table.)*
Antonia: Don't hurt me!
Ambrosio: We'll do it—
Antonia: Please!
Ambrosio: —like the dogs we are!
Antonia: I'll do anything you say! *(Enter ELVIRA, in her nightclothes, barely able to walk.)*
Elvira: Get away from her!! *(ELVIRA feebly hits at AMBROSIO.)*
Antonia: No, don't! *AMBROSIO grips both women by the throat, bending them over the table. A shaft of light, in which they all freeze. Music. Blackout.)*

Scene 17

(Prison of the Inquisition in Cordoba. THE INQUISITOR, with trial records, seated. Standing by him is LUCERO. AMBROSIO, on his knees before them.)

Lucero: You claim you were visited by a demon named Rosario.
Ambrosio: Yes, Father.
Lucero: Reply to His Grace.
Ambrosio: Yes, your Grace.
Lucero: In the form of a boy.
Ambrosio: Yes, your Grace.
Lucero: A novice in your monastery.
Ambrosio: Yes, your Grace.
Inquisitor: Ambrosio. Monks have testified there was no such person.
Ambrosio: Ah.
Lucero: The boy seduced you and led you to a meeting with Satan.
Ambrosio: Yes, your Grace.
Lucero: Who walks the earth disguised as a man, Don Pedro Juan de Lastanosa.
Inquisitor: While there is a Don Pedro Juan de Lastanosa, he is a widower from Murcia.
Lucero: With a family and records, and so on.
Inquisitor: He denounced you to us.

Lucero: As a heretic!

Inquisitor: Satan seduced you. He robbed you of your faith. He led you to attack Antonia Dalfa and Elvira Dalfa.

Ambrosio: Yes.

Lucero: It is now said in the streets they were your mother and your sister!

Ambrosio: What?

Inquisitor: Cordoba believes you raped and murdered your sister, then strangled your mother.

Ambrosio: I am an orphan.

Inquisitor: Elvira Dalfa did lose a son. Had he lived, he would be about your age.

Lucero: When you were left at the monastery door, monks say you were wrapped in a kind of cloth woven in the town of their birth. *(AMBROSIO nods. Pause.)*

Inquisitor: Will you confess to heresy, recant, and repent?

Ambrosio: Of course.

Lucero: But will you mean it?

Ambrosio: How can I tell? My love for the boy was not traffic with Satan. It was in me. My love for the woman was not traffic with Satan. It was in me. My violence was not traffic with Satan. It was in me! Who put it there? God put it there! Then he and Satan, who were lovers themselves, made a fool of me! God and Satan are lovers again! Burn me!

Lucero: He is pretending, badly, to be insane.

Inquisitor: You must demand of the Holy Office a final audience, which is your right.

Lucero: He has confessed! Why a final audience?

Inquisitor: Because I so advise him! *(To Ambrosio.)* You must say that while you are guilty of murder you were beset by delusions, not devils, and are innocent of heresy.

Lucero: I will not concur in this decision.

Inquisitor: Let us pray for him.

Lucero: I refuse.

Inquisitor: Then leave us, and do not return. *(Exit LUCERO.)* My old friend, let us pray for you. *(Lights out.)*

Scene 18

(GRAND COUNCIL. AMBROSIO, on his knees. THE INQUISITOR stands by him. LUCERO stands to one side.)

Inquisitor: Your Graces, the Holy Office in Cordoba must come to a

Council decision. A monk, of great reknown, caught by the Inquisition, and self-confessed, is a murderer. But he also says he is a heretic. You must decide if that is so, since I, your Inquisitor General find him a lunatic only, possessed by delusions of demons. The difference is crucial, since it must measure either human frailty or diabolical intervention. Fray Lucero does not concur, and will speak to you in his turn. *(Pause.)* Let us recall, for a moment, excesses of the past. Instance: Estella Manosa, of Burgos, testified that Christ removed her heart and replaced it with his own, and she therefore held the Trinity in her stomach. And she wouldn't give it back. Heresy. She was burned. Antonio Desplugas, Barcelona. He sucked the breasts of an angel named Trillias. Jesus Christ joined him in making love to Trillias while Satan sang sacred music, and danced. Heresy. He was burned. *(The INQUISITOR nods to LUCERO, who exits.)* These poor lunatics, along with witches and sorcerers, bandits and thieves, adulterers and all kinds of criminals, were swept to the stake by the zeal of our Holy Office. Murder we know this man committed. But heresy is a far different matter, with consequences not just for individuals, but for everyone alive. You have the testimonies before you. We summon two witnessess. *(Enter DON PEDRO and ROSARIO, followed by LUCERO.)*

Ambrosio: Ah!

Inquisitor: Is this Satan?

Ambrosio: Yes.

Inquisitor: Is this his demon, who seduced you?

Ambrosio: Yes.

Inquisitor: Your Graces, this gentleman is Don Pedro Juan de Lastanosa, a fisherman from Murcia. This is his nephew Rosario Cidan. Proof is in your records. Let them speak for themselves.

Don Pedro: I come from a very old family, living for centuries on the seacoast of this country.

Ambrosio: Devil.

Don Pedro: I came to Madrid to seek a wife. The woman I courted was the mistress of this monk. She agreed to marry me.

Ambrosio: Father of Lies.

Don Pedro: The next thing I knew this monk murdered her and her mother. I was not there, but I can reasonably suppose that when she told the monk she would marry me, he killed her in a jealous rage and then killed her mother to escape discovery.

Ambrosio: Prince of Darkness.

Don Pedro: I thank your Graces.

Rosario: I am Don Pedro's nephew.

Ambrosio: Lover.

Rosario: I am a novice, in a monastery, but not in the Monastery of the Capuchins. In the Monastery of the Benedictines, in Murcia.

Ambrosio: Demon.

Rosario: I visited Cordoba, with Don Pedro, a short time ago. We went to hear the famous monk, Ambrosio.

Ambrosio: Traitor.

Rosario: I was aware, while he preached about freedom and lust, he was staring at me.

Ambrosio: Fiend.

Rosario: Otherwise, I never met him.

Inquisitor: An unbalanced monk notices a handsome young man in church and the young man appears to him in his cell. His companion becomes the devil. Vanity, lunacy, and lust, but not heresy. You see it for yourselves. He thinks that man is Satan. Fray Lucero.

Lucero: I am shocked. I am appalled. If this is not heresy, I do not know what is. Yes, these men appeared to him, and seduced him. He came to think they were Satan and his demon and he was right! They were! Appearing in the forms of these innocent men! Do I have to remind our own Inquisitor General that Satan is not a prankster, but a supernatural force, second in intellect only to God? He walks the earth as he pleases, in what form he pleases, and no one, not the Pope in Rome, will say that is not true! But suppose Don Pedro Juan de Lastanosa denounced the monk out of his own jealousy, viciously seduced him with his nephew, to bring about his damnation. Has our Inquisitor General investigated that? No. I have. The Master of Novices here says that is impossible, the Master of Novices in Murcia says that is impossible. I had all four men arrested, and faced with torture. Shown the rack and the water bottle and the hoist, not one flinched. We could have broken their bones, but we didn't. Obviously, they were telling the truth. So. Lust for a boy, at first. Once begun, the desire is insatiable. He is overheard talking with a woman about rites with Satan, blowing into the Devil's mouth, and meeting Satan on a mountain. Ambrosio called the devil and he came, in the likeness of this man. And Ambrosio consorted with the devil, to commit bloody, heartless murder, very possibly incestuous murder, with his sister and his mother and even worse! Worse!! *(LUCERO holds up two pieces of the portarit of the Virgin.)* He made a painting of the the Blessed Virgin herself! WITH THE FACE OF HIS DEMON LOVER! HE TORE THAT FACE APART, BUT WE FOUND IT AND PIECED IT TOGETHER. HERE IT IS! *(LUCERO puts the two pieces of the portrait together.)* Does the Inquisitor General say THAT is innocent delusion? I say it is diabolical heresy, and what Ambrosio thinks he sees, though not true now, was true then! Gentlemen, tell him you're not the devils he thinks you are.

Don Pedro: *(To AMBROSIO.)* You poor man.

Ambrosio: Darkness clouds your face.

Don Pedro: I once believed you had a good heart and a clear mind.

Ambrosio: Over your shoulders I see two scarlet wings.

Don Pedro: But many who preach purity to others lose it in themselves.

Ambrosio: And in your hair serpents writhe.

Don Pedro: You thought that I was Satan.

Ambrosio: Lightning flashes around your face.

Don Pedro: While Satan was using you to kill the woman I loved.

Ambrosio: While your tongue reaches out for me, like a frog!

Don Pedro: With all my heart, I forgive you.

Ambrosio: You and God are lovers again.

Don Pedro: What?

Ambrosio: Why have you done this to me? Rosario!

Rosario: You are a madman. I never said a word to you in all my life.

Inquisitor: You may go. With God.

Don Pedro and **Rosario:** *(To AMBROSIO.)* With God. *(Exit DON PEDRO and ROSARIO.)*

Inquisitor: As is his right, the monk will make his final statement to you. *(THE INQUISITOR steps aside.)*

Ambrosio: Nothing I say or you say matters now.

Inquisitor: It does. Say what I told you.

Ambrosio: It doesn't matter that I had to love. It doesn't matter that I loved a boy and a young woman at the same time. It doesn't matter that I never meant to kill anyone. It doesn't matter that everyone says they were my mother and my sister. Only one thing matters now, and that is the truth. I was in love with what I was doing.

Inquisitor: Ambrosio!

Ambrosio: I still love everything I did. *(LUCERO steps forward.)*

Lucero: *(Quietly.)* Heresy, pure and simple.

Inquisitor: Heresy is never simple! Satan uses it to hit targets we don't know exist! A lunatic monk creates a scandal. It is nothing by itself, unless we make it into that greater arrow the Devil is aiming somewhere else. Put Ambrosio in a madhouse, or hang him, say no more, and avoid the Devil's trap, whatever it may be. Your Inquisitor General trusts to your wisdom and common sense. That is all.

Lucero: Not quite all.

Inquisitor: What? *(LUCERO takes a parchment to the INQUISITOR.)*

Lucero: Will you read it, or shall I?

Inquisitor: *(Reading.)* TO THE HOLY OFFICE OF THE INQUISITION

IN SPAIN, CORDOBA: FROM THEIR WISE AND GRACIOUS MAJESTIES OUR VALOROUS KING FERDINAND AND HIS BELOVED QUEEN ISABELLA: *(The INQUISITOR stops reading, and stares at the letter. LUCERO takes it back and finishes it.)*

Lucero: *(Reading.)* If the heretic will not repent, take his life and his property. Write it down in stone! Fray Diego Lucero is appointed Inquisitor General in Cordoba. Your King, your Queen. *(He smiles at the INQUISITOR.)* There!

Scene 19

Sounds: DIES IRAE, crowds, tumult, wind. Projections: the Procession of an Auto da Fe. Light on AMBROSIO, as he hears the voices of DON PEDRO and ROSARIO, amplified.)

Don Pedro (V.O.): Ambrosio!
Rosario (V.O.): Ambrosio!
Don Pedro (V.O.): Can you hear the people singing?
Rosario (V.O.): They celebrate the largest Auto da Fe in the history of Spain!
Don Pedro (V.O.): It is the action of Diego Lucero. *(LUCERO brings them two San Benitos, over-clothes for heretics. They are bright yellow, and on them are painted flames and black devils around the heretic's face. AMBROSIO and the INQUISITOR. LUCERO puts them on. LUCERO puts large concial caps on their heads, each marked, HERETIC. Exit LUCERO.)*
Rosario (V.O.): The most ferocious Inquisitor General ever!
Don Pedro (V.O.): Others will follow! In Seville!
Rosario (V.O.): Granada!
Don Pedro (V.O.): Valencia!
Rosario (V.O.): Badajoz!
Don Pedro (V.O.): Salamanca!
Rosario (V.O.): Valladolid!
Don Pedro (V.O.): Burgos!
Rosario (V.O.): Barcelona!
Don Pedro (V.O.): Madrid!
Rosario (V.O.): And who will burn?
Don Pedro (V.O.): Thousands and thousands of heretics will burn!
Rosario (V.O.): From the shacks to the castles!
Don Pedro (V.O.): Anyone!
Rosario (V.O.): Spaniards will burn!
Don Pedro (V.O.): Foreigners will burn!

Rosario (V.O.): Moors will burn!
Don Pedro (V.O.): Jews will burn!
Rosario (V.O.): Bishops will burn!
Don Pedro (V.O.): Archbishops will burn!
Rosario (V.O.): Saints will burn!
Don Pedro (V.O.): Endless chaos!
Rosario (V.O.): Endless violence!
Don Pedro (V.O.): Endless hatred!
Rosario (V.O.): Everyone is fighting again!
Don Pedro (V.O.): No one can stop what you have started!
Rosario (V.O.): The skies of Spain are dark with smoke!
Don Pedro: The wind will blow it across the world!
Rosario (V.O.): Now you are famous!
Don Pedro (V.O.): The lascivious monk who murdered his mother and his sister.
Rosario (V.O.): The Archbishop who defended him.
Don Pedro (V.O.): The Inquisitor who exposed them both.
Rosario (V.O.): Your ashes will cry out to all the world.
Don Pedro (V.O.): How well everything ends.
Rosario (V.O.): When evil is punished! *(AMBROSIO and THE INQUISITOR are left at the stake. Music, wind, voices, tumult stop.)*
Ambrosio: Are they coming?
Inquisitor: I can't tell. *(Pause.)* Yes! They're bringing the fire.
Ambrosio: I thought we would be last!
Inquisitor: Evidently not.
Ambrosio: The wind!
Inquisitor: It's blowing!
Ambrosio: The fire will burn us faster. Pray for me!
Inquisitor: I can't! Help me! Ambrosio knows the devil! I recant!
Ambrosio: Ah.
Inquisitor: I recant! I recant!
Rosario (V.O.): Your only friend deserts you! *(The INQUISITOR backs away into darkness.)* He will not feel the fire as you will.
Don Pedro (V.O.): They will strangle him to death.
Rosario (V.O.): Then burn you both. With God, Ambrosio.
Don Pedro (V.O.): With God, Ambrosio.
Ambrosio: With God. *(Enter LUCERO, now in the white hood of an INQUISITOR GENERAL, carrying a flaming torch which he places in a holder before AMBROSIO.)*
Lucero: Making an example of a heretical monk and a corrupt Inquisitor, we turn towards others. There will be no end to this. *(Exit LUCERO.*

AMBROSIO stands at the stake, fire burning before him.)

Ambrosio: If it is true there was no devil, no demon, and what I did, I did in madness, then why should I see them so clearly? I see them now, turning from me on shimmering wings, with faces so radiant! And I know they are terrible, but you my God, I cannot see at all. *(Light goes out on AMBROSIO. AMBROSIO steps back slowly into darkness. The fire burns for a moment. Spirited music. Curtain calls.)*

THE LOVE SUICIDE AT SCHOFIELD BARRACKS

C.O., a Brigadier General, thoughtful and sensitive.
CAPTAIN MARTIN, a capable young career officer.
SGT. BATES, a weathered, mature, sympathetic Sergeant in his 40's.
LORNA ANN BATES, his wife, a plainly dressed woman, once sexy and beautiful, 30's.
MISS NOMURA, a plain, hardworking Japanese secretary.
SGT. MAJOR RUGGLES, a blunt, ferocious career NCO.
LUCY LAKE, a down to earth, formidable New England poet, 60's.
COLONEL MOORE, a healthy, sardonic Chief of Staff.
EDWARD ROUNDHOUSE, a large, bitter, eloquent rich man.

Place: A conference room, Division Headquarters, Schofield Barracks, Oahu, Hawaii.

Time: 1970.

THE LOVE SUICIDE AT SCHOFIELD BARRACKS was first produced by Herbert Berghof at the H.B. Playwrights Foundation and by Cheryl Crawford at the ANTA Theatre in New York in 1971 and 1972. In one act, it was first produced at the Actors Theatre of Louisville in 1984. This version was produced by the Signature Theatre Company in New York, James Houghton, Artistic Director, in May, 1991, with the following cast:

CAPTAIN MARTIN................Kernan Bell
LORNA BATES.....................S.J. Floyd
SGT. BATES.........................James Seymour
LUCY LAKE.........................Mary Jane Wells
MISS NOMURA.....................Constance Boardman
COLONEL MOORE................Gordon C. Jones
SGT. MAJOR RUGGLES..........John Woodson
C.O.....................................Garrison Philips
ROUNDHOUSE.....................Fred Burrell

It was directed by Romulus Linney, music by Paul Earls, sets by E. David Cosier, costumes by Teresa Snider-Stein, lights by Jeffrey S. Koger, production stage manager, Ellen Melaver.

THE LOVE SUICIDE AT SCHOFIELD BARRACKS

A conference room at Division Headquarters, Schofield Barracks, Hawaii. Monday morning, November 1970.

Two small tables sit apart, one for Captain Martin and the other for the Commanding Officer. Between them is a rolling office chair. On a third table upstage are two wooden Japanese boxes. Seven chairs sit to one side.

Enter Captain Martin, a young career officer. He places files and papers on the two small tables and pushes the rolling chair to the center of the room.

He double checks the room. Then he opens the door and speaks to people outside it.

Martin: Please come in. *(Enter Sergeant Bates, Lorna Ann Bates, Colonel Moore, Katherine Nomura, Sergeant Major Ruggles, and Lucy Lake.)* Good morning. Thank you for coming. Please take a seat. As soon as the Commanding Officer arrives, we'll begin. *(They sit in the chairs. Martin sits, and checks them off his list. Enter the CO. He is a Brigadier General in his forties. Martin rises.)* The Commanding Officer of Schofield Barracks. *(The military personnel rise.)*

CO: Thank you for coming. Please be seated. *(To Martin.)* Are they all here?

Martin: Sir, all but one. A Mr. Edward Roundhouse.

CO: Who's he?

Martin: He owns several restaurants on Oahu.

CO: All right. We'll start. *(Quietly and politely.)* Ladies and gentlemen, this is an unusual and preliminary inquiry. It is authorized not by the Code of Military Justice, or by the Provost Marshall, but by a United States Army General Order, issued to me by my superior officer, the former Commanding General of Schofield Barracks. We will ask you some questions. You may answer or not. You may add whatever you wish. We thank you very much for whatever you have to say. Captain. *(He sits at his table.)*

Martin: Master Sergeant Norvel T. Bates, please. *(He indicates the desk chair. Sergeant Bates sits in it.)* Sergeant, you understand you are not required to answer under oath, or against your wishes?

Bates: I understand, sir.

Martin: You are on the General's staff?

Bates: I am the General's Enlisted Aide.

Martin: We have a note here, from the General, speaking of you very highly. You were aware of his esteem?

Bates: *(In sorrow.)* We knew each other pretty well.

Martin: You played a large part in his preparations. Can you describe that for us?

Bates: I'll do my best. Late Saturday morning, I was summoned to his quarters. He handed me a sealed manila envelope. In it was a General Order he had written out by hand and signed. I was ordered to process it myself, by myself. *(To the CO.)* I did, and that was the order you received, sir, to hold this inquiry.

CO: Right, Sergeant. Go ahead.

Bates: Then he asked me to sit down. He made me a drink. His wife joined us. Then he said something that surprised me. He told me he and his wife were writing a sort of skit. To do at the Officers' Club. I tried to show polite interest. But then they asked me to help them.

Martin: Write the skit?

Bates: No, sir. Be in it. They wanted me to read part of it aloud at the Officers' Club party. They said, "Here it is, look at it."

Martin: What did you think of it?

Bates: I thought it was silly. I didn't understand it. When I saw one of the last lines said, "I will wait for you in heaven, my noble husband," I thought, oh Lord. But, sir, I can't tell you how much I admire the General and his wife. And if what they wanted to do was make fools of themselves at an Officers' Club party, I was glad to help out.

Martin: What else were you asked to do?

Bates: On the porch, as I was leaving, the General gave me keys to his front door and verbal instructions. He told me no matter what happened Saturday night, I was to return to his quarters directly after the party and take possession of papers I would find on a card table in the living room. And I did that. In shock, but I did it.

Martin: Describe the papers.

Bates: First, the will. The General and his wife liquidated their estate. It was a lot of money, and they left it all to an Oriental-American orphanage in Honolulu. There is a certified check already in the mail to that orphanage now. I put it there, by his order.

Martin: How much was it?

Bates: Three hundred and fifty-five thousand dollars. They gave that orphanage everything they had.

Martin: What else did you find?

Bates: Many resignations, from all sorts of things he belonged to. On top, his resignation from the American Archery Association, and from the Army of the United States. I was to mail those, too. And then—of course, their bodies.

Martin: What about them?

Bates: Notarized document, donating their bodies to a civilian research hospital in Honolulu.

Martin: Thank you, Sergeant. Anything else?

Bates: Yes, sir. This envelope, sealed. It says on the front that I am to open it and read its contents at the end of this inquiry, if as the General directed, it is held here. If not, I am to destroy it. His signature is on it, there.

CO: Let me see that please. *(Martin takes the envelope quickly to the CO. He looks at it carefully, and gives it back.)* That's what you'll do, Sergeant. As ordered.

Bates: Yes, sir.

CO: Thank you very much. Is there anything you yourself would like to add?

Bates: Yes, sir. I want to say that I still admire the General. He was the best soldier I ever saw.

Martin: Thank you. Please remain in the room. Miss Katherine Nomura, please. *(Bates goes to his seat. A Japanese woman takes the chair.)* Miss Nomura, this is an informal inquiry, conducted along lines suggested by the General in his order. You may answer or not and we are obliged for your help. Do you understand?

Miss Nomura: Oh, yes.

Martin: How long have you been in the service of the General?

Miss Nomura: Four days.

Martin: How did you come to work for him?

Miss Nomura: I was sent to him from a commercial bureau. I fitted his requirements.

Martin: What were your duties?

Miss Nomura: Very light secretarial work, for his wife. I know now, of course, it was to read what was written. Which also explains his requirements.

Martin: What were they?

Miss Nomura: They were for a female with some knowledge of Japanese culture. Who should have one other qualification I prefer not to mention. He had trouble finding me.

Martin: And you read it aloud, with Sergeant Bates, on Saturday night?

Miss Nomura: Yes.

Martin: What did you think of it?
Miss Nomura: I thought it was very beautiful.
Martin: Why?
Miss Nomura: I knew what it was they had written. It was a shinju.
Martin: And what is that?
Miss Nomura: A love suicide. A kind of play, in which lovers, who cannot live together any longer, commit suicide together. There have been a great many of them.
Martin: Do you mean plays, or love suicides?
Miss Nomura: Both.
Martin: I see. Now, Miss Nomura—
Miss Nomura: Please. One other thing. It is not a sin or a disgrace. It is not an act of psychological selfhatred. It is release from illusion. It is embrace of eternal truth. Their life then becomes a poem they leave behind, and is considered a great achievement. Many believe they are taken directly into heaven and are reborn on lotus leaves. Thank you.
Martin: I see. Now, Miss Nomura—
CO: *(Breaking in.)* Miss Nomura, did you therefore have some idea of the actual purpose of the play?
Miss Nomura: Oh, yes.
CO: You *did?*
Miss Nomura: I said yes.
CO: You mean you knew Saturday night they were going to kill themselves?
Miss Nomura: I knew they were going to act out a shinju. It did occur to me they might be in earnest.
CO: Then pardon me, Miss Nomura, why didn't you tell anyone?
Miss Nomura: That would have spoiled a shinju. *(Pause.)* And who would have believed me? Would you?
CO: What else did they tell you about what they were going to do?
Miss Nomura: Nothing. I was to meet with Sergeant Bates at the Officers' Club at about ten o'clock. We were to read our parts while they performed on the dance floor.
CO: And you understood what they might really do?
Miss Nomura: I said yes. *(Pause.)* If a man and his wife decide the home they loved has become ugly, and seek a better one, is that impossible to understand?
CO: Thank you very much.
Martin: Is there anything you wish to add?
Miss Nomura: Oh, yes. I am glad I saw what I saw. *(She gets up and sits again in her chair. The CO stares at her for a moment, then nods to Captain Martin.)*

CO: Who's next?

Martin: Sergeant Major Reuben H. Ruggles, please. *(A calm, quietly arrogant soldier in his forties takes the chair. He carries a handsome swagger stick.)* Sergeant Major, do you understand the informal nature of these proceedings? That you don't have to answer a question if you don't want to?

Ruggles: I do, sir.

Martin: The General tells us here that you first served under him in Korea. As a platoon sergeant in a line company.

Ruggles: That's right.

Martin: His directive characterizes you as an outstanding combat NCO.

CO: And I can certainly agree with that.

Ruggles: I thank you, sir.

Martin: After giving us his opinion of you, Sergeant Major, what the General asks for now, is your opinion of him.

Ruggles: Yes, sir. *(Quickly.)* He was a great General, it was my privilege to serve under him.

Martin: There's a note here that you had a conversation with him, in his office, last week. Is that correct? *(Ruggles, surprised, pauses then nods.)* Can you tell us about that?

Ruggles: *(Slowly.)* If I have to.

Martin: You don't have to. The General asks you to.

Ruggles: Oh, he does, does he?

Martin: Can you tell us about your conversation with him?

Ruggles: To some degree, Captain, sir. A private, D Company, 19th Infantry Brigade, a black man, had a nervous breakdown on the rifle range Friday morning. Live rounds. It was dangerous. He was disarmed by big Georgia Sergeant with a big red neck, who fractured the black man's skull. There was going to be real trouble. The General took action.

Martin: What did he do?

Ruggles: Several ineffective things. Then he consulted me.

Martin: And what did you do?

Ruggles: I figured the racial incident, or whatever was going to happen, might happen on Saturday, the next morning, at the full Division parade. The General sent his black cadre around Friday night and posted all his bulletins. Saturday morning, at the parade, we'd see. Now, in two months, a black Sergeant, 12th Artillery, after his twenty years, was supposed to get out. Slated for a little parade. Two horns and a drum outside a quadrangle, where some Major would shake his hand, and that would be that. So, on Friday night, I had a chat with a Personnel Specialist and then another one with our black Artillery Sergeant. I told him he was going to retire the next morning. He really didn't want to retire the next morning, but I convinced him.

Martin: Of what?

Ruggles: To go home when he was told. Saturday morning, this Division massed for parade. Band started, flags unfurled and when seven thousand combat ready troops thundered past the reviewing stand, with tanks and artillery and choppers whirling in the air—wind, flags, the great Army in all its glory—who do you think was standing up there to receive all those salutes? The General and his black Sergeant, honored on the day of his retirement. Whose name, by the way is Caesar. That's right. Sergeant Nelson O. Caesar. Well, everybody saluted the colors and the colors saluted everybody and it was all just one big happy family.

Martin: In other words, Sergeant Major, what you did was put a black man in a window. Is that what you're so proud of? *(Ruggles stops laughing, looks mildly but dangerously at Captain Martin.)*

Ruggles: You best not talk to me like that, son, sir. I am nearing the end or a long and honorable career. You ain't, not yet.

Martin: After the parade, the General had a talk with you. What did you say to each other? If you please. *(Ignoring Martin, Ruggles speaks directly to the CO.)*

Ruggles: General, sir, what do I have to do here? Six weeks before I retire! I am only an enlisted man. I respectfully ask you to direct me.

CO: Follow your conscience and say what you please. Whatever you say will be to your credit.

Ruggles: *(Doubtfully.)* Yeah. Thank you, sir. If that's what you want.

CO: That's what we want.

Ruggles: After the parade, he took me into his office, closed the door, pulled out a bottle of Jack Daniels. And we had a drink together.

Martin: And that was all?

Ruggles: No, that wasn't all. He thanked me for the saving of his ass. Because putting Caesar up there probably stopped a race riot, and certainly saved his ass. He was grateful, or something. Anyway, he wanted to talk. Like we was chums.

Martin: What did he say?

Ruggles: Lots of dumb things nobody knows the answer to. If I really thought the new all-professional Army could become a black dumping ground. If the Army was getting like a big corporation that could plan but couldn't fight. Things like that.

Martin: What did you say?

Ruggles: I said I didn't know, what else? I reckoned a mostly black Army would have mostly black officers and mostly black parades, like in Haiti, and I reckoned men would always fight but I wasn't sure about officers. He didn't like any of that, and changed the subject.

Martin: To what?

Ruggles: Sergeant Caesar. "Good Soldier?" "Damn right," I said. "Just like his namesake. Julius Caesar served Rome, and so did Sergeant Nelson O. Caesar and so do I. We serve Rome for twenty years and Rome serves us for twenty years and we all got it made. "I don't see the connection, Sergeant," he said. "Well, General," I said, "maybe that's because you're not a Roman, really, and Sergeant Caesar is and I am. And if you're not, then I pity you."

CO: Sergeant Major, you spoke that way to your commanding General?

Ruggles: Why not, sir? I'd just saved his damned ass for him, hadn't I? One chance in twenty years to talk turkey to a General. Shit, I let go. I told him the Army he believed in didn't exist. That it was a god damned fairy tale he was told at West Point. That I found out what the Army really was in Korea. "Korea?" he said, politely, as if remembering the country was all I'd meant. "Yes, sir, Korea," I said. "When you and me was young, General, and we made our bargains with Rome." "I don't know what your bargain was, Sergeant," he said. "Mine was to serve my country." "Mine was to kill," I said, "and serve myself. To do what I was told to do, so my country would serve me. The trouble with you is, General, you just don't like what your country wants you to do." He didn't fancy that idea, neither, and changed the subject again.

CO: To?

Ruggles: Nostalgia. Maybe he thought that would be safe. "What I remember about Korea," he said, "is great long lines of marching men, ice cold nights, bleak Asian skies, and the hard, lonely duty of serving your country." "What I remember," I said, "is a damn good Roman soldier staying alive. White men, black men, Rome takes us on. Then murders us, if it needs to. But if we survive, we have earned our good name and we are honorably retired with it. 'Fair enough,' I said twenty years ago and so did Sergeant Caesar. Duty, honor, country, like they say at West Point. But hell fire, for me and Caesar, it wasn't to die for our god damn duty, it was to kill for the god damn Army! Kill for it and live! Tell me it's hard? You think I don't know that, General? I've seen a few people die in the war. My SON, my own SON, HE died in the god damn war, General! But not me. I'm alive, and I kill for this Army and live! Make money off the fucking P.X. for it, and live! Serve up slant-eyed pussy to Generals like you for it, and live! You don't have to tell me my duty, General. I know all about it. You give it to me and I done it, and so did my boy, whatever it was. He didn't live, but I did, to my honorable old age, and by God, I expect Rome to keep its bargain! I understand what the real Army is, and I would rather have the common virtue of a down-in-the-dirt, dog-face killer, than the glory of a fake like you!" *(Pause.)* And that was the end of the interview. Well, sir?

CO: It's a good thing you're retiring in six weeks. Anything else?

Ruggles: As a matter of fact, there is. When the General took over this Division, he gave me and the two other Sergeant Majors a swagger stick. This one here. He said he wasn't the smartest man in the world but he was smart enough to know who understood the Army: old time Regimental Sergeant Majors. He was always going to depend on us to tell him the truth when no one else would. Well, that's exactly what I did.

CO: Please remain in the room.

Ruggles: Thank you, sir. I prefer not to. *(He walks deliberately out of the room.)*

CO: Next.

Martin: Sir, next on the General's list is Lucy Lake.

CO: Is she here?

Lucy Lake: Yes, I'm here. *(An extremely plain, blunt, white-haired, down-to-earth old New England woman takes the stand.)*

CO: Miss Lake, in his directive, the General tenders you an apology for taking up more of your valuable time. And speaking for the rest of us, allow me to thank you very much for coming here today.

Lucy Lake: All right.

CO: Poets are not usually close friends with Generals. Am I right about that?

Lucy Lake: No. I knew Archie Wavell in World War II very well. He loved poets.

CO: A British General, I believe. In America, however?

Lucy Lake: America however, nope. Rare.

CO: You understand, Miss Lake, the nature of these proceedings?

Lucy Lake: I get the idea.

CO: How did you come to meet the General?

Lucy Lake: I didn't. He came to meet me.

CO: When?

Lucy Lake: Last summer.

CO: Can you tell us about this meeting please?

Lucy Lake: Breadloaf Conference, Middlebury, Vermont. Writers meet would-be writers, who pay to come, listen, and have their material read.

CO: Mike had been writing what—poetry?

Lucy Lake: Yep.

CO: And he went there on his leave?

Lucy Lake: Yep.

CO: Go on.

Lucy Lake: That's it. I was working with the poets. We all met.

Martin: What was your opinion of the General's poetry?

Lucy Lake: Not just his. His wife's too.

Martin: Their poetry, then.

CO: What did you think of it?

Lucy Lake: Oh, they were dilettantes, but not impossible. Bad, but not always completely. But, poets, you see, love very specific things, the concrete particulars of life, while Generals can be general. You could see that wrong with him. He didn't understand it at first, but he learned. And he did have a feeling for building, making a poem. Bringing disparate elements together. Yet I felt it was his wife who was truly remarkable.

CO: As a person, or a poet?

Lucy Lake: Both. Poets are people, General, even when they may seems mysterious to you as generals do to me. She was a lovely woman. It was my pleasure to know her.

Martin: Did they say or do anything unusual at this writers' conference?

Lucy Lake: No. He was very self-conscious. Said he was retired. He and his wife seldom came to the parties with everybody else. They worked on their poems. Took longs walks. Looked at Vermont, the mountains and the stars. They had a quiet, enriching cultural experience, just like it says in the brochure.

Martin: How about you, may I ask?

Lucy Lake: I was drunk most of the time. It's a fun two weeks.

CO: When did you hear from them again?

Lucy Lake: Just a month ago. Three lectures on American poetry, University of Hawaii. Money. I was in the newspaper, and the General called. So I spent the last two weeks with them in a little beach cottage they'd rented for me.

CO: Miss Lake, you have been seeing them for the past two weeks?

Lucy Lake: Yep.

CO: Well?

Lucy Lake: Well?

Martin: Well, haven't you any—didn't you notice—

Lucy Lake: I noticed a lot! Some of it I may tell you about, and some of it I may not. You ask the questions, and I'll make up my mind as we go along.

CO: Certainly. But the first question is this: You're hostile to everything here, aren't you?

Lucy Lake: Yep.

CO: Okay. In your meetings and conversations with the General and his wife, did they ever indicate anything unusual about themselves?

Lucy Lake: General, you are going to have to be more specific.

CO: I'll do my best. Did they talk about suicide?

Lucy Lake: Nope.

Martin: Criticize the Army? The country?

Lucy Lake: Never.

Martin: Did they exhibit psychological peculiarities? Show nervous strain? Act or think in strange ways?

Lucy Lake: No. I did all that. They were fine, always quite composed. We simply talked about poetry and watched the sea. They drank a little, I drank a lot, and exhibited psychological peculiarities.

Martin: I see.

Lucy Lake: Good.

CO: But Miss Lake, didn't anything about the General say anything to you—about his despair, his impending suicide?

Lucy Lake: Nope.

CO: Well, perhaps the man was trying, Miss Lake, and you were too drunk to pay him any attention! Is that a possibility?

Lucy Lake: They talked about writing something Japanese, using poetry and masks. I suggested they read Chickamatsu. They liked one of his plays in particular. From what I hear, their own was a copy of it.

CO: What play is that?

Lucy Lake: The Love Suicides at Sonezaki. Famous, in Japan. *(Pause.)* That was the last visit.

CO: Miss Lake, what did you think about an American Army General and his wife doing such a thing?

Lucy Lake: I thought it unutterably sad. Sobering. At their age, watching them try to find a life in poetry. They began like good children, slightly worshipful. Stealing quietly into the world of art, a magic forest they thought filled with mossy groves and dappled pastures and innocent living things. Finding instead the pits and swamps and the true difficulties of the animals within—ahh!

CO: Please take your time.

Lucy Lake: Well, Sheila. What a waste! She must have been so cheerful once! Not beautiful, but—radiant, whole, a good American girl! A Navy nurse, picked up by a young Army Captain, as they stood wondering in front of the great golden Buddha at Kamakura. They had just conquered Japan. So they shacked up, took a trip. Nikko, Nara, Fuji, the Inland Sea, everywhere. Then they married. They loved each other, Japan, and the Army. In twenty years, they managed to spend only seven west of Hawaii.

And then it all—well.

CO: And then?

Lucy Lake: Oh, Jesus, General! If you don't know, how can I tell you? Ask me another!

CO: Well, I don't know, Miss Lake! And, yes, I certainly will ask you another. The General and his wife killed themselves. Do you know why?

Lucy Lake: And if I do, and if I tell you, do you suppose I'd believe you would ever take me seriously?

CO: Well, why do you think you were asked to come here?

Lucy Lake: Oh, because my name was on that list. For the recording session.

CO: The what?

Lucy Lake: Recording session. That's all this is. We're his secretaries, scribes! The General has us here writing it all down for him, what he made happen through us. We were all used. Somehow. Still are. *(Pause.)* Bringing his disparate elements together.

CO: That may be.

Lucy Lake: Has to be. Why weren't you there, by the way?

CO: At the Officers' Club?

Lucy Lake: Sure. You were second in command. Number two, right?

CO: Yes.

Lucy Lake: Well, where were you?

CO: In the field. Inspecting a supply base, on another island.

Lucy Lake: And who sent you there?

CO: The General.

Lucy Lake: Sure.

CO: In any case, Miss Lake, believe me, whatever you have to say, I will take seriously.

Lucy Lake: Promise?

CO: Promise.

Lucy Lake: Okay. Ask.

CO: The General is dead. Why?

Lucy Lake: Because he came to believe, literally now, something dreadful. And his wife had the courage to agree with him.

CO: And what was that?

Lucy Lake: That he was a sort of child murderer. That he had murdered his son.

CO: Miss Lake, the General's son was a grown man. A combat Marine. He was killed in action in 1965, near Danang.

Lucy Lake: Precisely.

CO: The horrors of war? Well, my dear Miss Lake.

Lucy Lake: Well, my dear General. *(The CO laughs, throws up his hands.)* Yeah, you see?

CO: What?

Lucy Lake: You were going to take me seriously, remember?

CO: Well, I'm sorry, but I expected something more worthy of Lucy Lake.

Lucy Lake: And I expected you to keep your word.

CO: I beg your pardon. You say the General believed he'd murdered his son. How? And now let me ask you to be specific.

Lucy Lake: He believed he had done his duty. He believed his duty led to the useless death of this son. He questioned his duty and his country. He decided he had become a moral lunatic.

CO: A what?

Lucy Lake: Mo—ral lun—a—tic.

CO: What did doing his duty have to do with the death of his son?

Lucy Lake: It was the murder weapon. The instrument of homicide.

CO: You don't make sense.

Lucy Lake: Call it poison. He had poisoned his son. That help? *(The CO sits back in his chair, and looks at Martin.)*

Martin: Did the General ever say he'd murdered his son?

Lucy Lake: Not in words.

Martin: Did his wife?

Lucy Lake: No.

Martin: You never overheard them say that?

Lucy Lake: No.

Martin: And you still insist—

Lucy Lake: Insist the General believed he had murdered his son. And his wife did, too. Yes.

CO: How can you—with your book review platitudes—insult a good servant of his country, a wonderful father to his son? Mike and I both had sons killed in action. Mike never pushed his boy to the service and neither did I. They ran to it! They embraced it! Mike and his son, my dead boy and I, we were all proud of *any* life given for our country! And your pompous attitude here is obscene!

Lucy Lake: Bullshit, General! Don't you talk to me about dead children! Pompous am I? You son-of-a-bitch, you make those boys serve one solid year in that deathtrap. You watch them die from your helicopters, and then fly home to your bloody promotions! Don't call me obscene!

CO: Oh, please. What do you know about military life? It's Sheila you keep talking about. Just why were you here, messing about in her life?

Lucy Lake: Old dyke, General! Who's been through wars you would never survive! *(She holds up one hand.)* But. You seem like a decent man. I'm sorry about your son. We should speak to each other with respect. Mike and I did.

CO: So we should. I beg your pardon.

Lucy Lake: And of course you're right. I did stay to be with Sheila. I don't often find someone I like as much as I liked her. We became good friends. On those afternoons by the sea, we knitted, Sheila and I, and talked about poetry and children.

CO: I can't understand that. I knew them longer and better than you did. They grieved. But they knew why their son died. They loved their country as well as their child. They wouldn't write amateur romantic poetry about that. *(Lucy Lake opens her purse, takes out a piece of paper.)*

Lucy Lake: This is a sonnet. Written together. Shall I?

CO: Yes. *(LUCY LAKE reads it critically, like a writing teacher.)*

Lucy Lake:

ON MAKING LOVE AGAIN
But for this night and rain we wouldn't weep,
As that dear face fades slowly from our keep.
And we drink gallons, press our souls to sleep,
And in this world alone no harvest reap.
(She looks at the CO.)
Backs again should bend, old fists be furled,
As if from sperm and womb we'd simply hurled
His being, so deep in our ambition curled,
Away! Right now! Into some better world.
(She looks at the CO.)

It's dry, my love, to bear these dreams we seek,
And tears at night fit best the treacherous meek.
I've watched my heart, I know the blood-sharp beak
Run through it is my own: it mends next week.
But wet and heedless rain undoes the national spite,
And my corrupted love is yours through rain and night.
(Pause. Lucy Lake shrugs.)
Romantic poets today are all in the Army.

CO: Is there anything else you'd like to say?

Lucy Lake: I'd like to tell you something.

CO: Fire.

Lucy Lake: I was married, General. Three times, years ago. Before I learned what I know about myself now, that I destroy as much as I create. I, too, had a son who died. At Harvard, where he should never have been. A battlefield where he wanted to please me. Where he perished.

CO: I'm truly sorry. But that's more like it. It's your son you've been talking about here. I understand.

Lucy Lake: My son and yours, General. And Mike's. Ours. *(Pause. She looks around.)* Wait a minute. Has anyone else—called here today—lost a son—or a child—in any way?

Miss Nomura: That was the General's other qualification for his private secretary.

Bates: Yes.

Mrs. Bates: Our firstborn.

Moore: Me, too. And Sergeant Ruggles.

CO: And mine.

Lucy Lake: Building a poem.

CO: Thank you very much. Please stay.

Lucy Lake: Sure. It's my story, too.

CO: Next.

Martin: Colonel Robertson H. Moore, please. *(Colonel Moore, a thin, healthy, sardonic man, gets up and goes to the witness chair.)*

Moore: And I do understand the nature of this inquiry et cetera, et cetera, and I am Robertson H. Moore, Colonel U.S. Army, Chief of Staff, this Division, and I know exactly why the General got me down on his little list and why I'm here and what I'm supposed to say and I'll be just delighted to say it.

CO: *(Smiling.)* All right, Robie. Go ahead.

Moore: A pleasure. I suppose I'm here to give the minority report, my usual function. I really don't mean to dance on the man's grave, but I disagreed with the General on just about every idea he ever had. The only thing I approved was the way he played poker. That he knew how to do. And his archery, of course. But tennis, his mind collapsed every second set. And golf, a game of fidelity and endurance, well, to watch him go to pieces inside a constant framework was to realize that he was a profoundly childish man. It sometimes passes for intelligence. Sorry, ladies and gentlemen, but that's the freezing truth.

CO: And just what we want you to say, Robie. Go on.

Moore: You really don't have to call me "Robie." Little telegrams are no doubt replacing both of us at this moment: you as executive officer and heir apparent, and me as his ridiculous chief of staff. He appointed me above my time in rank, kept me there against my wishes. He also started calling me "Robie," with nauseating condescension.

CO: I beg your pardon, Colonel. Your record speaks for itself. You've been very effective.

Moore: Well, I do have my passion for details. Okay. But that isn't why he put me here, over the heads of at least five other officers. He made me his chief of staff because I was a thorn in his side. Due to the chemistry of our personalities, or whatever, I could never lie to him. Or flatter him. He kept me with him because I always told him what I thought of his decisions, and him. And I disapproved of that more than anything.

CO: You disapproved of a superior officer who allowed you to speak honestly to him?

Moore: Of course! That isn't the way this Army or any other Army works, and you know it and I know it and he knew it! As a matter of fact it isn't the way anything works, as everybody knows! But it was his perverse nature to be—well, illustration, please. May I? I mean, I can't be sued for slander, can I?

CO: You can't be sued for slander, Colonel.

Moore: Fine. That Italian place down the pike, you know, was his favorite off-post restaurant. It's pretty dependent on the military, so of course the waiters all peed in their britches every time he walked in the door. Okay, fine. But you see, he made them play it the other way around. They had to joke with him—ha, ha—and pick on him and kid him and bully him a little, you know—ho, ho—so he could just be one of the boys there. Another good fellow, who belonged, and who'd get it, just like anybody else, if he stepped out of line. Christ, you half expected him to go out and lay some bricks with them on weekends. Pals, real sports, and it was pathetic to watch him. Sickening. You might have respected the man if he'd made those flunkies bang their heads on the floor and run their tails off when they brought him his Chateaubriand—I think he hated Italian food—but watching him play that game with them made me want to vomit. Because that's what I was! Honest, outspoken, independent Chief of Staff, nothing. I was his flunky Italian waiter, and I hated it, and him.

CO: All right, Colonel Moore. You've filed your minority report. Did you have any specific confrontation with him just before the incident?

Moore: Well, I fought with him damn near every day, you know, so I hold out to you an embarrassment of riches. But the biggest fight we had, and the gem, was, of course, about the President.

CO: President?

Moore: Yes. Of the United States. Yes.

CO: You mean the conference?

Moore: That's right. That was called off. That's right.

CO: Well, what about it?

Moore: As everybody knows, on September 15th, the President of the United States announced another Hawaiian conference with representatives of our noble allies in Indochina. Word had come down to the General almost six weeks ago. September 25th. Same old thing. Three days of the President in Hawaii. The General had a fit.

CO: Why?

Moore: Oh, God knows. He was full of little explosions. He bitched and raved about the preparations involved, when he knew the President would never come within thirty miles of Schofield. Then he said the hell with it, and left the paperwork to me. Okay. Five days later, with steam coming out of his ears, he wanted to know why the hell our contingency plans for the arrival in Hawaii of the Commander in Chief weren't smoldering red-hot on his desk. "Because you said the hell with it," I said. So he hopped all over me, and I hopped and we both hopped.

CO: Why the sudden change in attitude? Duty?

Moore: Hardly. This General's idea of his military duty was much too sophisticated to include anything as simple as obedience. No, what happened was brand new. Army Headquarters had now scheduled the President, if he felt like it on Saturday night, to visit Schofield Barracks and attend a party at the Officers' Club. Now, the General thought that was just dandy, so we worked like hell.

CO: But that conference was called off.

Moore: Right. Poof. Fini. No Hawaii conference with Indochina. No Saturday night with the President. The General, surprise, after all that work, wasn't angry. No, he had a strange, dippy, far-off look in his eyes, as if he was dreaming about something impossible, and he said, "Well, we'll just pretend he came. We'll have a chair marked RESERVED, pretend he came, and have the party anyway." And that was that. *(Pause.)*

CO: Interesting.

Moore: Yes, isn't it. *(Pause.)*

CO: Well, Colonel, were there any other confrontations you wanted to tell us about?

Moore: You don't get it, do you?

CO: Get what, Colonel?

Moore: Never mind. Neither do I. But it's here, somewhere. Yes, there was another confrontation, of sorts. A day or so later. He came into my office and put a photograph from a newspaper on my desk. Of a Buddhist monk in flames. You saw the gasoline all over him, burning. You could see the suicide in the fire, looking out at you. "How about that?" said the General. I was mad at him. "Barbecued gook," I said. "So what?"

CO: Colonel Moore!

Moore: Sure I did. He looked at me with profound distaste while I so regarded him. And I thought, to hell with this. "It is a pathetic, useless gesture," I said. "It is utterly un-American. What does it accomplish?"

And he just looked at me a minute, and then, by God, he slapped me on the back. "You're absolutely right," he said. "There has to be something more. There has to be something more." And he walked out of the room.

CO: What did he mean?

Moore: Who knows? Maybe what he did. Maybe something we haven't got yet. Anyway, nothing more from me, except I was there Saturday night, and I find most extraordinary the justice of it. I still can't believe he did it, but the man gave himself exactly what he deserved.

CO: Now, Robie!

Moore: *(Quickly.)* Sorry! I didn't mean that. *(Pause.)* Oh, hell yes I did. You see? It's hard being a United States Army Colonel and an Italian waiter at the same time. Sorry. *(He steps down.)*

Martin: Mrs. Norvel T. Bates, please. *(A woman in her thirties takes the chair. She is very decorous and proper, dressed in a simple ladies suit.)* Mrs. Bates, this inquiry does not require you to answer if you don't want to. Is that clear?

Mrs. Bates: Yes, sir.

Martin: You are Lorna Ann Bates, married to Sergeant Norvel T. Bates, Headquarters Company, this Division?

Mrs. Bates: Yes, sir.

Martin: You live here at Schofield, in Army housing, with your husband and three children?

Mrs. Bates: Yes, sir.

Martin: Mrs. Bates, you are also in charge of the Schofield Day Care Center?

Mrs. Bates: Yes, sir. *(Enter Edward Roundhouse, a large man, with a tortured look, wearing casual, comfortable clothes.)*

Roundhouse: *(To Mrs. Bates.)* Excuse me. *(To others.)* I am looking for a Captain Martin.

Martin: I am Captain Martin. Please have a seat. I'll be with you in just a moment. *(He indicates a seat with the others, turns back to Mrs. Bates. Roundhouse sits down.)* Mrs. Bates, is it true that the expansion of the Children's Day Care Center was the General's idea?

Mrs. Bates: Oh, yes. And his wife's. There wasn't much to it until they came.

CO: And brought you.

Mrs. Bates: And brought me, yes, sir.

Martin: Mrs. Bates, we have no particular questions here to ask you. By your name the General noted that you would know what to tell us, and that he hoped you would. Do you understand what he meant?

Mrs. Bates: Yes, I'm afraid I do.

Martin: Are you willing, then, to talk about it?

Mrs. Bates: I guess I have to. If that's what he wanted. Like I say, everything at the Children's Center was just wonderful until about three weeks ago. Then they took to coming to the playground together, every day. Something was different about them. I don't know how to describe it. They just stood there by the fence, watching. Then, about ten days ago, they told me they wanted a child.

Martin: I beg your pardon?

Mrs. Bates: They said they wanted a child, for the Officer's Club party. A little boy who could be in a play.

Martin: What was your answer?

Mrs. Bates: To them? We have twelve orphans four afternoons a week. Mostly Eurasians, GI fathers, abandoned by both parents. They're sent to us for the chance to play with other children. So I called.

Martin: Called who?

Mrs. Bates: The Orphanage. They said as long as the General and his wife were responsible, of course. So I introduced them to a new little friend we have: Yoshida Robinson. Yoshi is six and a half.

CO: Mrs. Bates, are you telling us that a child, from an orphanage, was being prepared by the General and his wife to take part in an act of violence?

Mrs. Bates: No, of course they wouldn't do that! But—Yoshi was supposed to have been there, and was, except for me—

CO: Except for you?

Mrs. Bates: I took Yoshi away from there. When they came out with those masks on, I just took him home.

CO: Be glad you did.

Mrs. Bates: Yes, I am glad I did, but after all they had done for me, I—

Moore: All they did for you, Mrs. Bates, was use you. Can't you see that?

Mrs. Bates: That's not true!

CO: Well, Mrs. Bates, they did in fact involve you, and through you, a child. Why?

Mrs. Bates: I don't know why!

CO: Mrs. Bates, you prevented what looks like an act of cruelty.

Mrs. Bates: Cruel? Them? *(She jumps out of her chair, goes to her husband.)* Oh, Norvel.

Bates: Lorna, go on and say what you want to say.

Mrs. Bates: It ain't going to do no good.

Bates: That's all right. Say it.

CO: Please. *(Mrs. Bates sits in the chair. Sergeant Bates stands a few feet* behind her.)

Mrs. Bates: I met them first outside Miami, at a place called Slim's, on Route One. Dinah Shore and Jerry Lewis don't play Slim's, but I did. That was in the summer of 1962. I was twenty-six American years old, and I had seen all the ugly, low-down American things a girl like me could see. I wrote a song about that. Used to sing it, with my Star-Spangled Garter-Belt Guitar: "I'm Highway born and Highway bred, I'll be Highway shed, and Highway dead." I'll sing it for you sometime. Well, that night, I was just back from the Dominican Republic, where I'd been for a while, with a real nice man I knew. Brought back an act with a snake, and a few other things. Like smashing customers' beer bottles in a big towel and rolling around stripping in the broken glass, and not getting cut. Things like that I learned for a living, and playing with snakes, and men. I didn't even see them come in. They were just there, sitting at the piano bar. They were wearing plain old clothes, and just wanted a quiet, relaxing, low-down bar sort of a drink. They could get awful tired, you know, of Officers' Club parties they had to go to. *(She smiles, fondly.)* Oh, we had a time that night. They stayed; and we sang a lot, and drank a lot, and had the best time together. They even sent me a Christmas card that winter, and we wrote now and then, and about two years ago they wrote asking where I'd be that summer, and they came to see me. "Hello," they said. They didn't ask why I was at Freedom Ranch, in Calcutta, California, which is a western-style mental-encounter-group-type whorehouse, because they knew. I was working, like before. This time I was a masseuse. The house girl, Lorna. "Hello," they said. "Hello," I said. "You're looking fine," they said. "Oh, yes," I said, "I've come up in the world. High society, now." "Any different?" they asked. "No," I said. "Same old Highway trash. Better clothes, and the pimps have Ph.D.'s." And they laughed, and that was the night, because of so many things, I don't know, it came to an end for me, and I swallowed everything I had in the medicine cabinet, and went to sleep dreaming of my first husband, my childhood sweetheart I married in Plainfield, Kansas, who when he got mad at me used to fry my brassiere and panties in the oven, and I did sleep, and I was gone away from it all, a free American at last, at peace, and then, oh, God, I woke up in the hospital, with the General and his wife, who'd got worried about me, and come back that night, and saved my life. "WHY?" I asked them when I saw them at my bedside. He was dressed right then. It was the first time I'd seen him in his uniform, looking so—strong. "Because, Lorna," he said, "you are a decent woman, and we know that, and we're your friends." And they did what they'd come to see me about. They got me and Norvel together. Norvel alone with two children to care for, and so, after awhile, we was married. I was saved. Saved from the ditch, from the rock-bottom Highway trash of these United States! *(Filled with anger and anguish, she stands up.)* And now they've gone and done what they saved me from! They have killed themselves, like I tried to do. And everybody wonders why. Well, Jesus Christ on the Cross, I'll tell you why! They were too god damned good for their own stinking country, that's why! And after fifty years of believing in it, they found that out! *(She weeps.)* I could have told them that! They didn't have to die for that, god damn it! The good life they gave me, they couldn't keep for themselves. *(MRS. BATES stares at everyone with defiance.)* Because it is the Army that is the most decent thing about this country. Everything else I ever seen in it is shit. And the General, except for the husband he found for me, is the only top-to-bottom real man I ever met. My husband and our children, and me, we will be all right. What the General and the Army gave to me, this country cannot never take back again. That's what they mean to me, the General and his wife. *(They go to their seats.)*

CO: Next.

Martin: Are you Mr. Roundhouse?

Roundhouse: Roundhouse, Edward E. I wasn't coming, but I had a drink and changed my mind. You want me to sit there?

Martin: Please. *(Roundhouse goes to the chair, stands by it.)* This is an informal and preliminary inquiry, and we thank you for coming. The General left us notes, one saying you were an old and valued friend. That you would have something to tell us.

Roundhouse: I want to see the note. *(Martin looks at the CO, who nods. Martin gives Roundhouse the note. He reads it, hands it back.)* All right. *(He sits in the witness chair.)*

Martin: You are the owner of a restaurant on the island?

Roundhouse: Several now. Because Michael got me the first one, when he was a Major, stationed briefly here. Its title was Michael's idea, The Breeze and I. He found it for me, helped me buy into the place, where I washed the dishes and swept the floors until it became a lunch stop for tour buses from Waikiki. Now you must ask me what I did before sweeping the floors of The Breeze and I.

CO: Ask him.

Martin: What did you do before sweeping the floors of The Breeze and I?

Roundhouse: I was President of two American universities. After a scholar's education in classical studies, I graced several advanced faculties, and in due process, bored finally with Socrates and Plato, turned my hand to university administration. Then, in 1945, I became President of Triton College, in Ohio. In 1951, President of the University of the Southwest.

In 1952, I began sweeping the floors at The Breeze and I. Follow me? Never mind, don't try, just listen. In those lost days of my academic glory, I traveled often, up to my neck in liberal crusades. I met Michael and Sheila in August of 1951, on the great sweeping porch of the Zen temple that overlooks the Ryuanji Stone Garden, outside Kyoto. They were on a vacation, and we liked each other at once. On my way home, I stayed with them a week, here. We became good friends. I enjoyed their common sense, and respected their intelligent patriotism. They loved to hear all about the great figures in the wide world I journeyed in so freely. Then, time up, I returned home, to give my incoming freshman class my most stirring speech on the advantages of being an American, how lucky we were, of the endless possibilities thereunto appertaining, of their duty to the very best in themselves, and after that, there was a business trip to New York, where in a perfectly respectable hotel bar, over a glass of sherry, I met a young man who thought me equally charming. We adjourned to my room, where he turned out to be cruising for the Vice Squad. He arrested me, that little Benedict Arnold, whose legs, by the way, I can still remember. Those were the days of terror, you recall, when you were probably not merely a homosexual, debauching a poor, innocent policeman, but also most likely a Communist, since both vices were obviously intimately connected. When I got out of jail, what the Hearst papers in Chicago didn't do to me, the faculty and Board of Trustees of the University of the Southwest did. Never mind the honors and the service now, the friendships and the acclaim. As far as my country, which I loved, was concerned—just another fairy. *(Pause.)* All a kind of hideous joke now, except that it killed my mother. Contrary to what you are told, in the Dell edition of Freud, I was very fond of her. But there I was, Mama dead as mutton, and with her my distinguished career in higher education, which had educated in bitterness, alas, only myself. I vaguely supposed I would go to Paris, call myself Sebastian Melmoth, and die there like Oscar Wilde. But my little Major Michael from the summer, who had read about me in the newspapers, called me and said, "Come here." With Michael's help I bought my little restaurant by the sea. And as Michael foresaw, a tidal wave of tourists rolled over me. So here I am, better off than ever, a closet queen midwestern college President, turned into a rich, free comber of Somerset Maugham beaches, and boys. I am even a force in the economics of this state now, and believe me, where my sex life is concerned, nobody says a word. *(Pause.)* Michael didn't do it just for me. We made a deal. In return, I was to make The Breeze and I, in the evenings only, a place for certain soldiers of the Army this young Major loved. "They are good men, too," Michael said. "The Army should help them. You should help them."

So I put Offenbach and jazz in my jukebox, draped with fiendish cunning fish nets and sailcloth on the walls and ceilings, arranged booths for dignified semi-privacy, and created what Michael had wanted. At noon, of course, I made a killing, the place jammed with Los Angeles tourists and their screaming wives, bedlam but profitable, and at night, under an Oahu moon, something else. *(Pause.)* It's been that way now twenty years. Major Michael left Schofield for other assignments, passing through now and again. He would call me on my birthday, and at Christmas, like a good son. He wrote me letters from his battlefields in Korea and Vietnam. Then he returned to Schofield Barracks. Major General Michael, commanding. And once again, as it was in 1952, one night a week The Breeze and I was closed. Only two men drank the coconut rum, ate the bonito, listed to Offenbach and jazz and looked at the moon. But now it was the war he talked about, and what happened to him in it. About the jealousy of Generals, the panic over their careers, the maneuvers that turned what should have been counsels of war into tangles of vipers. About a President of the United States who so skillfully invited his Generals to lie to him, they finally didn't care when they were lying and when they weren't and neither did he. *(Pause.)* Three nights ago, he told me he understood now, what my country had done to me. "Me, too," he said, his face like slate. "We are going to lose this war, and rightly." He looked at his watch then, and my telephone rang. "I've had someone call me here," he said. "Is that all right?" I said yes. He talked briefly to the leader of a Washington protest organization, gave him some information, said, "Use my name," and hung up. *(Pause.)* And there we were. A disgraced college President and a defeated Army General. "I won't see you again," he said. "But let's kill the bottle first." And we did. We embraced. And that was the end of us. I watched him turn, warrior into priest. Religions come and go, conversion remains. I saw it touch him, burning away the soldier he had always been. I loved him. I admired him. In an age where everyone else is innocent, Michael chose the terrible right to be guilty!

Martin: And to betray his country, sir!

Roundhouse: His country, young man, betrayed him!

Martin: *(Coldly.)* Thank you, Mr. Roundhouse. *(To CO.)* Sir, that's the last of the witnesses.

CO: Right. Ladies and gentlemen, the last request the General makes is for a simple review of what they did. Captain Martin. *(Martin gives Bates and Nomura a few pages of a play.)* Mr. Roundhouse, please stay with us. *(Round- house goes back to his seat.)* Sergeant Bates, Miss Nomura, would you please read what you did Saturday night? And Captain Martin, do we have the masks they wore?

Martin: Yes, sir.

CO: Let's see them, please. *(Martin moves the table holding the masks to center. He opens the wooden boxes and sets the masks up against them. They are Noh masks. We see the faces, a suffering Japanese warrior and a beautiful woman, staring. The CO nods to Sergeant Bates.)*

Bates: *(Reading.)*

The sky is lit
with fires of war

Miss Nomura: *(Reading.)*

The smell of death infects the world
and blood rains down from heaven

(Lights change, dimming, while a circle of light comes up on the two masks.)

Bates:

But today I leave the field
And with my wife
I make this pilgrimage
Evening falls
Night comes upon us

Miss Nomura:

Birds fly up and vanish
in the darkening sky

Bates:

We have reached the river
that leads to the mountain we seek
We step into our boat
to cross the swift waters

Miss Nomura:

And I remember
when long ago
down these same rivers
once we sailed

Bates:

Now they stream with blood
choked on the bodies of the young
my soldiers dead in the war

Miss Nomura:

And I see in the currents below
beneath my child
beneath his hanging arms
and drifting hair

my husband's face
and mine

Bates:

Now we have come
to the Mountain of Death

Miss Nomura:

Where young lovers come to die
a grove of pines
a bed of stones

Bates:

It is hard to think of ourselves
climbing this mountain
as a suicide of lovers

Miss Nomura:

For happiness and youth were ours
We married in joy and pleasure
We had many victories
and great powers
but now we are here

Bates:

O my country farewell
You once were all the world to me
what you taught me I became
and served you far too well
I am yours no longer

Miss Nomura:

O great compassionate Buddha
before your beautiful face
shining down upon us
I met my brave husband
years go
Husband!
Now!

Bates:

The knife may part the flesh
but miss the heart
I must use my bow

Miss Nomura:

Use your bow
and your arrow tipped in steel
Kill me! Kill me!

I will wait for you in heaven
my noble husband!
(Pause.)
Wait! Look there!
Ah! Our child!
Look there!
(The light on the masks fades.)

Martin: And that was it. They waited a minute and—did it. With the General's wife pointing—where, Sergeant Bates?

Bates: Toward the door.

CO: What was she pointing at?

Martin: Nobody knew.

Lucy Lake: I know. The child.

CO: You mean the orphan?

Lucy Lake: Yoshida Robinson. Yes.

Mrs. Bates: No! I took him home.

Lucy Lake: But they expected him.

Mrs. Bates: That's right.

Lucy Lake: Then the General meant to do so something with the child.

Moore: I know what we've forgotten! The chair! RESERVED! For who? The man who didn't come, but who damn near did, and who almost sat there Saturday night. The man that lunatic General pretended HAD come! The President of the United States, that's who! I don't know why that man committed suicide, but I do know what he really wanted to do! Shoot the President!

Lucy Lake: No, that's not it!

Mrs. Bates: Never!

Moore: The President of the United States, shot to death, right here!

Lucy Lake: No. You're forgetting the child. Yoshida Robinson. A bequest to an orphanage. That was the heart of it. *(Lucy Lake steps forward.)* The President? Where would he have been?

Moore: In his chair! In his chair!

Lucy Lake: The General and his wife, at the close of the play?

Martin: On the dance floor.

Lucy Lake: And the little boy would have come in—

Mrs. Bates: The door. To them.

Lucy Lake: The General was going to kill the child.

Mrs. Bates: Do WHAT to the child? *(They all react, in a quick explosion.)*

Moore: *(Simultaneous.)* No, the President was the target! That's who he wanted to kill!

Miss Nomura: *(Simultaneous.)* It was a shinju! You don't understand!

Lucy Lake: *(Simultaneous.)* The child! That was the poem! The child!
Bates: *(Simultaneous.)* Lorna, please. Calm down.
Mrs. Bates: No! No! It's wrong! You're all wrong! *(The CO stands up.)*
CO: That will do! *(Pause.)* We have not finished. Is there a medical report?
Martin: Yes.
CO: I want to hear it.
Martin: *(Reading.)* The General's wife died, unresisting, from the intrusion into her throat of a steel-tipped archer's arrow, shot from a sixty pound bow. It severed the right carotid artery. She herself grasped the arrow in both hands, wrenched it back and forth in her throat. The General then took off his mask, drew his Army automatic pistol, placed it against his ear and pulled the trigger. The force of the explosion, at that range, removed the entire cranial vault. Both deaths were suicide. That is all, sir.
CO: No, it isn't. Sergeant Bates, you have a sealed envelope from the General?
Bates: Yes, sir.
CO: Open it and read it. Let him speak for himself. *(Sergeant Bates opens the envelope, takes a sheet of paper and reads from it.)*
Bates: *(Reading.)* General. Plan A. To cut the throat of an Oriental American child, and throw his blood on the President of the United States. Plan B. To make that intention known to you, to others, and if possible, to public record. Goodbye. *(Bates gives the paper to the CO. The CO stares at it a moment.)*
CO: Thank you. *(Captain Martin goes to the door and opens it. They all go out. The CO stands staring at the masks. Captain Martin comes back in briskly. The CO holds up a hand. Martin turns and goes back out. The CO stands before the masks for a moment, then goes behind the table and slowly, deliberately, returns the masks to their boxes and replaces the lids. He stands for another moment, very uncertain. Then he lifts his hand in a slow salute. He turns and goes briskly out of the room. Lights fade on the wooden boxes.)*

SAND MOUNTAIN

for Robert Levy and Karl Jenson

SAND MOUNTAIN MATCHMAKING

REBECCA TULL, a spirited young widow, 20's.
CLINK WILLIAMS, a muscular mountaineer, 20's.
SLATE FOLEY, hard-faced and deadly, 50's.
RADLEY NOLLINS, a plump, genial fanatic, 40's.
LOTTIE STILES, a weathered mountain woman, 50's.
VESTER STILES, a curious mountain boy, 10.
SAM BEAN, a mature mountaineer, 30's.

WHY THE LORD COME TO SAND MOUNTAIN

SANG PICKER, a weathered mountain woman, 50's.
SAINT PETER, a balding, energetic apostle, 40's.
THE LORD, a friendly, engaging traveler, 30's.
JACK, a hardscrabble, alcoholic farmer, 50's.
JEAN, his young, alcoholic wife, 20's.
FOURTEEN CHILDREN, one spirited boy, 10.
PROSPER VALLEY FARMER, a well-fed, sure of himself farmer, 30's.

Place: Sand Mountain

Time: Awhile ago.

SAND MOUNTAIN was first produced by The Whole Theatre Company, Olympia Dukakis, Artistic Director, in 1985, directed by Romulus Linney, with the following cast:

REBECCA TULL & JEAN.......................................Kari Jenson
CLINK WILLIAMS & PROSPER VALLEY FARMER...Kevin Carrigan
SLATE FOLEY & JACK...William Hardy
RADLEY NOLLINS & SAINT PETER......................Ron Lee Savin
LOTTIE STILES & SANG PICKER...........................Kathleen Chalfant
SAM BEAN & THE LORD.....................................Leon Russon

Sets were by Michael Miller, lights by Richard Moore, costumes by Sigrid Insull, and the production stage mangager was Kathleen Cunneen.

SAND MOUNTAIN MATCHMAKING

A back wall of wood, against sky. At center, a rosewood dining room bureau, well made and polished, with silver candlesticks, a pewter bowl, and a Bible lying on it. On the wall, at each side, oil portraits of a grandfather and a grandmother, circa 1840's.
Darkness. Music: an introductory phrase for a folksong, played on a guitar or dulcimer, or perhaps, whistled. This short phrase will be repeated on various entrances throughout the play.
Lights up.
In two handsome wooden chairs sit Rebecca Tull and Clink Williams, who is courting her. They are both in their early twenties.
Pause. The phrase of music ends.

Clink: So.
Rebecca: So.
Clink: I seen you watching me work.
Rebecca: Did you?
Clink: Whilst we was a-raising this house.
Rebecca: Is that a fact?
Clink: Hit purely is.
Rebecca: I recollect near thirty men a-raising this house. I watched 'em all.
Clink: Me a tad more'n tothers.
Rebecca: Modesty in a man is everlasting welcome to the lady receiving him.
Clink: You ain't modest. Neither am I. This house warn't easy, neither. Hard hard work. We scored these logs off flush, se 'em level on a rock foundation, and chinked 'em in with riverbottom clay. Four rooms, a loft, moved in yore fine Virginia furniture, silver goblets, and painted pictures of Momma's Momma and Daddy's Daddy on the wall. And whilst yore Daddy was gitting his house built, you was twelve places at onct, man looking. And you looked at me a tad more'n tothers, and you plain let me know it.
Rebecca: You've a right to your opinion, however loony it may be. I've heard it and that's all I have to do about it.
Clink: One man after another's what you was a-doing, speculating on us all and looking hard. Back muscles, front muscles, sweat and swearing, hands and fists and legs, tongue, lips, shoulders and top, Lady, and bottom, Lady, all of us, all of that. You are plain ready to marry agin, and let me say it, the man fer you is me. I tolerate a woman's carnal nature. You let a man

know about it. I know what to do about it.

Rebecca: Lord God four or five times. You strong men hereabouts, you jest don't mince words, do you?

Clink: Honey, if the shoe fits, wear the damn thing. When you looked at me, raising up and laying in at log wall yonder, thangs were happening.

Rebecca: What a muscle-headed man like you sees happening, and what is truly a-going on, can be a great big two-piece sod-busted difference. I got no need to marry a man whose preference is forever at the front of his pants.

Clink: And I got about as much use fer a blueblooded Virginia sweetheart as a pig fer a Bible. But you've come to live on Sand Mountain, your husband died on you, you're jest as hot as a horseshoe in a forge, and you'll marry again. Any woman looks at a man the way you've looked at me, got to marry or bust.

Rebecca: That may be, and a body can bust all right, but they're other men in the world to bust over than you!

Clink: You ain't been here long enough to sort us all out, Honey Bunch. Rub yoreself agin some other legs here, b'grannies, you'll commence thinking better about me.

Rebecca: I doubt it.

Clink: I don't. *(He gets up.)* Ponder this. I am the only growed up young man on this mountain who ain't never married. You may be a high-born, well-off widderwoman with a famous preacher fer a Daddy but you're twenty years old. Men here commence low-rating wives the day after they hit fourteen. Maybe I'll be back, maybe I won't. So long. *(Exit Clink Williams. The phrase of music again. Enter Slate Foley. He is in his forties. He sits in Clink Williams' chair. Music ends.)*

Slate: So.

Rebecca: So.

Slate: Told ye I'd come a-courting.

Rebecca: You best speak to my Daddy about this. He's in the church.

Slate: Ain't studying yore Daddy, in or out of church, I'm a-studying you. Jest like you are a-studying me, and was all during this house-raising.

Rebecca: More modest men. Run plumb into 'em, ever time a body turns around. What makes you think I am a-studying any man?

Slate: Come outside with me. Walk a little ways. We'll find out.

Rebecca: Hush. You reckon all you got to say to me is, "Lady, lie down," and I'm so dizzy I'll do it?

Slate: You was displaying the sign of it. Has been known to happen.

Rebecca: To a bubble-headed milkmaid in a storybook, but not to me. If ever other man on Sand Mountain is as cow-sheep clumsy and corncob coarse as you, I look forward to a by myself happy old age.

Slate: None of us hyar plays Virginia reels, Sweet Potato. No man hyar's got the time fer sech stammering and stuttering around. You looked at me enough, and more than enough. My first wife died of pneumony, my second of distemper, but I am still feisty and will consider you. I speak plainly. You know what I want, outside right now or next week when we're married, either one. How about it?

Rebecca: *(Smiles.)* What can a woman say, when a man puts it to her like that?

Slate: She can say yes.

Rebecca: How kin I ever resist? Fine figure of a good honest man, sneaking in when you know my Momma's a-visiting and my Daddy's in church, doing me the honor to figure I got nothing better to consider than throwing my life away on some blackslope cowpath, with a split-britches-hasty, shaller-headed fool twenty years oldern me! Then expecting me to wait around like a strollop to git married! No, sir! *(Pause.)*

Slate: You ain't a-coming outside, are ye?

Rebecca: You have finally and at last said one thing that's true. Pore young widder, what choice does she have? The ugliness of him, or nothing. Well, so be it. Before I give over my days on earth to a clod-faced, bark-faced, slit-eyed roughneck like you, I'll live alone ever last day of my creation!

Slate: *(Quietly.)* No, you won't.

Rebecca: I will, too!

Slate: You can't.

Rebecca: Meaning whut?

Slate: Meaning that here on these slopes the nights are cold and blood gets hot. Spit out all them stinging words you've a mind to now. Come three or four hard winters on Sand Mountain, you'll take the man will have you, take him fast and gladly. There's worse than me.

Rebecca: I don't believe it!

Slate: Hm. Old boy I know, name of Ollen. Took him a well-off wife, who could read and write and talk, jest like you. She didn't come to care for him, and after awhile, she told him so. He put her through a little school of his own. She don't talk to nobody now. She tends his younguns, and his—

Rebecca: HIS younguns?

Slate: And HIS meals, and HIS clothes, and HIS house and HIS yard and everythang else that's HIS, afore she even commences pondering arythang that's HERS. It will happen to you, you keep on talking and strutting.

Rebecca: I'll die first.

Slate: That could be. I won't lie about it. There's another old boy around here, named Skeets. He shot his wife. And the next day her brothers come and shot him, and their six chillun and his grandaddy too. That's the kind of real trouble flighty women git everybody into around here, when they don't know what they're talking about. Watch what you say to men. They live powerful lonely here. Fires kin bank up inside 'em, a-smouldering meanness. You don't know what you're a-fooling with, in this country. *(He gets up.)* What you need ain't flowers or lace. You need a man who knows the life we live and kin be hard but fair and old as he may be, keep you safe. And I might never hit ye atall. Might never have to, onct the flirting is over, and you lie down and like it. Ponder what I've told ye. I'll be back. *(Exit Slate Foley. The phrase of music again. Enter Radley Nollins. He sits in Slate Foley's chair. Music ends. Pause.)*

Radley: So.

Rebecca: So.

Radley: I do comprehend how you must feel. A woman new here, with sensitive complexions and dainty ways. You let me see that in you, how fine you are. Not many here much prize sech qualities, but I do. I'm not afraid to say so, neither.

Rebecca: I will confess it is good to hear a man admit it.

Radley: A bull goose gits ramptious. Fractious. Not ever man rides a woman that hard, though some, telling the Lord's flat truth, get that way. They don't have no reliable guide. They burn and then marry, marry and then burn. I am protected agin sech fritter-minded misery.

Rebecca: By what?

Radley: By that there. *(He goes to the bureau, holds up its Btble.)* "And from the rib, which the Lord God had taken from man, made He a woman, and brought her unto the man." Genesis Chapter Two, Verse Two. *(Pause.)*

Rebecca: Oh.

Radley: There is no doubt with me. A man of God I have always been and always will be. Any wife I have can take refuge in that. "For Adam was first formed, and then Eve." Timothy Two, Verse Thirteen.

Rebecca: What a comfort.

Radley: "A virtuous woman is a crown to her husband, but she that maketh him ashamed is a rotteness in his bones." Proverbs, Twelve and Four.

Rebecca: You've been married before.

Radley: I have. Satan called my wife. She ran off with him, in the shape of a scoundrel called Buzzmore. "But she that liveth in pleasure is dead while she liveth." First Timothy Five, Verse Six. *(Rebecca closes her eyes.)*

Rebecca: "And men shall be lovers of their own selves, covetous, boasters, proud, blasphemers, unthankful, unholy, truce breakers, false accusers, incontinent, heady, high-minded and lovers of pleasure. From such turn away, for they creep into houses and lead captive silly women." Second Timothy Three, Verses Two through Six.

Radley: You know yore Bible, too.

Rebecca: A tad, yes. I would make you a misery of a wife.

Radley: Why?

Rebecca: Because I quote scripture good as you and better!

Radley: "Temper in a woman is like—"

Rebecca: Shut up, Radley! Just go home!

Radley: You are mocking me.

Rebecca: I'm not mocking you, I just do not want you!

Radley: "Favour is deceitful and beauty is vain, but a woman that feareth the Lord, she shall be praised." Proverbs Thirty-one and Thirty.

Rebecca: Radley? You know what that is. That is a great heavy hunk of last month's lard is what that is, and in her bones, Radley, a woman knows it, and you know it and I know it. Favour is good, Radley, and beauty is jest plain sun-ball wonderful, and the woman what goes about eternally a-fearing the Lord is scared of her own husband and I ain't going to live thataway, so go home! *(Pause. Radley gets up.)*

Radley: Then why play the pore soulful widderwoman hyar? Not jest to me, neither, but to any man come near you, and you not so picky and choosy you don't bat eyes at all of 'em! Amen! I understand Clink Williams and Slate Foley have been here courting you. Along with me, they're all you can expect hereabouts. Tother men who'd have you, compared to us, are razorback hogs. Don't be a fool. Praise God, pick a man and live with him. I'll be back to find out which. *(Exit Radley. Music. It ends. Pause. No one else comes. Music. It ends. Pause. Rebecca shakes her head, clenches her fists, beats her knees, then bows her head.)*

Rebecca: *(Praying.)* Lord Jesus Christ. I am in the wilderness, here on this dreadful mountain. Forgive me, Lord, but I can't abide these people. I know I'm yet willful and too frisky for a decent widow like my Momma and Daddy say, but dear Lord, must I live in ignorant meanness and hateful con tention like this? Help me, Lord. Deliver me from this place. Or if you won't, give me some sign, it ain't crazy I'll be on Sand Mountain. In Jesus name. Amen. *(Music. Enter Lottie Stiles, with her young grandson, Vester Stiles. She sits in the other chair, with Vester standing beside her, staring at Rebecca. Music ends.)*

Lottie: Then you pull the laurel leaves out of the snow, wrap 'em tight, and scrub the baby's face. For teethin', rub his gums with a cool minnow. For the colic, make him some chimneysoot tea.

Rebecca: Truly?

Lottie: I recollect ever cure in these mountains. You comprehend walnuts?

Rebecca: I know what one is.

Lottie: Then you know the shell is like yore skull and the meat is like yore brain. So eat it, when ye got woobles in the head.

Rebecca: *(Doubtfully.)* Woobles, in the head.

Lottie: If you break your bed, a relative's coming to visit. Dream about catching a fish, you'll get pregnant. Black chicken blood helps shingles.

Rebecca: At a fact?

Lottie: Some reckon so, some don't. Do you?

Rebecca: *(Smiling.)* No'm. I don't.

Lottie: That's all right. You'll learn. Stale cabbage helps boils, but best keep them cabbage leaves wet and steamy, now, or no good. You commence growing a goiter—

Rebecca: Oh!

Lottie: Happens. Bathe it in the blood out of the tail of a grey cat. Powerful high fever? Ye split a trout. Lift out the bones. Tie each half of at trout to the soles of yore feet. Walk around. You think I got woobles in the head?

Rebecca: I do.

Lottie: Jest try it. Cure a fever blister, kiss a dog. Pick a husband, talk to me. *(Pause.)*

Rebecca: Oh.

Lottie: Hit's common knowledge you're being powerful pestered. By three peckerwoods powerful horny. You comprehend, now, whut's horny?

Rebecca: Yes, I comprehend what's horny.

Lottie: Cagey, pruney, rollicky, horny, all the same. Nothing wrong with it, long as hit's pleasant. But I misdoubt you bottomland like them men, ary one of them, at's why you tease and play with them all. The one who ain't pruney here, cagey, rollicky or horny, is you, whatever you pretend. Truth to tell, you're nightowl scared. I still got woobles in the head?

Rebecca: No.

Lottie: Pleasure an old woman who means you well. You was married before this?

Rebecca: Yes.

Lottie: Yore husband. A man content?

Rebecca: No.

Lottie: A scoundrel?

Rebecca: No.

Lottie: Whut wus he then? *(Rebecca sighs.)*

Rebecca: Jest a man.

Lottie: Oh. *(Pause.)* And to make what's worse, rockbottom, yore Momma and Daddy want you married agin. Mournin's done with, hit's time to breed. You got three men saying marry me, religion, and time's running out. Pick one. Shore. *(Pause.)* Tell me this. You know, at all, the man you'd have?

Rebecca: No.

Lottie: Um-hm. You fancy ary man you ever met?

Rebecca: No.

Lottie: Didn't reckon ye could. Now, when you was the littlest girl, as pleasant as the flowers are made, you ever dream and ponder that boy a-walking around that minute, the man who'd grow up to take you, the man you'd gladly have? Who was he? Walking around whar?

Rebecca: Yes.

Lottie: Do ye fancy him still, at boy ye never met? In yer head?

Rebecca: Yes.

Lottie: There is a way to make him appear. And tothers, disappear.

Rebecca: *(Smiling.)* How?

Lottie: With a charm. A spell.

Rebecca: Fer me? Woman, I'm a preacher's daughter!

Lottie: I know that.

Rebecca: Make a potion? Grind up frog's bones, pour in bat's blood?

Lottie: Jest say something. About men, to their faces, and all at onct.

Rebecca: Say what?

Lottie: Something about their noses.

Rebecca: Their noses?

Lottie: Hm.

Rebecca: Well, what about their noses?

Lottie: Onct this is heard, hit can't git unheard.

Rebecca: So tell me!

Lottie: To find the man for you, in a bunch of God awful puddlejumpers, you say this. To them. A man's horn is times three the size of his nose. *(Long pause.)*

Rebecca: Now what was that?

Lottie: A man's horn—you comprehend a man's horn?

Rebecca: Yes, I comprehend a man's horn! Is what?

Lottie: Times three the size of his nose. *(Rebecca stares at her.)* You say that to all them men.

Rebecca: I do?

Lottie: You do.

Rebecca: What'll happen?

Lottie: That's the charm, that's the spell. What it'll do, I can't tell.

Rebecca: You think I'm a fool?

Lottie: At's whut everybody's waiting to discover.

Rebecca: I'll pick a husband my own way. Thank ye kindly. *(They both rise.)*

Lottie: Don't say nothing about it. If ye change yore mind, don't worry none, jest say it to them three men, right out. Come on, Vester.

Vester: Yes, m'am.

Lottie: Vester? With yore little eyes a-googling out of yore head at this fine lady?

Vester: Yes, ma'am?

Lottie: Whut do you have to say? *(Pause. Vester thinks.)*

Vester: Cat looks big till dog shows up.

Lottie: Fer sartin. *(To Rebecca.)* You bother men cause they bother you. You ain't never seen a man you truly want. Hit will end in misery. Don't settle fer a man ye can't fancy. Use the spell. Call Vester's dog. *(Exit Lottie Stiles, followed by Vester. Pause. Rebecca stares after them. Music. Enter Radley Nollins.)*

Radley: I trust you been a thinking me over. You know what I got to offer you. A life anchored in the sure and certain ways of the righteous God. Do you have ary thang to say to me?

Rebecca: Yes, sir. I have.

Radley: Well? *(Pause.)*

Rebecca: A man's horn is times three the size of his nose. *(Pause.)*

Radley: Say whut? *(He thinks.)* A man's.... times three .... his nose? That ain't the Bible! Are you a runion, woman? A-mocking the word of God? Speak!

Rebecca: I jest did.

Radley: "She that winketh with the eye causeth sorrow, and a prating fool shall fall." I bid you good day. *(Exit Radley Nollins. Music. Enter Slate Foley.)*

Slate: I trust you been a-thinking me over. You know what I got to offer you. A life with a man who knows the world is a damn mean place, and who's mean enough hisself to keep you safe agin it. Have you ary thang to say to me?

Rebecca: Yes, sir. I have.

Slate: Well?

Rebecca: A man's horn is times three the size of his nose. *(Pause.)*

Slate: Aye, God, woman. Making fun of a man's horn, at's a damn deadly thang to do. Hit ain't smart, Lady, not in no way, size, shape nor form. I bout made a mistake here. So long! *(Exit Slate Foley. Music. Enter*

Clink Williams.)

Clink: I trust you been a-thinking me over. You know what I got to offer you. Hot blood and high jinks, the way it ought to be when a man and a woman are young together. Have you got ary a thang to say to me?

Rebecca: Yes, sir. I have.

Clink: Well?

Rebecca: A man's horn is times three the size of his nose. *(Pause.)*

Clink: *I'd fancy me a wife, now, be a mite more delicate, who don't spend her time pondering horns. A woman say a thing like that ain't got manners enough to tote guts to a bear. Goodbye. (Exit Clink Williams. Music. It ends. No one comes. Music. It ends. No one comes. Pause. Rebecca sighs, lowers her head, closes her eyes. Silence. Music. Enter Sam Bean. He is a man in his thirties. Rebecca opens her eyes, sees him. Music ends.)*

Sam: My name is Sam Bean.

Rebecca: Oh.

Sam: I've done spoke to yore Momma and Daddy. They allowed as how I might come set a spell. You recollect me atall?

Rebecca: Yes, sir. You helped raise this house. But you didn't never stay for no play parties after work. And you never talked to me.

Sam: That's exactly so.

Rebecca: I didn't reckon you cared a straw what I said or did.

Sam: At's exact. I figured you flighty, genteel, and snakey.

Rebecca: So what're ye doing here now?

Sam: Did you really say to Radley Nolins, Slate Foley, and Clink Williams, a man's horn is times three the size of his nose?

Rebecca: I did.

Sam: Hm. *(He Sits.) Why?*

Rebecca: *None of your business why. I said what I said, and I will say what I please, and if you don't like it, go home.*

Sam: *You been married afore?*

Rebecca: *That's what widder generally means.*

Sam: *What happened to yore husband?*

Rebecca: *God Almighty, Mister Bean, he died. Widder? Died?*

Sam: *I mean, how did he die?*

Rebecca: *Oh, I pizened him, of a sartin. Left him to perish, crying fer his Maw, pore man. I'd do it agin, too, if'n I had to marry a Clink Williams or a Slate Foley or a Radley Nollins or a Sam, God help us, Bean!*

Sam: *You don't have to marry me. You content with yore husband?*

Rebecca: *What kind of a judge and jury are you? I don't downhome have to answer no skin-close, out of line preesumption like that!*

Sam: I figured the woman bold enough to make sech talk about the size of a man's horn, wouldn't be afeared to. She might even talk turkey with a man who's ready to talk squirrel. *(Pause.)*

Rebecca: Talk turkey, talk squirrel, is it? You been married, Bean?

Sam: Onct. My wife died, too.

Rebecca: You content with her?

Sam: Only when she died.

Rebecca: Grannies, what does that mean?

Sam: Hit means I'm a-telling ye the truth. Her stomach is whut killed her. Milk-sick, was all the doctor said. She was poorly deathly over a year. She didn't like being sickly and we had us a hell of a time fighting. My chillun—got two, boy four, girl three, lost a girl one—scared to death. Hit was like she faulted me fer her getting sick ready to die. Then bout three weeks afore she died, all that stopped. What had been meanness and spite, went away. There wasn't nothing left of it. There wasn't nothing mean betwixt us. We got so close, there wasn't nothing, not plumb line, not stob measure, not yardstick ruled in our way. Thar wus not one hard thang betwixt us. Then she died. *(Pause.)*

Rebecca: My husband got hisself gored by a bull. *(Bean laughs.)* What's so damn funny?

Sam: Can't say bull up hyar. Say cow-brute instead.

Rebecca: What?

Sam: Wimmen here can't abide it. Can't say stallion, neither. Say stable-horse. Ram? Sheep-male. Cock? He-chicken. What do you think's wrong with wimmen like that? They modest?

Rebecca: They scared.

Sam: Of horns?

Rebecca: Of a body gitting their pleasure easy.

Sam: Reckon so. Gored by a bull, was he?

Rebecca: Whole side tore open, like his flesh was jelly and his bones paper. We had a doctor, too, poured a whole jar of store-bought medicine in him. That fixed him. He was a preacher, like his Daddy, and mine. He went eternally about with his Bible and his stop-watch, calculating hourly wages of sin, minutes left in a day bodies had to repent, and all sech as that. But when he got sick, to face God hisself, he didn't fancy no stop-watch then, he wasn't keen on his Bible even, what the man wanted then, was me. I did my best to comfort him, but I didn't do no good atall. And he died, and this is squirrel now and turkey, I'm glad he died and I'm free of him, but I dread the way it had to come about, and what I jest didn't have to give my husband. *(Pause.)*

Sam: Was his horn three times the size of his nose?

Rebecca: On occasion. *(Pause. They almost smile at each other.)*
Sam: This here is why I stopped by.
Rebecca: To talk turkey whilst I talk squirrel?
Sam: Exactly so.
Rebecca: You'd expect me to raise your younguns?
Sam: And those we'd have. I would.
Rebecca: Where do you live?
Sam: Halfway up the mountain. I ain't rich, with no bottomland farm, or pore, wandering up above the waterfalls. I got seventeen acres, tolerable ground. Log house with rooms, and a wood floor.
Rebecca: What kind of bed?
Sam: Seven foot long. Rope-held feather-down mattress, and a Cumberland Quilt.
Rebecca: How long you calculate hit'd be, Mr. Bean, afore you got plumb tired and familiar with me in that grand feather bed, and did it jest to ease yeself on cold nights, turning away from me and my comfort, to your own?
Sam: Turkey, now?
Rebecca: And squirrel.
Sam: No man can prophesy how long he'll treasure his wife. Hit ain't in his power to do so. Love grows old and waxes cold and we both know it. Fast. So might mine fer you, if hit could ever come about in the first place. I might have to leave ye, one day, and set alone other side of the porch. But I would never disgrace ye with that, nor would ary other living soul hear of it.
Rebecca: Squirrel, now?
Sam: And turkey. How long would you pleasure yeself with me, and recollect bold widder sayings about the sizes of horns, afore ye commence saying cow-brute fer bull, cross them legs when other wimmen low-rate men, and press them hot purty lips into parched-out thread-stiches at the pull of my hand? Turkey and squirrel, Rebecca.
Rebecca: No woman can say how long she will pleasure at the hand of her husband. Hit ain't in her power to do so. Hit may be, in my fashion, I too will want that other side of the porch. But if you don't disgrace me with yore distain, I'll abide you with mine. Friendly and pleasant, as the flowers are made. Turkey and squirrel, Sam. But if you yell Bible scripture at me, like Radley Nollins, if you strut about big, tough and mean, like Slate Foley, or if you talk nothing but randy foolishness, like Clink Williams, then I'll make you wish you'd never been born.
Sam: Well, I won't talk randy, onless hit's both our foolishness and I won't strut about onless hit's both of us big, tough, and mean, but I will quote scripture.

Rebecca: You will?

Sam: Give me the Bible there. *(She gets it, warily.)*

Rebecca: Here. Now what you fixing to do? *(He opens the Bible, studies it.)*

Sam: Married to a preacher was you? Got one fer a Daddy as well, have you?

Rebecca: Sam Bean, don't you mortify me with scripture.

Sam: Hesh, woman.

Rebecca: I'll put a lump on yore head your hand won't cover!

Sam: Here, now. Gen-e-sis, Chapter Two. At's when man and woman God creates.

Rebecca: I know that, Sam! I know that!

Sam: So what's the day of the month you was borned?

Rebecca: Huh?

Sam: Jest tell a man, fore he dies!

Rebecca: Twenty-fifth. *(Pause.)*

Sam: Is at so? Me, too. *(Pause.)*

Rebecca: That a fact?

Sam: Purely is.

Rebecca: So. What about it? What does the Bible say?

Sam: Let's see. Book of Gen-ee-sis. Chapter Two, Verse Twenty-five. "And they were both naked, the man and his wife, and they were not ashamed." *(Sam gets up, hands her the Bible.)* Shall I come here again, to expound this further?

Rebecca: Do so.

Sam: Till then. *(Exit Sam. Music. Rebecca sits thinking. Enter Vester.)*

Vester: Ma'am?

Rebecca: Vester?

Vester: Grandma sent me. T'ask how you are a-gitting on.

Rebecca: Tell her I still live. I used her spell, and your dog did show up. I will admit, there is some power, though just how much I've yet to see. I'm glad she came to see me. You tell her that.

Vester: Yes, ma'am. I will. *(He starts to go, stops.)* I know a riddle. You want to hear it?

Rebecca: All right.

Vester: Why is a tongue like an unhappy girl?

Rebecca: I don't know, Vester. Why?

Vester: They are both down in the mouth. I know anothern too. What colors would you paint the sun and the wind?

Rebecca: Tell me, Vester.

Vester: The sun rose, and the wind blew. *(Pause. Vester hesitates.)*

Rebecca: Number three?

Vester: How can I tell you what you are, in six letters?

Rebecca: I don't know. How can you do that, Vester?

Vester: U-R-A-B-U-T. *(Pause.)* I'd marry you, if I could. Bye. *(Exit Vester. Rebecca opens her Bible and reads, smiling. Music. The lights fade slowly.)*

WHY THE LORD COME TO SAND MOUNTAIN

Mountain music, which fades into a man whistling.
The stage is backed with aged wood, suggesting the Smoky Mountains. There is a platform at center, representing the interior of a mountain cabin. In darkness, three figures sit turned away, before a large battered cupboard. On the wall or next to the cupboard hang two extra slat chairs.
The lights fade and narrow into one light down center. Into it steps the Sang Picker, a mountain woman. She wears a long black coat-like dress, carries a hoe, a barlow knife, and a burlap sack. She holds up the sack.

Sang Picker: Gen Sang. Grows wild on Sand Mountain but powerful hard to find. Bring ye one whole dollar a dried pound. And why not? Hit'll keep yore body young. Gen Sang is China language. Hit means root of life. *(She reaches into the sack and pulls out a genseng root. She rubs the dirt off it, slices a piece from it with her knife, chews it.)* Mmmmm. Good. Make ye tingle. *(She looks up. Sound of wind.)* Ravens. Sailing the updrafts. Wings out, like that. Yore raven was the firstest creature Noah let out of the Ark, to go fly-see if tar was ary thang a-growing after the flood. And that bodacious bird, hit never come back. Bible says so. But don't say why. I'll tell ye why. Noah and them ravens just didn't get along, that's why. Ever soul on Sand Mountain knows yore raven will jest downright dispute with ye. We are like that too, herabouts. Can't read no Bible, but love to dispute the thang anyhow. *(She looks about.)* Big these mountains. I never seen the end of them, never will. Lived here all my life. Pleasant baby, purty woman, and what ye see now. Had three men. All died farmers. Firstest one all right, second a mite bettern that, the third God-awful. He was the disgust of the world, he was, half man, half buzzard. Worked four wives to death, figured I'd be the fifth. Fooled him. How? Gen Sang and Bible Stories, that's how. Roots of life. Yes, sir. Chew Gen Sang, ponder Bible Tales. Keep yore body alive in spite of debts, doctors and even husbands. *(Pause.)* I reckon you've heard Smoky Mountain head benders a-plenty. How Little Jack Killed the Giant and The Ghost of Daniel Boone, all that. And Bible Tales a-plenty, too. Noah in the Ark, Jonah in the Whale, Daniel in the Den, Moses Up the Mountain, all that. Ain't no disputing them. But around here, we fancy 'em all mixed up up tegether, something a body ain't heared four hundred times, something a body kin dispute. Like Why The Lord Come To Sand Moun tain. *(Thunder, far off, Wind. Lights change.)* Hit was a day powerful gusty, some years back, when the top of Sand Mountain was all a forest. Clouds had black bellies, rain wus in the air, and something up thar downright mean, a-figuring whut to do. *(Enter The Lord and Saint Peter. They wear long dark coats, mountain hats and kerchiefs, and carry small packs on their backs. They move toward the Sang Picker.)* Outlanders. I seen them afore they seen me. *(She steps back. The Lord moves forward, and looks around. Saint Peter follows.)*

Saint Peter: Lord, are you sure you know where we are?

Lord: Well, just about. *(He sees the Sang Picker. He takes off his hat.)* Hidy.

Sang Picker: How do.

Lord: That river called Little Scataway?

Sang Picker: Hit used to be, yes, sir. *(Pause. The Lord smiles.)*

Lord: Is it still?

Sang Picker: Is by me. I don't speak for nobody else.

Saint Peter: Lord, she's not going to tell us anything. Why waste time?

Lord: Hush. *(To Sang Picker.)* We're looking for Sand Mountain.

Sang Picker: From whar?

Lord: We just came down the Shenandoah.

Sang Picker: Over Roan Ridge? And Little Snowbird?

Lord: *(Enjoying her.)* That's right.

Sang Picker: Through Torn Britches Woods, Stand Around Gap, and Dog Slaughter Creek?

Lord: Yes, m'am.

Sang Picker: You willing to pass through Odd Bottom Cove, Hell Fer Breakfast, and Prosper Valley?

Lord: I am.

Sang Picker: Then I suspect you'll come to Sand Mountain about dusk.

Lord: You saying it's just down the river?

Sang Picker: I ain't saying hit's not.

Lord: I thank you kindly.

Sang Picker: Don't say nothing about it. *(The Lord moves away. Saint Peter, with a doubtful look at the Sang Picker, follows. Thunder again, and wind.)*

Sang Picker: I tell ye plank flat, them men are Saint Peter and the Lord Jesus hisself. Come to the Smokies a-looking fer Sand Mountain. But when they come on Prosper Valley, with a mountain night at their heels, and the sky all a clabbering up fer a storm, Saint Peter wanted to stay thar. *(The Lord and Saint Peter have walked around the stage. Now Saint Peter breaks away from The Lord and comes to the edge of the stage, looking out over Prosper Valley. The Sang Picker moves to one side of the stage and* sits on a crate.)

Saint Peter: Come here, Lord! Look down there! Must be Prosper Valley. *(The Lord comes up beside him. From the valley below, we hear voices singing a hymn: "What A Friend We Have In Jesus, or, if at Christmas, "Silent Night." A figure enters from behind the Sang Picker. He is a Prosper Valley Farmer, a large well-fed man. He listens.)* Look at that good bottom land, Lord!

Prosper Valley Farmer: *(To himself.)* Lord?

Saint Peter: Black dirt crops. Pens, fences and barns. Timber and plaster houses. Good solid folks down there. Listen to them sing your praises, Lord Jesus!

Prosper Valley Farmer: His praises? Lord Jesus?

Saint Peter: I know we'd be welcome. Let's go down there and spend the night. *(The Prosper Valley Farmer, hat in hand, comes to Jesus and Saint Peter.)*

Prosper Valley Farmer: Begging yer pardon, Outlanders, but am I a-visualizing little sort of circle-thangs over yore heads?

Saint Peter: You might be. Some see them, some don't.

Prosper Valley Farmer: Then could you really be the Lord Jesus and—

Saint Peter: Saint Peter, beloved of the Lord. That's right. *(The Prosper Valley Farmer falls to his knees.)*

Prosper Valley Farmer: Well, Halleluia! Lord! Saint Peter! I'm from Prosper Valley, down yonder! Please come set a-spell, and spend the night, too! A storm's clabbering up, and we'll take good care of ye, and feed and rest yore bodies. We all love ye, Lord, and to worship ye day and night, why, that's what we love a-doing most! Come set a-spell. *(Saint Peter smiles broadly.)*

Saint Peter: We certainly thank you kindly. We will. Let's go, Lord! *(He turns to The Lord, who abruptly turns away.)* Lord?

Lord: This way.

Saint Peter: What?

Lord: Follow me.

Saint Peter: But where?

Lord: Up there. Up Sand Mountain.

Saint Peter: But it's almost dark! And those clouds! I think there's a storm coming.

Lord: There is. And we're going up there. *(The Lord begins to walk around the stage. Saint Peter follows him.)*

Saint Peter: All right, Lord. Whatever you say. *(To Prosper Valley Farmer.)* Sorry, Mister. So long. *(Thunder, loud. Wind and rain. Lights flash as lightning strikes around them. They move from one side of the* stage to the other. The Prosper Valley Farmer, at a distance, follows them.)

Sang Picker: Storm commenced to break on their heads, powerful ornery. They climbed Sand Mountain purt near two mile. Cold and bone-marrow damp, hit was. Raw wind, gusts sweeping the slopes. Hit was plain uncomfortable. *(Saint Peter and The Lord struggle through the storm, followed by the Prosper Valley Farmer.)*

Saint Peter: Lord, wait a minute! *(He sneezes.)* Where are we going? *(He sneezes again. The Lord points to the center of the stage.)*

Lord: There. Right up there. *(In the cabin, a dim figure of a woman lights a candle.)*

Sang Picker: Now pon my word and deed, through the wind and the rain Saint Peter seen a little tee-ninesy light in what was jest the worst kind of slattery old cabin. Timber all warped, held together it was by sticks, and mud. There wasn't even a dog around the place to bark at them. *(The Lord and Saint Peter approach the cabin. They stand before the platform at stage center. The Prosper Valley Farmer hides and watches.)*

Lord: Knock. *(Saint Peter knocks upon an imaginary door. Nothing happens.)* Again. Harder. *(Saint Peter knocks again, harder.)*

Saint Peter: If I knock any harder, it'll fall down. *(The figure of a man picks up the candle and comes to the door. With him is Fourteen Children, played by one child, a boy as young as possible, who is dressed very poorly, dirty and ragged. The man's clothes, hair and beard are all unkempt and his eyes are feverish. He opens the door a crack.)*

Jack: Whatchu men want here?

Saint Peter: *(To The Lord.)* Lord, this is pitiful.

Lord: Ask.

Saint Peter: *(Sighs.)* All right. *(To Jack.)* I am Saint Peter and this is The Lord. Can we come in? *(Pause. Jack and his child stare at them.)*

Jack: Yer who?

Saint Peter: Saint Peter and The Lord. We've been walking all the day long. We're tired, hungry, cold, and rained on. We'd appreciate a place to spend the night. *(A woman in the cabin turns around. She is much younger than the man, but gaunt and pale. She calls out.)*

Jean: Who is it?

Jack: Two men. Allowing as how they're The Lord and Saint Peter. They want in.

Jean: Well, tell 'em to possess their souls in patience. *(She goes to the door, lurching unsteadily. She is also dressed in rags, unkempt as her husband. She stares out, squinting and weaving. Saint Peter turns away from her.)*

Saint Peter: Whew! Lord, this woman's drunk. Smell her breath?

Lord: They both are. *(Thunder crashes down on them. The rain pounds down. Lightning flashes. The wind howls.)*

Jean: Why, shore. I kin tell. At thar's The Lord and at thar's Saint Peter. Of a sartin. Ask 'em in.

Jack: Reckon we should?

Jean: No, but whut difference do hit make? Whoever they be, if they figgur on cutting our throats, all they have to do is kick down the door. *(Thunder, rain, wind and lightning. Jean takes the chairs down from the wall.)*

Saint Peter: I'm sorry to trouble you, but we're getting wet. *(He sneezes again.)*

Jack: Well, come on in.

Jean: *(Laughing.)* Jest in time fer supper. *(Jack and Jean step back. Lights come up on the interior of the mountain cabin. It is stark and primitive. Outside, the Prosper Valley Farmer has seen The Lord and Saint Peter enter the cabin. With a gesture of disgust, he exits.)*

Sang Picker: Hit wasn't much more'n a shack. A stone fireplace, some slat chairs, an old battered cupboard, a split log fer a dinner table, some corn-shuck mattresses, and that was all. Saint Peter seen what this was. A hard time family.

Jean: All right, then. The Lord gets the head of the table, I reckon, and Saint Peter sits the foot of it, or something like that. Shore. At's right. *(They sit around the table. The Lord at right, Saint Peter at left. Jean goes to a pot hanging in the fireplace, over a meager flame.)*

Sang Picker: The woman give them what she had. Shaller clay bowls of thin corn soup. A thumb of cornbread apiece. And now, friends, that there was all. There wasn't no more. *(Saint Peter and The Lord look at what they have to eat, and then they look at the child, who gets the same, sits and eats greedily.)* An old man and his young wife, the way men do in these mountains, her having babies one a year since she was a little girl herself, fourteen children now, none of 'em too happy mealtimes. They took what they got, sat down and fought over it.

Fourteen Children: *(Fighting.)* Gimme that! No, I won't! Yes, you will! No, I won't! Let that be! I'll bust you upside the head! I'll tear out yore gizzard! No, you won't! Yes, I will! Ow! Ow!!

Jean: Hush, chillun! Eat yore supper!

Sang Picker: Hit was jest plain squalid. Saint Peter had a hard time a-choking down at soup. This kind of thang got on his nerves. He appreciated one thing at a time, calm at the dinner table and quiet chillun. And at soup was hog slop. *(The Lord finishes his soup, with relish.)*

Lord: Hmm. Very good. *(He reaches for his switch. He twitches it.*

There is a sudden glare and blaze of fire in the fireplace. The Lord smiles. Fourteen Children, finished, erupts again.)

Fourteen Children: I won't neither! Ow! Give at back! I'll bust ye open! I'll funeralize ye! I'll kill ye graveyard dead! Ow! Owww!!! *(The Lord stands up. He goes to Fourteen Children.)*

Lord: *(Quietly.)* Hush. Listen to me. *(He holds out his arm. Fourteen Children goes to The Lord, leans against him and listens to him.)*

Sang Picker: The Lord told Fourteen Children a story about a sad, worried peacock. Then he turned around and told anothern about a fat mountain lion. Then he told a story about chillun like them, all lost in the dark forest, what couldn't get theirselves home. They smiled at the first two stories, but not at the last un. The Lord waved his stick and the fire blazed up agin and Fourteen Chillun commenced to yawn. Afore a grown man kin spit, they got drowsy and stayed that way. *(The Lord gets up, leaving Fourteen Children settled peacefully in the chair. They all stare at Fourteen Children, then Jack and Jean stare at The Lord as a bright light glows around him.)*

Saint Peter: You see? I told you he was the Lord. He can do anything.

Lord: *(Smiling.)* He's right. What you're seeing now are halos. *(The light glows brighter, on him and on Saint Peter.)* That is Saint Peter. I am the Lord. *(Clumsily, Jack and Jean get to their knees before The Lord.)* No, now don't do that. You're not used to it, for one thing, and you're both drunk for another. Just be yourselves. *(The light fades. Jack and Jean stand before The Lord and Saint Peter, hanging their heads.)*

Sang Picker: Hit was a plain embarrassment. Neither soul thar knowed whut to say. *(Pause.)*

Saint Peter: *(Sternly.)* What are your names?

Jack: Jack, Saint Peter.

Jean: Jean, Saint Peter.

Saint Peter: Jack and Jean. Old man, young woman. Whiskey. You two married? *(They look at each other, then shake their heads.)* You go to church? At all? *(Same.)* Well, no wonder you're in such a mess.

Jack: Lord. Saint Peter. Hit warn't always thisaway. We figgered we wus like everbody else, fer a time. But we can't farm no moren a passle of corn, land here above the waterfalls is powerful sandy, last year our cow died, and whut with the chillun being so puny and poorly, we stopped going places much, and afore we knowed it, we wus living up here alone.

Saint Peter: Up here by yourselves, with fourteen children and a jug of whiskey, drinking until the world looks little.

Jack: Yes, sir.

Jean: Not at much at first, then the littliest bit more, and then some more *and now all the time. We've come to that.*

Saint Peter: *And when you drink, do you fight? Get mad, yell and shout, hit each other? The children? (They nod.)*

Jack and Jean: *(Quietly.)* Sometimes. Yes, sir.

Jack: *(To The Lord.)* Whut happened to us, Lord?

Saint Peter: I just told you. Old man, young woman, no wedding, no church, and too much corn liquor.

Lord: *(To Saint Peter.)* Hush. *(To Jack.)* We can't really tell you. Life can be mysterious, sometimes, and sad. *(Pause.)* Let me put it this way. I have no sermons on the matter. *(With a look at Saint Peter.)* And neither does he.

Sang Picker: Well since the Lord ruled that plumb out, Saint Peter didn't know whut else to say, and give up a-wondering why they wus there. Hit wus another embarrassment. The onliest question left hanging wus whut sort of tribute at miserable shack could pay to the Lord and his Apostle Peter, who'd been good enough to visit. Jack figgured he only had one thang. *(Jack, making a decision, goes to the cupboard and gets a clay jug and some clay mugs. He sets them down before The Lord and Saint Peter.)* Sand Mountain brandy, Lord. Ain't very much and ain't very good, but hit's the best thang we got here, and hit's yours.

Saint Peter: Man, put that away. That's what's caused all your trouble in the first place.

Lord: Hush. *(To Jack.)* That will do. We thank you. *(Jack pours brandy for them and for himself, to Saint Peter's exasperation. When he is finished, we see he has poured out the last drop in the jug and there is nothing left. The Lord lifts his cup.)*

Lord: To this house.

Jack and Jean: Thank you, Lord.

Saint Peter: Whew. To this house. *(They sip the mountain brandy. Saint Peter makes a face, and The Lord glares at him, kicks him under the table. Then he holds out his switch, swishes it slightly. The fire, with a whoosh, flares up again. They drink and watch it burn. Pause.)*

Sang Picker: At brandy wus hair raisin'. But, in the least little while, they wus all feeling powerful improved, like that pore corn soup had been nourishment a-plenty, and the awful brandy good fer a body, too. At fire, which wus almost burned out, flared up agin, and they found theirselves sitting around the place in tollable comfort, drinking and pondering the fire. *(Pause.)* Hit wus The Lord what commenced it.

Lord: Know what it means when you stumble over a stone?

Jack: No, Lord. Whut?

Lord: *(Slowly.)* It means on that spot a fiddle player lies buried. *(Pause.*

Jack and Jean look at each other.)

Jack: Know whut's the onliest thang kin cure the deadly curdles of leper sickness?

Lord: No. What?

Jack: Ye have to wash yore skin in the blood of a man who's life you have saved. *(The Lord nods.)*

Sang Picker: The Lord pondered at. So did Saint Peter.

Saint Peter: Now, where did you hear that?

Jack: Here on Sand Mountain, awhile ago. I know a feller around here, too, says he onct taught cats to hold candlesticks. *(Pause.)*

Saint Peter: Oh, stop. What for?

Jack: So he could turn a mouse loose, and see whut'd happen.

Lord: What did?

Jack: Them cats dropped them candlesticks and went after at mouse. *(Pause.)* Ye learn, but ye fergit.

Saint Peter: What?

Lord: You learn, but you forget.

Jack: I reckon. *(They acknowledge each other's approval.)*

Sang Picker: Now you know Saint Peter, pon my word and deed, he couldn't comprehend why Jesus had at littliest piece of a smile on his face, or why Jack and Jean did too. Hit wus like the three of them wus taking a few throws and tosses afore some kind of a ball game. *(Pause.)*

Jean: A humpback and blind man, down around Hazel Creek, robbed a traveling salesman. They set down to divy up the goods. And fell out. "You damn scoundrel," said the blind man, "you're a-cheating me." "You miserable lint-head," said the humpback, "you ain't blind at tall." "Yes, I am," said the blind man and "No, you ain't," said the hump back, and then they both said, "You son of a bitch." The humpback rubbed dirt in the blind man's eyes, and that give him back his sight. The blind man hit the hump back with a stick, and that broke his hump. The blind man seen the humpback standing thar tall and handsome-bodied, and the humpback seen the blind man a-looking at him with two big shiny-smart eyes, and they fancied each other so much, they lived together happy and pleasant all their lives. *(Pause.)*

Sang Picker: This time Saint Peter jest looked out the one winder of the cabin, at the rain a-coming down. He did his best to put it together some way, the blind man and the humpback, and make some sense out of 'em, but he couldn't and gave up. *(The Lord holds out his cup.)*

Lord: Could I have a drop more of this good brandy?

Jack: We're sorry, Lord.

Jean: There ain't no more. That wus all we had.

Lord: Take a look. *(Jack picks up what he is sure is an empty jug, and finds it heavy and full.)*

Sang Picker: Shore enough, the jug was full, so Jack poured them all a big fat dollop. And hit didn't taste like no sulfur this time, no, sir, hit tasted like the bestest gum tree mountain brandy a body ever had. I mean, hit wus smooth as cedar and warm as a cat. *(Thunder, wind, rain and a surge of flames in the fireplace.)* And while at storm broke open above 'em, big logs, thick and fat, jest plain grew in the fireplace, a-sizzlin and a-poppin. Outside at pore miserable shack, goobers and gusts of rain passed right over the roof, and never touched it nowhere. *(Saint Peter makes a show of stretching and yawning.)*

Saint Peter: I sure am sleepy. That brandy. This fire. All the rain. Lord, isn't it about time we turned in?

Lord: Not yet. *(He smiles, sips his brandy and waits.)*

Jack: One day, near Hangman's Gap, a deef man went to see his sick neighbor. *(Saint Peter sits back, groaning.)* He set down by his neighbor's bed and said, "How are ye?" Sick man said, "Dying." Deef man said, "Thank God fer that! Who's yer doctor?" Sick man said, "Doctor Death! Now git out and leave me alone!" Deef man said, "At's wonderful! Whut medicine is he a-giving ye?" Sick man said, "Poison! Now will ye plain damn go away and let me die?" Deef man said, "Why, shorely, and I'll come see ye tomorrow, too." *(Pause. Jack, Jean, and The Lord relish the story. As before, Saint Peter shakes his head.)*

Sang Picker: Right about here Saint Peter plain decided Jack had woobles in the head. He looked over at The Lord to sort of shrug but there The Lord was, a-smiling agin. And then, whut floored Saint Peter, The Lord was a-telling one! *(The Lord leans forward in his chair, and tells a story, inaudible to us, to Jack and Jean. Saint Peter stares at him, open-mouthed.)* Some story about folks he'd heared of near the Cumberland Gap, where the men were so contrary, if ye throwed them in a river, they'd float upstream. Where the women wus so ugly they had to blindfold babies to git 'em to suck. *(Jack and Jean nod their approval, without smiling more than they need to, and The Lord turns to Saint Peter, nodding. Thunder. Lightning.)* Logs burned. At jar stayed full of brandy. Rain and wind flew past the shack, leaving it dry. Jack told—

Jack: The Moon Frog—

Sang Picker: Jean told—

Jean: The Water Man—

Sang Picker: The Lord told—

Lord: The Child Who Could Not Shudder. *(Thunder, lightning, rain and wind.)*

Sang Picker: Then Jack told—
Jack: The Breaking of the Stone of Patience—
Sang Picker: Jean told—
Jean: Sherrif Unexpected and the Bony Bandit.
Sang Picker: And The Lord told—
Lord: Flowering Cholera, Phantom Funerals, and Sleeping Kings. *(Pause. Saint Peter smacks a fist into the palm of one hand, decisively.)*
Sang Picker: Saint Peter figgured this'd gone fur enough. Crazy wild stories, well, he'd fight fire with fire, and give 'em something strong, human, and down to earth sensible. With a meaning to it!
Saint Peter: Once upon a time, there was a Sailor and a Parrot. The Sailor sold his Parrot to the Queen, who was beautiful and proud. She kept him in a golden cage in her castle bedroom. One day the Queen stepped naked out of her bath. The Parrot whistled and said, "Whew-o! I see your ass!" This made the Queen furious. She opened the golden cage, pulled out that Parrot by the throat, choked him, banged him on the floor, and threw him out the window. He landed on a pile of garbage. He was lying there when a scrawny Chicken came sailing out of the kitchen window, neck wrung too, and landed on the garbage pile next to the Parrot. The Parrot thought a minute, and then said, "Whew-o! Whose ass did you see?" *(Saint Peter laughs at his own story, slapping his knees.)*
Sang Picker: Jack, Jean and the Lord were real polite about it.
Jean: That wus plain interesting.
Jack: Hit wus, of a sartin.
Sang Picker: Then Jean told—
Jean: The Lady Who Gave Birth To A Rat! *(There is a terrific burst of thunder, wind and lightning. Saint Peter shrinks back in his chair.)*
Sang Picker: Saint Peter's skin plain crawled. In the rain outside, at Sand Mountain wind howled like bobcats. Then Jack and Jean together told—
Jack: Goforth Baines.
Jean: And his devil son, Stamper.
Saint Peter: Oh, really.
Jack: And how he died. You want to hear it, Lord?
Lord: We do. *(A low rumble of thunder.)*
Jack: First you must know Stamper Baines got a Sand Mountain girl named Sally Newell pregnant.
Jean: Sally loved him fer that. She come a-running with shining eyes, to tell him about the baby. When did he want to marry her?
Jack: Stamper jest laughed. Whut kind of a fool did she take him fer? At baby's got as many daddys as a pickle's got warts.
Jean: Sally hated him fer that. When Stamper went off from her still a-

laughing, hit were a mistake.

Jack: She got her three brothers, Jack, Zack and Mack Newell. They waited fer Stamper Baines behind a chincapin tree, fell upon him graveyard deadly with barlow knives, cut him all apart, throwed the pieces in a totesack, and give it to Sally Newell. From his bones—

Jean: She made her a chair.

Jack: From his skin—

Jean: She made her a mattress.

Jack: From his skull—

Jean: She made her a goblet.

Jack: Wine from his blood.

Jean: Candles from his fat.

Jack: Candlewicks from his hair.

Jean: Stew from his fingers.

Jack: And soup from his balls.

Jean: Then she invited his father, Goforth Baines, to supper. *(Saint Peter chokes and coughs.)*

Jack: But Goforth Baines had his doubts. He come to Sally Newell's cabin, but with eyes in the back of his head. When she laid out the big meal afore him, he asked her what she'd been a-doing lately. Sally smiled at that.

Jean: She answered him with a riddle, and a song. *(She sings.)* I BEEN A-SITTING WITH MY LOVE-O-

Jack: *(Speaking.)* The chair—

Jean: I BEEN A-DRINKING WITH MY LOVE-O—

Jack: The goblet—

Jean: I BEEN A-SLEEPING WITH MY LOVE-O—

Jack: The mattress—

Jean: I BEEN A-READING WITH MY LOVE-O—

Jack: The candles—

Jean: I BEEN A-EATING WITH MY LOVE-O—

Jack: The soup and the stew—

Jean: I'LL GIVE YOU SOME WINE-O—

Jack: The blood—

Jean: IF YE GUESS ME A-RIGHT-O!

Jack: But all fer naught, cause Goforth Baines guessed her hateful riddle, unsheathed his own great barlow knife, and called her she-devil. In rushed Jack, Zack and Mack Newell, to cut Goforth apart too, but mighty Goforth Baines, in a tantrum, killed them all, afore he cut off Sally Newell's head. *(Jack and Jean sing lustily, with mountain harmony, stamping their feet.)*

Jack and Jean: *(Singing.)*

HE SWUNG AROUND HIS BARLOW KNIFE

THEM BAD MEN THEY DID FALL,
HE CUT SALLY'S HEAD FROM HER SHOULDERS
AND HE THROWED IT AGIN THE WALL.

Jack: Then Goforth Baines, he stood thar in mortal dread at the dinner table. Stamper Baines, his evil boy. He wept his bitter tears, a-touching the bone chair, a-lifting the burning candles, and a-smelling the simmering soup. *(Saint Peter, watching, shakes his head.)*

Saint Peter: Really.

Sang Picker: Now you know Saint Peter didn't begrudge nobody no story, but he did figgure hit ought to have some mortal point to it. I say, be about life as hit really is. He did mislike jimcracky tales about people eating other people, rats born in place of babies, and wooble-headed heroes with names like Stamper and Goforth. So he stopped listening. Fer awhile.

Jean: Lord, you strike a body dead, they tell a Jesus Tale?

Saint Peter: Tell a what?

Lord: *(Smiling.)* No. Which ones you know?

Jean: All of 'em, purt near.

Lord: Tell some.

Jean: You plain positive?

Lord: I'm plain positive.

Saint Peter: Lord, what's this now? Jesus Tales?

Lord: That's right. Hush.

Jean: *(To Jack.)* Whut'll we tell?

Jack: Well, thar's Saint Peter's Divorce.

Saint Peter: Saint Peter's what?

Jean: That's whar Saint Peter is womberjawled miserable cause his wife talks too much, and he asks the Lord to git him a divorce, and the Lord says well, all right, but only if Saint Peter will marry the next woman coming down the road.

Saint Peter: Now, Lord. Wait a minute.

Lord: Tell it.

Jack: And the next woman down the road is decent looking and nods yes she'll marry Saint Peter, and be grabbies hit turns out she can't talk at all, so Saint Peter gets right happy until the Lord takes a nail pulled out of a coffin, sets it agin her back tooth, knocks the tooth out—

Jean: And at woman commences to talk and talk and she can't stop, so Saint Peter gives up and goes back to his good decent wife and forgets about divorce.

Sang Picker: And Saint Peter got up then, right stiffly, stood thar resenting all at. But the Lord was smiling, so whut could he do? *(The Lord leans forward and starts telling Jack and Jean another story. Fourteen Children* wakes up and listens, too.) Then The Lord told Jesus, Saint Peter, the Goose and the Bean, which they hadn't never heard. *(Saint Peter turns away, offended.)* And Saint Peter, he wondered then, jest a mite bitter about it, why it wus he wus forever the dummy in these doings. *(Saint Peter looks at The Lord, rubs his head.)* Why does The Lord treat me this away? When I love him and always have and always will. Why are we a-setting here in this miserable shack with these crazy people got woobles in their heads? Why ain't we down thar in at Prosper Valley we seen, with them good healthy Christian farmers, singing hymns. None of this makes no sense. *(Scratching his head, Saint Peter sits again. The Lord finishes his story, which goes over big. Jack and Jean laugh and applaud. And Fourteen Children likes it, too. Smiling, The Lord fills their cups again with brandy.)*

Lord: Well, one more.

Jack: What'll hit be, Lord?

Jean: You pick it out this time. *(Pause. The Lord is suddenly serious. He speaks very softly.)*

Lord: Tell Joseph the Carpenter.

Jean: Old Man Joseph?

Lord: And his family. You know it?

Jack and Jean: *(Together.)* We all do. *(They look at Fourteen Children, who nods.)*

Lord: Good. Tell it.

Jack: All right.

Jack and Jean: We will.

Sang Picker: And they did. Before the Lord and Saint Peter, this man and his young wife told the old story The Lord needed to hear, and to hear it, from them, is Why The Lord Come To Sand Mountain. *(Change of light, spilling out over the stage, expanding it. After consulting each other, Jack, Jean, and Fourteen Children sing.)*

Jack, Jean and Fourteen Children: *(Singing.)*

O JOSEPH WAS AN OLD MAN
AN OLD MAN WAS HE,
HE MARRIED VIRGIN MARY,
THE QUEEN OF GALILEE.

Jack: Joseph was an old man when he met Mary.

Jean: He wus eighty-nine, and she wus fourteen.

Jack: His wife of sixty years'd jest died. He wus about ready to pass on, too. Then he met Mary this young girl, who didn't want no young man. *(They move D., out of the shack. Fourteen Children stays in his chair. Their scenes will be played around a tree stump at R., a clump of logs at*

L., and in front of the cabin.)

Jean and Jack: *(Singing.)*

O JOSEPH WAS AN OLD MAN
AN OLD MAN WAS HE,
HE MARRIED VIRGIN MARY,
THE QUEEN OF GALILEE.

(Jean, as Mary, turns to Jack.)

Jean/Mary: If you want me, Joseph, take me.

Jack/Joseph: At my age?

Jean/Mary: Yes.

Jack/Joseph: Honey, whut would I do with ye? Be sensible.

Jean/Mary: All right. *(Pause.)* You were the perfect man.

Jack/Joseph: Sorry.

Jean/Mary: At's all right. *(She sighs, looks away bleakly. Jack/Joseph watches her.)*

Jack/Joseph: Now whutchu thinking about?

Jean/Mary: Hot boys. Goodbye, Joseph.

Jack/Joseph: Now, wait a minute. *(Jean/Mary weeps.)* Stop a-crying!

Jean/Mary: I ain't crying! *(She weeps.)*

Jack/Joseph: I might could use me a housekeeper.

Jean/Mary: You could?

Jack/Joseph: Fer awhile. I'll be gone soon. So we'll have no talk of marriage.

Jean/Mary: Why not? I'll marry you. I want to!

Jack/Joseph: Well, iffn ye still don't want no hot boys a year off, and I'm still here, maybe then. How's at?

Jean/Mary: At's jest fine.

Jack/Joseph: Now, Mary, I'm a plain country man, at's all.

Jean/Mary: Yes, sir. I'm glad. *(Pause.)*

Jack/Joseph: My children, my grandchildren, my great grandchildren, when they see you, they will piss green. I beg yore pardon. I swear sometimes. That bother you?

Jean/Mary: When other men swear, I see darkness. When Joseph swears, I see light. *(Joseph holds out his arm. Mary takes it and they walk together across the stage.)*

Jack/Joseph: You'll think agin, about hot boys. I won't keep'em away.

Jean/Mary: You won't have to.

Jack/Joseph: Oh, yes, I will. Whut'll ye do, in a year?

Jean/Mary: Marry you.

Jack/Joseph: On my ninetieth birthday? Hush.

Jean/Mary: I will, though. Joseph?

Jack/Joseph: Whut?

Jean/Mary: Hit ain't the ending what's important. Hit's the beginning. *(They move to the clump of logs. Joseph gives her his coat, and she shakes and brushes it.)*

Sang Picker: And two year later, Joseph wus ninety-one, married to Mary, and looking thirty years younger.

Jean: *(Singing.)*
O MARY AND JOSEPH
WALKED THROUGH A GARDEN GREEN,
THERE WERE APPLES AND CHERRIES
A-PLENTY TO BE SEEN.
(Mary helps Joseph put on his coat, happily.)

Sang Picker: She kept his house, give him hot meals, washed his clothes and cut his hair. He told her all them thangs he'd seen in his long life, and whut life wus all about and she felt safe.

Jack and Jean: *(Singing.)*
O MARY AND JOSEPH
WALKED THROUGH A GARDEN GREEN,
THERE WERE APPLES AND CHERRIES
PLENTY TO BE SEEN.

Sang Picker: He even commenced working agin, as a master carpenter, and acause of his great long age and experience, he wus in demand, too. One day, he wus a-going on a trip.

Jean/Mary: Joseph.

Jack/Joseph: *(With a little jig.)* They want four cabins and a general store. How about that?

Jean/Mary: Joseph.

Jack/Joseph: *(Dancing.)* This is going to be some junket, I tell ye.

Jean/Mary: Joseph.

Jack/Joseph: *(Dancing.)* Honey, whut is it?

Jean/Mary: I'm pregnant.

Jack/Joseph: You're whut?

Jean/Mary: I'm fixing to have a baby. You care about how it happened?

Jack/Joseph: I reckon I kin figure that out by myself.

Jean/Mary: No, you can't.

Jack/Joseph: Didn't I give ye a whole year? Say, git ye a hot boy when ye want one?

Jean/Mary: I never wanted one.

Jack/Joseph: Ye want one now.

Jean/Mary: No, I don't. *(Pause.)* Joseph, I am still a virgin. *(Pause.)*

Jack/Joseph: Honey, I have reached the age of ninety-one year. Jest don't talk to me like that.

Jean/Mary: It's the truth! Three months ago, you went off fer four days. The first afternoon, I got sleepy. I took a nap, and I dreamed a young man was standing outside my winder. He opened the winder. He clumb in the winder. Sunshine come in and mountain air. He stood by my bed. He told me something wonderful was fixing to happen to me.

Jack/Joseph: Yes, by grabbies, I reckon he did.

Jean/Mary: He had big wings on his back. Dark-green and copper-colored they were, Joseph, and they wus moving up and down like big fans. Ever so gentle, he blew in my ear. He told me I would have a holy child. Then he flew out my winder, into sunshine. I felt so peaceful. I slept awhile. I dreamed a star fell into my mouth. Then I woke up. Now I'm pregnant. *(Pause.)* What do hit mean?

Jack/Joseph: Hit means ye git pregnant through yer ear!

Jean/Mary: Joseph, Almighty God kin do anythang!

Jack/Joseph: Maybe He kin, but He don't! He made the rules! He sticks to 'em! Virgins don't have no babies! *(Pause.)*

Jean/Mary: Whut do ye want me to do? Go way?

Jack/Joseph: Be best. *(Pause.)* But if ye did, child, I'd die.

Jean/Mary: Then I won't. Go on yore trip, Joseph. But I have to ask ye this.

Jack/Joseph: No, you don't. What kin I say? At child ain't mine, hit's a green-winged angel's!

Jean: Will you allow hit's yore'n?

Jack/Joseph: I won't say hit ain't.

Jean/Mary: All right, then. Bye. Be careful.

Jack/Joseph: Yeah. You, too. *(He moves away from her, taking a file from his pocket and sitting on the tree stump, begins to work a piece of wood.)*

Sang Picker: When the baby wus born, Joseph never believed them wise men or shepherds or that star wus ary thang but accidents. He'd get fired up whenever Mary allowed as how Jesus was ary sort of special child at tall. *(Jack/Joseph turns to Fourteen Children, who comes to sit beside him, watching him quietly.)*

Jack/Joseph: Hit'll be up to yore Daddy, Least One, to tell ye. Yer nothing special. Git at through yer head. Be the worstest thang I could do to ye, son, to say ye are. Puff ye up like a fool, send ye out into the world a Momma's boy, a-thinking ye hung the moon. No, sir. Ye gonna be like my Daddy and his. Yer gonna know straight plumblines and honest buildings. Yer gonna know square scored off beams set so flush an ant can't get between, the fireplace drawing strong and the home whut's built to last. Hit's my duty, Jesus, to teach you all at. Take ye to town, show ye good men up and doing, a-building and a-sweating, opening the stores, swinging hammers, banging horseshoes, and working like men! I'll set you straight in this life, my boy. Yes, by God, I will! *(Jack/Joseph finishes his work. He holds a wooden toy out to Jesus. When one part of it is rubbed, another part spins.)* Here. This is fer you. Rub hit right thar. *(Jesus does. The primitive toy spins.)* Hit's a whimmy-diddle. Play whilst ye kin, son. *(Fourteen Children goes back to his chair.)*

Sang Picker: Now because Mary believed the boy was a holy child and old Joseph didn't, Jesus had passles of trouble as a boy. He acted up. Wouldn't mind nobody. Talked back. Got into this fix and that with other chillun. *(Jack/Joseph and Jean/Mary meet at C.)*

Jack/Joseph: Where is he? Whut's happened?

Jean/Mary: They were all on the river bank, making animals out of clay. One little boy was making a sparrow. They say Jesus took it away from him, blew on it, and it flew away!

Jack/Joseph: More crazy talk. Hit's all them stories told about him. Holy child. Wise men and stars and all that. See what happens? People commence gitting outlandish ideas about somebody and hit won't never stop.

Jean/Mary: When I got thar, he had all them chillun setting at his feet. He wus telling them all stories.

Jack/Joseph: Where is he now?

Jean/Mary: I don't know. When he saw me, he ran off. *(Fourteen children/ Jesus, stands before them. Jack/Joseph gets up, stares at him coldly.)*

Jack/Joseph: Well. Come home fer supper, did ye? Hm. *(He turns away from him. Jean/Mary sits by him.)*

Jean/Mary: I should have stopped him a long time ago. Making you a man too soon. He's wrong. You're not a man yet, you're still a boy. He shouldn't be so hard on you. All that work. Hit's no way to treat a little boy. No wonder you run away and tell stories. I won't have it. My son will never be a ditchdigger. Or some lackey. Or some carpenter. We don't make too much of ourselves, you and me. You are better than all this. There is more to life than what we know. You will find it. *(Jack/Joseph stands before them. Jean/Mary turns away.)*

Jack/Joseph: I should have stopped her a long time ago. She's kept you a child too long. You aint' the sun and the moon. We're dust, Jesus. You, me, yore Momma, yore little friends, all the world. Don't stir it up. *(Pause.)* I dreamed about all at when I was a boy. My kingdom. But I had to go to work, like a man, with a hammer and saw. I did the best I could. Try to do more, is crazy. So git hit straight. Please me, ye'll cross her. Please her, ye'll cross me. Take yore pick, and never mind kingdoms. You ain't a baby no more. *(He turns away. Pause. Fourteen Children/Jesus lets out a cry of frustration and rage and runs away.)*

Sang Picker: That little boy become a little demon that night. Run through the town, breaking winders, turning thangs upside down. Folks yelled at him, called him a Child Terror, and the whole town chased after him. They caught him, cornered him. Joseph and Mary had to come git their boy, and when they did, there was a plain squalid, pore-ways family fight, right there fer everbody to see. *(Jack/Joseph and Jean/Mary face Fourteen Children/Jesus.)*

Jack/Joseph: Tell these people yer sorry and come on home.

Fourteen Children/Jesus: I won't.

Jack/Joseph: Oh, yes, you will.

Fourteen Children/Jesus: You go to hell.

Jean/Mary: What did you say?

Fourteen Children/Jesus: *(Shouting.)* You, too!!

Jack/Joseph: Ah! *(Jack/Joseph strikes Fourteen Children/Jesus.)*

Fourteen Children/Jesus: Ah! *(Fourteen Children/Jesus grabs Jack/Joseph's staff and hits him with it, knocking him down. In the cabin, The Lord suddenly stands and moves forward. Frightened, Fourteen Children/Jesus drops the staff and runs to his mother. They go to Jack/Joseph, who holds up one hand, warding them off.)*

Sang Picker: He wouldn't go to bed. He hobbled to his workshop, sat there in the dark and wouldn't talk to nobody. *(Jack/Joseph sits by himself, on the edge of the cabin floor, The Lord standing just behind him.)*

Jean/Mary: Joseph. *(No answer.)* Joseph.

Jack/Joseph: Burning up. Burning up.

Jean/Mary: Come to bed, Joseph.

Jack/Joseph: On fire, like wood.

Jean/Mary: Jesus is here. He's sorry for what he done.

Jack/Joseph: And the wind a-blowing. I'm burning up. *(Pause. He looks at a wall.)* Ah! I see him! There he be! *(He points at the wall.)* He's come!

Jean/Mary: Who's come, Joseph?

Jack/Joseph: Angel of Death, that's who! I see him, all in black, with at shining sword! With a littlest drop of gall on hit's tip I got to drink, afore he cuts my soul from my body, and throws me away. Jesus!

Fourteen Children/Jesus: Yes, sir.

Jack/Joseph: You look. Tell me what ye see.

Sang Picker: Jesus looked outside. There wasn't nothing thar. Not one blessed thang. *(Fourteen Children/Jesus stares out the window.)* At young boy's hands, what struck his father, ached. His tongue, what cursed his mother, ached. He wus powerful scared but he knowed what he wus a-going to do. *(Fourteen Children/Jesus sits by Jack/Joseph, takes his hand and holds it. The Lord speaks for him.)*

Lord: Yer right, Daddy. At angel is thar, and on the tip of his sword hangs the gall you got to drink. He's fixing to cut yore body from yore soul and throw hit away.

Jack/Joseph: Jest like I said?

Lord: Jest like ye said. But I'm here, too. Yore boy. I tell ye, magic is mine, powers whut stretch beyond this earth. Kin ye hear me? Ain't nothing stronger than my love fer ye. Kin ye hear me? *(Fourteen Children/Jesus gets up, looks out the window.)* I'm a telling at black-dress angel, put up ye great sword, and step aside. Angel of Death, ye going to wait. I got to talk to my Daddy. I got to tell him goodbye. *(Fourteen Children/Jesus sits again, holds Jack/Joseph's hand.)* The rivers of fire are cool water. The mountains of hell are sweet bottom land. Nary thang burns ye. Nary thang kin hurt ye. Everythang is all right. Go in peace, Daddy. *(Jack/Joseph dies. Fourteen Children/Jesus lets go of his hand, bows his head.)*

Sang Picker: When Joseph died, Jesus wept.

Jean: *(Singing softly.)*

O JOSEPH WAS AN OLD MAN
AN OLD MAN WAS HE,
HE MARRIED VIRGIN MARY
THE QUEEN OF GALILEE.

Sang Picker: When at story got told, the fire was a-going out, and The Lord didn't make it burn no more. He'd come to Sand Mountain to hear tell about his Daddy, and Mary and hisself as a child, and he had. *(Pause. Saint Peter, who some time before fell asleep, now wakes up.)*

Saint Peter: Ah. Well. Some story. But now, Lord, none of that really happened, did it?

Sang Picker: And the Lord loved Saint Peter, the fisherman he knowed as a man, who reminded him of the carpenter he'd knowed as a boy.

Saint Peter: I mean, what's the use of a story about things that never happened? What's the point of it? *(The Lord looks at Jean. Jean looks at Jack.)*

Jean: Hit ain't the ending whut's important. Hit's the beginning.

Saint Peter: What?

Lord: Never mind. *(Smiling.)* Let's turn in. *(They all sit in their chairs and go to sleep. Very short pause. They wake up, and stir themselves.)*

Sang Picker: In the morning, when the Lord and Saint Peter were fixing to move along, Jean was about to wash the family rags in a beat-up old tub.

(Jean sets a battered wooden washtub on the table.)

Saint Peter: Wash day, Jean?

Jean: Yes, sir, shore is. We'uns are pore but clean.

Saint Peter: Well, we appreciate your hospitality.

Jack: Don't say nothing about it. *(The Lord faces them. He holds up his hands.)*

Lord: Now's the time for your knees, if you like. *(The family kneels before The Lord.)* What this morning you first begin, will not stop until tonight. *(They look at each other, puzzled. The Lord makes the sign of the cross over them. They get up and all shake hands.)*

Jack, Jean and Fourteen Children: Goodbye! Goodbye, Lord! Goodbye, Saint Peter!

Saint Peter and Lord: Goodbye! Goodbye! *(Saint Peter and The Lord leave the cabin, turning their backs and walking in place. Jean goes back to washing clothes. Enter Prosper Valley Farmer.)*

Sang Picker: Hit didn't take long.

Jean: Oh. Oh!! Ohhhh!!!! *(Spotlight on the tub. Beautiful, magical music. Jean begins pulling clothes out of the tub.)*

Fourteen Children: Momma! Momma!

Jean: Looky here! Looky here!

Sang Picker: Work clothes, Sunday clothes, hunting clothes, sleeping clothes, lace kerchiefs and colored bandanas, purty dresses, sheep-wool coats, big thick socks, everthang like that! *(Jack, Jean and Fourteen Children hold the clothes. The Prosper Valley Farmer watches.)*

Jack, Jean and Fourteen Children: Thank you, Lord! *(They put the clothes back in the tub and set it aside, turning their backs. The Prosper Valley Farmer runs around to the other side of the stage, waiting for The Lord and Saint Peter.)*

Sang Picker: Now pon my word and deed, when at fat Prosper Valley Farmer seen at, he skittered after The Lord and Saint Peter and jest plain faced them down. *(The Prosper Valley Farmer stops The Lord and Saint Peter.)*

Prosper Valley Farmer: Hold on! Both! Come see us, we'd a give ye real comfort. Bean-bacon soup, goat barbecue, corn, black-eyed peas, feather beds, holiness hymn-singing and powerful preaching in yore sacred name. Ye didn't care fer it. All right! But at least do fer us the same ye done fer them shiftless no good cornsqueezers ye spent yore time with. All we ask, if you are really The Lord and Saint Peter, is jest be fair!!

Saint Peter: He's right, Lord. You have to.

Lord: Have to what?

Saint Peter: You know. What you did for Jack and Jean and their children.

Lord: I won't do it. *(He turns away. Saint Peter gets mad.)*

Saint Peter: Well, why not?

Lord: Never mind. I just won't.

Saint Peter: Now listen! I stayed up half the night listening to lunatics tell crazy stories, when we could have been down in Prosper Valley with the faithful and the devoted. I tolerated your kind of folks, now you tolerate mine!

Lord: You sure about that? The faithful and the devoted?

Saint Peter: Yes!!

Lord: All right. *(He turns to the Prosper Valley Farmer, who quickly falls on his knees before The Lord.)* What-this-morning-you-first-begin-will-not-stop-until-tonight. *(The Prosper Valley Farmer jumps up.)*

Prosper Valley Farmer: Thank you, Lord!

Saint Peter: Thank you, Lord.

Lord: Follow me. *(Saint Peter does, and they exit. The Sang Picker moves down to the edge of one side of the stage.)*

Sang Picker: Well, at farmer lit out fer Prosper Valley like a scaulded dog, and got everbody tergether.

Prosper Valley Farmer: "What this morning you first begin, will not stop until tonight." So! Everybody git yer purse! Open 'em up! We'll commence now, a-counting silver dollars! We'll not a body stop all day long, and like them clothes, them silver dollars'll keep on a-coming til hits dark! Let's go! *(He turns away, stops, turns back.)* No, hold it! Everbody best light into the woods thar and relieve yeselves. At way we won't never have to stop all day long! *(He runs off. The Sang Picker moves to the center of the stage and looks at the audience.)*

Sang Picker: Yep. Like the preachers say, "The Lord he moves in mysterious ways." *(We hear a whistle, offhand, the tune of the Joseph and Mary ballad. In the cabin, Jack and Jean hang up the two extra chairs on the wall again, and sit with Fourteen Children in their mountain home, amid the colors of the clothes, and the lights go down on them.)* The top of Sand Mountain is a bald now, in timothy grass. Hits peak is a sunshiney meadow, with wildflowers pleasant as a scenery of children, some say the wind keeps clear, some say ghosts of run-off Indians tend. But some on Sand Mountain say hit's a bald because the Lord hisself won't let nothing overgrow it. That thar was onct an old mountain shack up thar he set a spell in one night, laughing and telling tall tales, and he liked the way he wus treated. *(The light focuses on the Sang Picker's smiling face. The whistling ends.)* Course, a body kin deny it. Say The Lord never did laugh or tell no tall tales. Well, I never heared him laugh, but everbody knows he liked a story, and I'll dispute that anywhar. At's whut I think. *(Pause.)* Now. *(She leans forward, smiling.)* Whut do you think? *(Blackout.)*

THREE POETS

KOMACHI for Scott Powers
HROSVITHA for Adrienne Thompson
AKHMATOVA for Kathleen Chalfant

KOMACHI - from the Komachi Noh Plays of Japan

KOMACHI, a poet, young, beautiful and brilliant, who wears a Noh mask.
KOMACHI'S VOICE, a woman speaking KOMACHI'S lines, dressed in black.
SHOSHO, a warrior Prince, passionate and physical.

Place: A seashore in Japan.
Time: 9th century.

HROSVITHA - from her play ABRAHAM

GERBERGA, Abbess of Gandersheim, a mature and powerful Canoness Mother Superior.
HROSVITHA, a talented and creative nun.
BROTHER WILLIAM, a furious monk.
ABRAHAM, a hermit, ascetic and troubled.
MARY, his niece, young and beautiful.

Place: The free convent of Gandersheim, in Saxony.
Time: Toward the end of the 10th century.

AKHMATOVA - from the poetry of Anna Akhmatova and Osip Mandelstam

PECDOV a Minister of Culture, urbane and deadly.
MARYA, a school teacher, young and frightened.
RUDINSKY, a policeman, ruthless and rough.
KLARINA, a poet, elegant and sick at heart.
ANNA AKHMATOVA, a regal woman, a great poet.

Place: Moscow
Time: 10 a.m. March 6, 1953

THREE POETS was commissioned by the New York Foundation for the Arts and The Theater for the New City, Crystal Field and George Bartenieff, Artistic Directors. It opened there in November, 1989, directed by Romulus Linney, with sets and costumes by Anne C. Patterson, lights by David Finally, production stage manager, Ellen Melaver. The cast was as follows:

KOMACHI

KOMACHI......................Adrienne Thompson
KOMACHI'S VOICE........Kathleen Chalfant
SHOSHO........................Scott Sowers

HROSVITHA

GERBERGA...................Kathleen Chalfant
HROSVITHA..................Mary Fosket
BROTHER WILLIAM.......John MacKay
ABRAHAM....................Scott Sowers
MARY..........................Adrienne Thompson

AKHMATOVA

PECDOV........................John MacKay
MARYA.........................Adrienne Thompson
RUDINSKY....................Scott Sowers
KLARINA......................Mary Fosket
ANNA AKHMATOVA......Kathleen Chalfant

KOMACHI

Sound of waves and sea birds.

A seashore tree stump. Below it, three seaworn rocks, and lying across them, a medieval Japanese sword in its scabbard.

Darkness. Silence. A flute plays.

Light appears, very slowly, on Komachi, who is wearing a Noh mask of a beautiful young woman. She wears a black kimono and has a white scarf around her waist. Komachi's VOICE, another actress, dressed in black, speaks for her.

Beside her stands Prince Shosho. He is not masked. He has a red scarf over one shoulder. He now has the sword and scabbard in his belt.

Flute stops.

Komachi
In the spring
young men come running
to love
and kill
young women.

Shosho
In the spring
young women wait
like spiders
to trap young men.

Komachi
Only the poet
who writes about love
when young—

Shosho
can write about life
when old.

Komachi
It takes one
to understand the other.

(The flute plays again. Komachi moves downstage and sits on the tree stump. Shosho follows, and formally addresses her.)

Shosho
I have come
beautiful Komachi
to pay my respects.
Shosho
Third Son of the Emperor
Prince of this kingdom.

(Komachi nods.)

Komachi
It is good of you
to visit me.

Shosho
Komachi!
You are the greatest beauty
in Japan!
One of the Six Poetic Geniuses
of our age.
I love you!
I will have you
and no one else!

Komachi
Prince, be careful.
When you know me
You might not want me.

Shosho
In love with you
I too am a poet!
You have inspired me!
I have written this!!

(Shosho kneels and declaims passionately.)

I see you in my sleep!
I hold you in my arms!
Let me love you now
Like I do in my dreams!

(Shosho looks at Komachi. She shakes her head slightly.)

Komachi
I slept, in love with you,
and oh, you appeared before me.
Had I known
it was a dream
Nothing could have waked me.

(Shosho nods.)

Shosho
That is better.

Komachi
Yes it is.

(Shosho declaims again, even more passionately.)

Shosho
I am on fire!
My body burns for you
And you won't have me!
I am filled with pain
All this moonlit night!

(He looks at her. Komachi shakes her head.)

Komachi
Through these dark nights
I sleep and wake
my passion rising
face on fire
a heart charred wood

turning black.

(Shosho sits up, nods.)

Shosho
That too is better.

Komachi
Yes it is.

Shosho
Very well!
Since you know
so much about love
tell me what it is,
in one poem!

Komachi
Very well.
He forgot about me.
And I was so sure he wouldn't.
Now all I do is wonder
if I exist.

Shosho
That is a poem?

Komachi
Yes it is.

Shosho
You think that is love?

Komachi
Yes I do.

Shosho
No! Love is a storm, a thunderbolt!
It strikes and crushes!
You are trying to make my desire foolish.
My passion ridiculous.

Komachi
Your passion is military not amatory.
Lovers without poetry
are trouble enough.
With it
they are exhausting.

Shosho
You take this disdainful attitude
toward those who love you?

Komachi
Yes I do.

Shosho
And write poem after poem about love
yourself?

Komachi
Yes I will.

Shosho
And you alone
know what love is?

Komachi
I alone
know that I alone
will love freely,
and not be conquered
by anyone's passion,
no matter how deeply felt
they think it may be.

Shosho
This only means
you love someone else.
The man who forgot about you.
What about him?

Komachi
Oh.
Outside it stays the same
inside it crumbles away
that is the flower
of a man's heart
in this world.

Shosho
Then forget him!
Forget every man you have ever met
but me!
I would die for you!

Komachi
No one
dies for love.
Some live for it,
falling in love
over and over and over,
as I do,
happy only then
but we die of other causes.

Shosho
How can you
make fun of me,
of this fire blazing
inside me!

Komachi
You want something you can't have.
and it burns.
You call it fire,
but I think
it has more to do
with impatience
than with passion.

Shosho
And you will write poems
insulting me.

Komachi
Yes, I will.

(Pause.)

Give in? Lie down?
Like a ripple on a lake
to a passing wind?
There are no fish in these waters.
I'm not here either.
Can't you see that?
Coming here
on your fisherman feet.

Shosho
You will refuse me,
a Prince of this Kingdom?

Komachi
Yes I will.

Shosho
I can take you by force!

Komachi
And disgrace yourself forever?
In this life and the one to come?

Shosho
But in the life to come
those who perished
enraged with passion
must linger
between life and death,
to wear out their humiliation
and take their revenge.

(Komachi moves away from Shosho.)

Komachi
Horrible man!

(Change of light: the stage is streaked with sharp-edged slants of light and

shadow. Sound of waves. Komachi goes to the seashore rocks, standing on the other side of them from Shosho.)

I will run from you,
to a house in a forest,
on an island
in the sea.

Shosho
And I will follow you!

(He follows her.)

Komachi
Here, across the waves
I turn and watch
To see if you will really come.

Shosho
There is no bridge.
How will I find you?

(He looks at the rocks.)

The rocks! I will pick them up one by one
and one by one with bloody hands
build a bridge to your door.
Up! Down! Bend! Work!

(He moves the rocks about.)

Tearing the land from itself
until the earth itself reaches out
as my pathway to your bed.

(He stops, looks at her.)

The bridge is finished.
Now you know I will find you.

Komachi
Now I know you will find me!

Shosho
Is the moon down?
Yes, darkness!

Komachi
Now you can come to me.
In the moonlight you can lead
your horse through the shadows.

(Shosho puts the red scarf around his neck.)

Shosho
Look how I go to you!
My scarf at my throat!

Komachi
Black wind, rising waves,
They will not keep you from me.

Shosho
On I journey
across my bridge
to your island forests
through showers of leaves.
Leading my horse
I see you watching from your window—

Komachi
As the storm breaks!

(Shosho struggles against an imaginary storm.)

Shosho
Waves pound the shore!
The wind rises—

Komachi
Blowing your scarf
out behind your throat—

Shosho
Lightning flashes!
I see you
beautiful and scornful!
Mocking me!

Komachi
The wind! The waves!

Shosho
The storm!

Komachi
The rocks are wet and slippery!

Shosho
My horse is frightened!

Komachi
He rears up!

Shosho
His hooves thrash in the air!

Komachi
His hooves strike your face!

(Shosho falls to his knees. He screams. Then he holds out the red scarf.)

Shosho
And my scarf is red with blood.

(Shosho tosses the scarf on the rocks. He sits back and looks at it. Komachi goes to Shosho. She kneels beside him. Together they look at the scarf. Sound of waves.)

Komachi
Your head was torn
from your body.

Shosho
My blood washed away
in the waves.

(They sit, staring at the scarf. Lights up. Waves stop. They look at each other.)

Komachi
How was I guilty
of your ridiculous death?

Shosho
You laughed at me.
But could you forget me?

Komachi
No.

Shosho
You live!

Komachi
I live!

Shosho
Badly!

Komachi
Badly!

Shosho
Write a poem about that!

(Komachi holds out her white scarf. The flute plays again.)

Komachi
Alone and miserable
I cut my roots away,
and float like a reed on a stream.
When water asks me
I follow it anywhere.

(She puts the white scarf over her head, and bends over, an old woman.)

Shosho
You become famous
You live for a hundred years.

Komachi
Like a beggar.
My black hair turns white.
Skin coarse, face wrinkled.

Shosho
At a Festival
you watch a child dance.
Those watching you
are enlightened.
You are still beautiful,
but do not think so.

Komachi
Aching and stinking
I am filthy among outcasts
who look at me with disgust.

(Komachi bends over, walks about.)

Shosho
In the great cities you hide yourself
afraid someone will see you.
"Look! There she is!
Beautiful Komachi!"

Komachi
No! No!
Age and guilt want silence,
and no one to ask
who I am
traveller so wretched.

Shosho
Because you destroyed
the man who loved you!

Komachi
But I did not!
I did nothing to you!

Shosho
You laughed at me!!

(Komachi journeys, painfully.)

Walking, walking, behind the trees,
past lovers tombs and autumn hills—

Komachi
Above rivers flowing beside you
like this one—

Shosho
You see the boats rise and fall
on the currents
in the moonlight.

(Komachi stops at the rocks, leans forward. She bends over further, seeing something in the water.)

What's that?

Komachi
There, in the water!

Shosho
What's floating toward you there?

Komachi
It crawls down the yellow river
like a snake in a stream!

Shosho
Like a scarf!

(Shosho stands up. Komachi stares, kneeling.)

Komachi
A red scarf!

Shosho
And you see—

Komachi
I see
floating on a scarf of blood,
your head and mine.

(Shosho draws his sword and scabbard from his belt.)

Shosho
Legends of Komachi say
your head was struck from your body
by a bandit robbing graves.

Komachi
He was in fact
a Prince returned to earth
for that moment.

(Shosho holds up his sword.)

Shosho
Above you I stand,
your death in my arms.

(He lays the sword in its scabbard on her shoulder.)

Komachi
An icy fist
hits my neck
and I am gone!

Shosho
Your hair I cut off for pillows.
Your skull I throw to the river.

Komachi
Where it washes out into the sea
and then to a rocky beach
and there it stays
forever.

(Sound of waves.)

Shosho
And through your eyes
the tall grasses grow.

Komachi
So when the wind sweeps in
from the sea—

Shosho
They move and bend in your skull—

Komachi
And oh, how that hurts!

Shosho
Now with a bandit sword
in the shock of an instant
I deliver you from earth to eternity
and to me.

Komachi
Only the poet
who writes about love
when young

Shosho
Can write about life
when old.

Komachi
It takes one
to understand the other.

The flute plays again. Komachi rises and takes the red scarf to the seashore stump. Shosho follows her, sword in hand.

Both turn their backs. Komachi takes off her mask and sets it on the red scarf, staring upward. Shosho now draws the blade of his sword from its scabbard and holds it up. It flashes in the light.

A heavy burst of drums and Japanese music.

Komachi and Shosho move quickly into darkness, leaving one shaft of light falling on the mask of the poet, staring at eternity.

HROSVITHA

Shadows. Nuns sing Ave Maris Stella, a Benedictine chant, or some other medieval chant, perhaps without words, sung by one woman. It is quiet and beautiful.

A thick carpet is unfolded, and set down. On each side of the carpet, facing each other, are set two wooden Gothic chairs.

Light falls on the rug, shafts of light on the two chairs. Above them, a stained glass rose window appears.

Enter Gerberga, Abbess of Gandersheim. She is a regal figure, in a white medieval cowl, with a surplice of scarlet over her black robes. With her is Brother William, a monk in a plain robe, whose hood hides his face.

Gerberga walks with Brother William to one of the chairs and indicates that he may sit there. Then she moves, slowly, formally, to the other chair. They both sit.

The Nuns stop singing.

Gerberga: Most dearly beloved Brother William. Of all the nuns in this convent, our Sister Hrosvitha is the only one whose behavior any Bishop might consider questionable. She is a writer. She composes devotional poems, all of them above reproach. But she is also writing a play, based on pagan Roman models, and I can see how your Bishop, since he has heard of it, may be alarmed. Let us see if there is anything to be alarmed about. Will you hear our Sister describe her work? *(Brother William nods.)* Sister. *(Enter Hrosvitha. She is composed but she is thrilled by this event. She stands above the rug, and speaks to Brother William.)*

Hrosvitha: My play is called Abraham. It is written to be performed by the Sisters of the Convent, with music composed for it here. I will gladly tell you its story. It is very beautiful, since I wrote it for God and his glory, and I know that you will like it. *(She smiles, excited by her tale.)* Abraham is a hermit. He has a niece called Mary. *(Around her, the lights change. They bathe her in a warm storytale glow, and light the rug brightly.)* When she is a child, Mary's parents die. Abraham adopts her. He builds a little cell for her, near his own, where he watches over her, hears her prayers and instructs her in divine law. *(Enter Mary, dressed in white and seen only by Hrosvitha. She kneels.)* Under his care, Mary becomes beautiful and devout. Abraham hears her prayers and her hymns every day, and thanks God for the happiness she gives him, for he wants her to enter a convent and become the bride of Christ. *(Enter Abraham, in a hermit's robe, holding a cross. Over his back hang a cloak and a large brimmed hat. He also is only seen by Hrosvitha. He kneels.)* "I am happy," says Mary. "My Guardian Abraham means—"

Mary: everything to me. I love to worship and study and pray and be near him.

Hrosvitha: "I am happy," says Abraham. "My niece Mary means—"

Abraham: —everything to me. I love to worship and study and pray and be near her.

Mary: I will always do whatever he says.

Abraham: I will send her to God, in heaven. *(Mary turns her back.)*

Hrosvitha: One day, when Mary is seventeen years old, Abraham has a vision. *(Abraham moves in front of Hrosvitha, throws his arm in front of his eyes and kneels.)*

Abraham: Ah! *(Hrosvitha stands behind him, seeing his vision with him.)*

Hrosvitha: A huge, dragon-like monster, with a horrifying stench—

Abraham: —rushes violently toward me! He wants to eat a little dove I have tied to my wrist. *(He acts it out.)* He knocks me over, seizes my little bird in his jaws and devours it!

Hrosvitha: Then he vanishes, in smoke!

Abraham: When I open my eyes, I am blind. I throw myself into prayer, for two days. Then, exhausted, I fall asleep. *(He does.)*

Hrosvitha: And he dreams he sees the beast again. But now, it is lying at his feet, no longer terrible or frightening. Just a huge, sleeping animal.

Abraham: And the dove is flying to heaven, safe and free! I awake, weeping, and I can see again!

Hrosvitha: He wonders what the vision means!

Abraham: Oh, the most awful uneasiness takes hold of me. Thinking of the monster asleep, and the dove free, I remember Mary, my little niece, my pupil. For three days, I haven't heard her praying or singing.

Hrosvitha: He goes to her cell! He knocks at her window! *(Abraham moves to an imaginary cell.)*

Abraham: Mary? My child? Mary? Why won't you answer me? Mary?

Hrosvitha: She's gone!

Abraham: Mary! *(He paces back and forth in anguish.)* What wolf has stolen my Mary? What devil has defiled her?

Hrosvitha: A hypocrite!

Abraham: In a monk's robe?

Hrosvitha: He came to her with prayers and sugared words! He made the girl fall in love with him!

Abraham: Mary, in love?

Hrosvitha: He seduced her and he abandoned her! When Mary realized what she had done, she tore her hair, dug her nails into her face and ran away!

Abraham: Oh, Mary!

Hrosvitha: She is gone, Abraham.

Abraham: Where?

Hrosvitha: Into the world. She has fallen.

Abraham: Fallen? How?

Hrosvitha: It hurts me to tell you this.

Abraham: Please!

Hrosvitha: She lives in an inn, where she sells herself to strange men.

Abraham: Strange men? My Mary?

Hrosvitha: It comes naturally to whores. There is nothing you can do.

Abraham: There is! I can go to that place!

Hrosvitha: They won't let you in!

Abraham: If I pay them, they will! As a *lover* they will let me in!

Hrosvitha: That will break your vows! *(He hands her his cross.)*

Abraham: Then I will break my vows! *(Abraham holds up a wide-brimmed hat that has been hanging from his shoulders, and spreads his cloak around his hermit's robe.)* With my face hidden by this hat, and my robe by this cloak, I will go to that place and bring her back to me, and to God! *(He turns away.)*

Hrosvitha: Mary! Come at once. You have a visitor. *(Mary turns around. She sweeps a colorful and sensuous shawl over her white dress. She moves down to the carpet. Abraham turns and comes onto the carpet. Hrosvitha, holding the cross, stands above and between them.)*

Mary: You wanted me?

Abraham: That's right. I've paid for you and for some women to sing for us. What's your name?

Mary: Mary.

Abraham: Give me your hand, Mary.

Mary: Take off the hat, Mister.

Abraham: Later.

Mary: You can keep it on in bed for all I care. *(Mary meets Abraham at the center of the carpet, and takes his hand.)*

Abraham: Mary!

Mary: Oh! *(Holding hands, they turn from each other.)*

Abraham: My Mary!

Hrosvitha: His hand is strong!

Mary: What's happening to me?
Hrosvitha: He feels like silk!
Abraham and Mary: Ah!
Hrosvitha: They remember happiness.
Abraham: *(To himself.)* Talk to her! Say something!
Hrosvitha: He tries to play the lecher!
Hrosvitha: She the whore!
Mary: Nothing! *(She turns away and weeps.)*
Abraham: Now what's the matter? I want to go to bed with you, not watch you cry!
Mary: I'm all right now. A little thing moved me, very silly. Come on, my friend. Let's go.
Abraham: Where's the bedroom?
Mary: This way, Mister. *(Leading Abraham by the hand, Mary takes him in a circle.)*
Hrosvitha: She takes him by the hand! They pass through a dark hallway, climb some stairs, and enter her bedroom! *(Mary leads Abraham to the center of the rug.)*
Mary: So lie down.
Abraham: All right. *(He lies down on the carpet.)*
Hrosvitha: Music! *(The quiet and beautiful chant is heard again.)*
Mary: Is that the music you want to hear?
Abraham: Yes.
Mary: While we make love, Mister?
Abraham: Yes.
Mary: No accounting for tastes. Well, you ready?
Abraham: Yes. *(Mary moves toward him, smiling.)*
Mary: Now I get to take off that hat! *(Mary takes off his hat, and kisses him, eyes closed. Abraham does not move. Mary opens her eyes. She sees the face she is kissing.)* Oh!
Abraham: Mary! It's me! I'm here! *(Mary throws herself down, away from him, head in her arms.)*
Mary: Oh! Oh!
Abraham: Don't you know me?
Mary: God!
Abraham: The man who loved you! Who wanted to marry you to the King of Heaven!
Mary: Leave me alone!
Abraham: I *bought* you, remember? You're mine!
Mary: Ah! *(Mary curls up on the carpet, knees drawn up, arms over her head, crying.)*

Abraham: Who was he?

Mary: Oh!

Abraham: Who did this to you? A devil?

Mary: No, a man!

Abraham: Why couldn't you trust me?

Mary: Oh!

Abraham: If you'd told me, I would have prayed for you! I would have done penance for you!

Mary: Oh, stop!

Abraham: No one but Christ lived without sin! We all sin! We fall! But we can repent, and rise again! Mary?

Mary: Go away!

Abraham: I love you!

Mary: NO!!

Abraham: What else but love could make me leave my cell, and break my vows? What else but love could make me, a hermit of God, come to this dreadful place and act like a lascivious fool? Mary, look at me!

Mary: I can't!

Abraham: Come back to me! Ask God for his mercy! Or I will take your sins upon me! Anything! I've been a dead man without you!! *(The Nuns stop singing. Mary raises her head, and looks at Abraham.)*

Mary: I can't say no to you. I can't disobey you, or hurt you. *(She goes to his embrace, her head on his chest.)*

Abraham: Mary!

Mary: I will come back to you! I want to! *(Abraham holds her in his arms.)*

Abraham: I can see the window of your cell. That blessed place, where I come to see you every day. You smile at me and listen to me.

Mary: I pray and sing!

Hrosvitha: She will do it all again! *(Abraham stands, picks up his hat. Mary casts off her shawl.)*

Abraham: I will take you to a convent, to be the bride of Christ.

Mary: Yes! I want to go there! Take me! *(Hrosvitha steps between them, with the cross.)*

Hrosvitha: Praise to the Son of God, and to His Mother the Queen of Heaven, who will never abandon those they love! Amen!

Abraham and Mary: Amen! *(Abraham takes the cross. Exit Abraham and Mary. The lights change again, back to what they were when Hrosvitha began her story.)*

Hrosvitha: That is the end of my play. There will be music and the Sisters playing the parts will leave the stage.

Gerberga: So. Brother William? *(No response. Gerberga gets up, walks about, thinking.)* I will admit, it's not quite clear. A sinner, Mary, is returned to God. But how? Under the persuasion of a holy man, who is a father to her, but who certainly does, like any other man, seduce her. This might suggest that women are seduced not only into sin and degradation but into sanctity and convents. And not just by holy men either, but by God, the greatest of Fathers. By Jesus, our perfect bridegroom, to whom we entrust our souls. I can see how a Bishop would be upset. *(Gerberga looks at Brother William. No response. Gerberga goes and sits in her chair again.)* Brother William? *(No response.)* Brother William? Are you asleep, sir?

Brother William: I am *not* asleep! *(Brother William throws back his cowl, revealing his face.)* I have looked and I have listened. And I too am upset, but not about the play.

Hrosvitha: I am so relieved. My little play only echoes God's great love!

Brother William: Your little play is hysterical female nonsense! No one in their right mind could care about anything so ridiculous!

Hrosvitha: Oh!

Brother William: But what isn't ridiculous, and what I have waited patiently to talk about, Gerberga of Gandersheim, is that music!

Gerberga: Music?

Hrosvitha: *Ave Maris Stella?*

Brother William: A hymn to the Virgin, composed by you, which you will sing not only here, but outside your convent walls, in public worship!

Gerberga: Brother William—

Brother William: Your Bishop knows what you are doing.

Gerberga: Brother WIlliam, do not speak to me like this.

Brother William: He doesn't like it!

Gerberga: Brother William, I beg you.

Brother William: Secure in your wealthy convent of Canoness Nuns, you think you are a law unto yourselves! Your Bishop is deeply offended, and by you!

Gerberga: And I, by him. Gandersheim is a free Abbey, given me by my King and my Pope. Who do you think you are talking to?

Brother William: To a fool!

Gerberga: Why am I a fool?

Brother William: That music!

Gerberga: What *about* that music?

Brother William: It is blasphemous!

Hrosvitha: Oh!

Gerberga: It is *what?*

Brother William: You compose your own chants. You play them on the harp, the psalterium and the trumpet! Women, tooting trumpets to the glory of God? It is obscene and it is grotesque! In the words of the blessed Saint Paul: "Let the women keep silence in Church!"

Gerberga: And why should we keep silent? Because we sing better here, write better here, LIVE better here, than you morose ugly men, with your dismal chants and your eternal hankering for domination and revenge? *(Brother William gets up.)*

Brother William: You insolent and insubordinate nun! You will write no more Ave Marias!

Gerberga: *(Gets up.)* I will go to the King!

Brother William: And he will strip you of your authority!

Gerberga: I will write to the Pope!

Hrosvitha: William Please, stop!

BROTHER WILLIAM: And he will empty all of Gandersheim! Music in Church is for MEN and BOYS, as God's Holy Scripture plainly decrees! WOMEN! WE sing the chants! It is OUR voices and not YOURS that will be heard in the vaults of heaven! WOMEN!! BE SILENT!! *(Exit Brother William.)*

Gerberga: A mad monk. Really. *(Hrosvitha falls to her knees, weeping.)*

Hrosvitha: What have I done?

Gerberga: Nothing.

Hrosvitha: But the Bishop?

Gerberca: If we followed every decree of every Bishop, we would live like soldiers, not like sisters. Depend on me. I will not abandon you. Continue your work! *(Hrosvitha kisses the hem of Gerberga's robe.)* As for this play, well. It can't be performed now. We will bind it, and put it in the Library. If the future should wonder what we did here, it will find your plays here. You are surely the first Sister, and perhaps the first woman, ever to write a play. And I am the arrogant Nun who preserved it. Yes, I like that idea very much. *(Pause. Gerberga starts to exit.)* Of course, I do have a few criticisms. Some of that language is very harsh. Smooth it out. And Abraham can't say out loud that he wants a woman. Change that. He just goes to get her, that's all. And that kissing. Do something about all that kissing! Ugh! *(Exit Gerberga.)*

Hrosvitha: Oh! *(She sits on the carpet, in frustration.)* OH!! *(She weeps. Lights change. Enter Abraham and Mary. They stand awkwardly watching her, looking at each other.)* OHHHHH! *(They sit with her on the carpet.)*

Abraham: What's the matter?

Mary: Why are you crying?

Hrosvitha: Oh, be quiet!

Mary: She doesn't like us anymore.

Abraham: Praise to the Son of God and the Queen of Heaven, who never abandon those they love.

Mary: Goodbye, stupid Abraham.

Abraham: Goodbye, crazy Mary.

Abraham and Mary: Not very nice!

Hrosvitha: Of course I love you! I danced and sang when you came to life! You know that!

Abraham: Then what's wrong? *(Pause.)*

Hrosvitha: That horrible monk called you nonsense. My mother in Christ says you mustn't kiss. They don't understand who you are!

Abraham: We are yours.

Mary: Just as you are God's. He made you. You made us.

Hrosvitha: Badly.

Mary: Why?

Hrosvitha: *(Thinking it out.)* I don't know. I tried to write about love—

Mary: How love brings us to God!

Hrosvitha: What did you say?

Abraham and Mary: How love brings us to God.

Hrosvitha: That's what's wrong! God is not always so simple, and love is not always so—beautiful. Go back!

Abraham: Where?

Hrosvitha: I don't know! Father in Heaven! Help me! Abraham! A huge, dragon-like monster! *(Mary moves aside kneels and prays. Abraham and Hrosvitha take up their positions at that moment in her play.)*

Abraham: —rushes violently toward me! He wants to eat a little dove I have tied to my wrist. He knocks me over, seizes my little bird in his jaws, and devours it!

Hrosvitha: Then he vanishes, in smoke!

Abraham: When I open my eyes, I am blind. I throw myself into prayer, for two days. Then, exhausted, I fall asleep.

Hrosvitha: And you dream you see the Beast again. But now— *(Hrosvitha stares at Abraham.)* just a huge, sleeping animal.

Abraham: And the dove is flying to heaven, safe and free. *(Hrosvitha steps back. Abraham goes to Mary.)* Mary? *(Mary is praying.)* Mary!

Mary: Ah, Father Abraham! I am praying.

Abraham: You may interrupt your prayers. Come with me.

Mary: Where are we going?

Abraham: On a journey?

Mary: Where?

Abraham: To another country. *(He puts on his hat and cloak, which* *disguise him.)*

Mary: Why are you doing that?

Abraham: So no one will see who I am.

Mary: But why?

Abraham: Hush. Trust in me. *(He takes her by the hand and they go into the brothel. He seats her on the carpet, and leaves her. Hrosvitha continues to revise her story.)*

Hrosvitha: *He* takes her to the brothel! He pays a great deal of money to keep her there, for him! *(Mary puts on again the colorful harlot's shawl. Abraham moves away.)* She lives in the brothel. At first she still prays, but then she just waits, for his visits. *(Abraham goes to Mary.)* She is always glad to see him. *(Abraham creeps up behind her, puts his hands over her eyes.)*

Mary: Father Abraham!

Abraham: My darling Mary!

Mary: It has been such a long time!

Abraham: Have you missed me?

Mary: You know I have!

Abraham: Mary!

Hrosvitha: Whorehouse! Music! Kiss! *(The Nuns sing once more. Abraham and Mary throw themselves into each other's arms, embrace wildly, and fall down on the carpet, kissing avidly.)*

Abraham and Mary: Ah! Ah! *(With his cloak lying over them, crying out in sexual pleasure, they make vigorous love.)*

Hrosvitha: Better! *(There is a great deal of graphic pumping and heaving under the cloak, completed by a satisfying mutual orgasm, loudly proclaimed.)* The Beast devours the Dove!

Abraham and Mary: Ahhh! *(Abraham and Mary uncouple, and fall heavily away from each other, gasping until they get their breath. Then they look back at each other in amazement and fall back into each other's arms.)*

Abraham: Oh, God!

Mary: How wonderful!

Abraham: I love you!

Mary: I love you! *(Mary and Abraham lie exhausted together, in passionate contentment.)*

Hrosvitha: And lies there, a huge sleeping animal.

Abraham: *(Groaning.)* Ahhh.

Mary: *(Groaning.)* Ohhhhh.

Hrosvitha: While the dove, safe and free, flies to heaven.

Mary: Ahhhh!

Abraham: Ohhhh! *(Pause. The Nuns stop singing.)* Mary?

Mary: Yes, my darling?

Abraham: I was a dead man without you.

Mary: *(Smiling.)* I remember.

Abraham: I did not know what love was.

Mary: Neither did I.

Abraham: It is the most wonderful thing in the world. *(Pause.)* But— *(He sighs.)*

Mary: But what?

Abraham: I may not be coming here again.

Mary: You mean never? Why not?

Abraham: *(Shrugs.)* Money.

Mary: Money?

Abraham: To pay for you. Didn't you wonder where I got it?

Mary: Sometimes.

Abraham: I steal it. From churches, who let me in to pray. From fools, who trust holy men. An Abbot found me out. He won't condemn me, if we stop now.

Mary: And if we don't?

Abraham: I leave the Church. Take you, and go live—in the world.

Mary: Oh.

Abraham: Man and wife, like other people. *(Mary sits up, frowning.)* Would you like that?

Mary: I'm not sure.

Abraham: To tell you the truth, as much as I adore you, I rather like living around men. The discipline, the prayers. Marriage and babies and listening to women, I don't know.

Mary: Well, to tell you the truth, as much as I adore you, I like living with women. Marriage and babies and listening to men, I don't know.

Abraham: I guess it's settled.

Mary: I guess it is.

Abraham: We have to decide what to do with you.

Mary: Don't leave me here!

Abraham: I thought you liked it here.

Mary: They'd put me in the bull pen.

Abraham: Bull pen?

Mary: Men standing in line. Ten, sometimes twenty an hour!

Abraham: Where do you want to go then?

Hrosvitha: There is only one place.

Mary: Where women are. If not a whorehouse, a convent.

Hrosvitha: Of course.

Mary: Can you arrange it?

Hrosvitha: *I can.*

Mary: *Thank you, Abraham.*

Abraham: *You're welcome, Mary. (They look fondly at each other.)* I will miss you.

Mary: I will miss you, too. *(Abraham reaches out to her.)*

Abraham: I will pray for you. *(Mary takes his hand.)*

Mary: And I will pray for you. *(Hrosvitha moves between them, a hand on each shoulder.)*

Hrosvitha: *(Fondly. To Mary.)* You will live with women. *(To Abraham.)* You will become an Abbot. And I will write more plays. *(Blackout.)*

AKHMATOVA

A red flag against a black wall.

An elegant carpet. A sturdy table with two chairs on each side. On the table is a cigarette box and ashtray, matches. Two other chairs downstage on each side.

Morning light. A deep bell tolls.

Pecdov stands in the light at ease, relentlessly cheerful. Marya sits. She is terrified, trying not to show it.

Pecdov: Stalin, dead. Difficult to believe. Hard to grasp. *(He mimes closing a window. The bell is shut out. He turns to Marya.)* It is about ten pages long. Divided into many sections. A poem. We don't know the title.

Marya: I see.

Pecdov: It is about a woman standing in front of a prison.

Marya: I see.

Pecdov: She is waiting.

Marya: I see.

Pecdov: *(Smiling.)* Please say something beside "I see." You sound pedantic.

Marya: I'm sorry.

Pecdov: Such poems, given out in pieces for different people to memorize, exist like that. Unwritten. To be assembled. The existence of this one is alarming. Why? We'll see. *(Pause. He stares at her a moment, smiling.)* Well, old woman, standing in line. Thinking, probably, poetic thoughts. Anything wrong with that?

Marya: If her thoughts are a danger to the state, yes.

Pecdov: How could they be? Some old bag of bones? But then, another woman becomes involved. She is also standing in the prison line. What does she say?

Marya: How should I know?

Pecdov: Guess.

Marya: How the old women could threaten the state?

Pecdov: That's better.

Marya: They know something. State secrets?

Pecdov: They have no knowledge of anything about the government. Try again.
Marya: One old woman is the poet?
Pecdov: Brilliant.
Marya: And the other is like the reader. Audience. You and me.
Pecdov: You are capable of marvels.
Marya: They have made someone in the government angry.
Pecdov: Exasperated, better word. Would you like a cigarette?
Marya: No, thank you.
Pecdov: Do you mind if I smoke?
Marya: Please do.
Pecdov: Well, maybe I won't. *(He doesn't smoke.)* Try again. Personal life. Husband, say.
Marya: The poet is married to the wrong person.
Pecdov: She was once but he died. You're getting close.
Marya: She is accusing someone of something.
Pecdov: Stay where you were. Not marriage, but what comes next?
Marya: Children?
Pecdov: Children. Exactly. This old woman, well, maybe not so old as I've made out, late forties, let's say, and in an oriental sort of way, quite handsome— she has a child. In the prison.
Marya: Oh. *(Pause.)* Akhmatova.
Pecdov: Good for you. *(Smiling.)* Ever met her?
Marya: You know I have.
Pecdov: I'm glad we're being straightforward with each other. One of the women in line: Anna Andreyevna Akhmatova. The other an old hag. Then, ten pages of poetry, saying we know not what, and at the very end, something overwhelming. Stupendous. But that's all we know. Ever meet Gumilev, her son?
Marya: After he was in prison.
Pecdov: The first time? That was in the thirties.
Marya: When I was a child.
Pecdov: Set free to fight in the Army. War over, his grateful nation puts him in prison again. In and out and in, like that. I wonder why?
Marya: His mother.
Pecdov: Um, and out of her son's tragedy she makes yet another poem, possibly treason. Poets are persistent, I'll say that for them. Now what? *(Pause.)* Do you like this room? It has always been used for these polite discussions. One of my predecessors, years ago, had Turgenev here. He was a young man then. So handsome, enormous shocks of hair. So rich. Mama's enormous hunks of the motherland. A thousand slaves. He had

written a story. Do you know what he was told? Right here?

Marya: No.

Pecdov: Given a brandy first. A Minister of Culture, no doubt quite like me, congratulated him. "Welcome, Ivan Sergeevich, to Russian letters!" "Thank you." There was a moment. Turgenev waiting to hear what was to be cut from his story, and the Minister like me waiting to strike to the heart of the matter. Which he did.

Marya: I see.

Pecdov: *(Quickly.)* You see?

Marya: I beg your pardon! I don't see! What happened then?

Pecdov: Turgenev finally blurted out, "Well, come now! What do you want cut?" Would you call that rude?

Marya: Uh, yes.

Pecdov: I wouldn't. He asked an honest question. He got an honest answer. "We don't want to change a word of what you have written," said the man like me. "We just want to break its spirit." *(Pause.) You see? (Pause.)* Do you have any idea of what I'm saying?

Marya: Not quite, no.

Pecdov: Well. We sit here in this same room, almost a century later, and I am saying the same thing, this time about a woman who stood in a line in front of a prison and then didn't write down a poem about it. Whatever that is, I want to break its spirit, but I don't know what that spirit is, or what it says. I only know who possesses it.

Marya: Akhmatova.

Pecdov: But why should I call you in, someone who knows her only slightly?

Marya: You know I know her very well.

Pecdov: Yes, I do know that. But still, why? To ask you what she wrote?

Marya: To ask if it threatens you.

Pecdov: Absolutely, and not just in the spirit. A real threat, in revolutionary terms. You love your country, don't you?

Marya: Yes.

Pecdov: You wouldn't do anything to hurt her, would you?

Marya: Never.

Pecdov: Do you think Akhmatova would?

Marya: No, I don't.

Pecdov: How do you know?

Marya: Her patriotic poems mean what they say. She wrote poems in praise of Stalin, too.

Pecdov: I know she wrote them and I know why and it wasn't for the love of Comrade Stalin. It was to keep her son from being executed. At the end of this poem, there is something else. What? Don't know. But whatever it is, people weep at the thought of it. So moved, they give Akhmatova money. Food. They help her live. What is it?

Marya: I don't know. *(Pause.)*

Pecdov: In her early poems there are always lovers. Lovers, lovers. Zhdanov called her half nun, half whore. Do you know many writers like that?

Marya: I know many writers who would like to be like that.

Pecdov: Artistic wit is so delicious when a country needs patriots. *(Pause.)* Anna Akhmatova is a relic of the Russian past. Living on, because of a talent, gift, yes, remarkable, for writing artistic ditties. Impressive as verse, perhaps: accurate, specific, surprising, melodious in her blunt way, sticking in the mind. But what is it about? Personal superiority, that's what it's about!! Nostalgia for a childhood in the city of the Tsars, and how beautiful were the pine trees! Young lieutenants committing suicide! Great artists, mysterious doubles! All this bunk steaming in the rotten fumes of sick Christian mysticism, and the stink of Great Art. What could be worse for a Working People than a self-absorbed Nun/Whore Artiste! Our Soviet children, studying her in school? Today? Unthinkable! Stalin would get right out of his coffin. *(Smile.)* But I am always ready to learn. *(Pause.)* Who is the other woman in her poem?

Marya: I don't know.

Pecdov: I have asked you two questions. What revelation is at the end of the poem and who is the old woman at the beginning. You say you don't know. Can you anticipate the next question?

Marya: No.

Pecdov: Simple. Have you read the poem? But, wait, I haven't asked you yet. I don't want to, because then if you say you haven't, we face real difficulties. I haven't asked you anything yet. Nothing can be done to you yet. All right?

Marya: Yes.

Pecdov: You're shaking. You've said nothing wrong. You are a valued worker, a teacher, respected by your students. However, once I ask you that question, then—we're in the soup. Your job, husband, children and so on. Do I have to ask? *(Long pause.)*

Marya: She gave me five words to remember. And I know the title. Requiem.

Pecdov: Requiem? *(Laughs.)* Not for Stalin, that's certain. For her son? Maybe. For our government? Maybe. Only five words?

Marya: That's all.

Pecdov: Do you expect me to believe that?

Marya: It's the truth!
Pecdov: Why only five words?
Marya: I don't know. Maybe she didn't trust me.
Pecdov: What are the five words?
Marya: River. Cows. Doves. Rain. Statue.
Pecdov: What?
Marya: Key words, maybe. I think for the ending of the poem, but she didn't say that.
Pecdov: This is all you have to tell me?
Marya: It's all I know.
Pecdov: Statue. Whose?
Marya: I don't know that, either.
Pecdov: Statue, statue. There is no statue in front of that prison.
Marya: I didn't think so.
Pecdov: What else? What *else?*
Marya: Anna Andreyevna told me nothing else. I swear it.
Pecdov: *(Smiling.)* I see. Wait outside, with the others.
Marya: You're smiling.
Pecdov: I begin my day with joy, and end it with joy. In between, I smile a lot. Wait outside. *(Exit Marya, as fast as she can.)* Hm. *(Blackout. Lights up on Pecdov with Rudinsky, a man in shabby, worn clothcs.)* You'll have to do better than that!
Rudinsky: He just won't talk about his mother.
Pecdov: But does he know about it?
Rudinsky: You mean her poem?
Pecdov: No, *the end of the world.* Sit down!
Rudinsky: You mean her poem?
Pecdov: *(Sighs.)* God damn it.
Rudinsky: Forgive me, but I have been given very peculiar instructions! Go to prison! Get to know a man! Find out about his mother! I am performing this duty to the very best of my ability but I can't threaten him! I can't work him over! I can't get *at* him! God damn it yourself! I beg your pardon.
Pecdov: Frustrated, are you? Have to know why you are doing what you are doing? *(Pause.)* All right. Stalin died Sunday, after an all night dinner with Beria, Bulganin, Khrushchev, and Malenkov. A purge was on. At the top. At the *very* top. Put it together. Well? *Well?*
Rudinsky: *(Aghast.)* They murdered Stalin?
Pecdov: It's possible. Cerebral hemorrhages can be brought about. Now, a rising Minister of Culture, in my position, does what?
Rudinsky: Something threatening none of them.

Pecdov: Of course, but what?

Rudinsky: Nothing?

Pecdov: Fatal. It would be like I was waiting.

Rudinsky: Some—ah—useful activity? Involving some general security? Like that?

Pecdov: Maybe. One of them will take over, but who? Everything is in the whirlwind. Anything can happen. Even a revolution, a real one this time. Zhdanov always said Anna Akhmatova was a traitor. Now she is writing an invisible poem about prisons and old women with endings that make people weep. What could it mean?

Rudinsky: My God, another revolution?

Pecdov: Maybe. Maybe. Does the son know about her poems?

Rudinsky: He knows she writes about him. But he doesn't know what.

Pecdov: Does he still hate his mother?

Rudinsky: Well, some. She farmed him out to his grandmother. He remembers her with bitterness. I did get that out of him.

Pecdov: Did you tell him Stalin is dead?

Rudinsky: Yesterday. He won't talk to me at all now.

Pecdov: Did he believe something would happen upon the death of Stalin?

Rudinsky: I think so.

Pecdov: Did he say anything about any specific poem? With something overwhelming at the end of it.

Rudinsky: No. *(Long pause.)*

Pecdov: Ah! Damn!

Rudinsky: I did the best I could. With my hands tied behind my back!

Pecdov: I know that. Wait outside. *(Pecdov shakes hands with Rudinsky, claps him on the back. Exit Rudinsky. Blackout. Light on Pecda and Klarina, a well dressed woman in her forties. She is fierce and intelligent. She suffers from many psychological wounds.)* And the title of it, evidently, is "Requiem." What I need to find out is what happens at the end of it.

Klarina: *(Paces.)* And you think I can find out?

Pecdov: You of all people. Do you understand why?

Klarina: Because she loved me, and doesn't know what I did to her.

Pecdov: *(Smiles.)* Yes. Anna Andreyevna was so popular. The plainest people loved her steamy little verses, and I'll admit it, her. Stalin is dead. I want you to put those two things together? Can you?

Klarina: No.

Pecdov: My dear woman, our great, vast, enormous land, our Soviet Russia, never had a revolution. Not a real one. Powers shifted. The backbone similarities between our government and the Russia of the Tsars are too obvious to need comment. We changed, yes, but not like France, or

America. The thought of a truly popular revolution in our colossal country is not to be endured. Those who might bring it about must be dealt with. Now Stalin is gone. The one man who made a real revolution unthinkable is dead. And it is thinkable now. *(He stares at her.)* Are you all right?

Klarina: Yes. I have a headache.

Pecdov: Four popular artists. Friends. Mandelstam, Marina Tsvetaeva, Pasternak, Akhmatova. Only she survived. Why?

Kiarina: she is a great poet.

Pecdov: Of a sort, maybe.

Klarina: People *love* the poems. Half Russia recites Akhmatova.

Pecdov: Good. Defend her.

Klarina: She refused to emigrate. She wrote passionately about staying with her country. She wrote a war poem praising Stalin.

Pecdov: All right. Mandelstam, labor camp. Tsvetaeva, suicide. Pasternak, muzzled. But Akhmatova remains, cooking up some deadly invisible opus called Requiem, of what, we may well ask! Do you follow me?

Klarina: A revolution *after* Stalin? That's very doubtful. We loved Stalin. Didn't we?

Pecdov: *(Quickly.)* Of course we did! But a group begins now. Establishes something. Keeps on. In a year, five, twenty? I want you to talk to her again.

Klarina: *(Paces.)* You can't ask me to do that.

Pecdov: Why not?

Klarina: When she stood outside the prison walls, in those awful lines, she had time to think. She knows it was somebody's idea.

Pecdov: Which worked very well.

Klarina: Do you know why I did that to her?

Pecdov: You love your country.

Klarina: Yes, but something else.

Pecdov: She took a man away from you?

Klarina: She is Dante!

Pecdov: And you are a Russian patriot. That's better than being Dante. You will try again. Right now.

Klarina: She's *here?*

Pecdov: In the next room. Waiting, she thinks, to see her son.

Klarina: Oh my God.

Pecdov: When she comes in, she will find you here instead. Her friend who put her son away in the first place. Elegant.

Klarina: What do you have to know?

Pecdov: The old woman. That ending. Listen. Troops surround Moscow this instant. Tanks at every crossroad. This city is sealed off, but by an army ready to do God knows what under orders from God knows who!

Klarina: Remember, she had a husband shot! She has a son in chains!

Pecdov: Oh yes, I know that. If Russia faces chaos, who cares? Here, smoke. If you get nowhere, don't worry. I'll be listening. *(Exit Pecdov. Blackout. Lights up on Anna Akhmatova. She has just entered the room. She is staring, stricken, at Klarina. She sinks into a chair. She is a middle aged woman, once a slim, imperious beauty, now growing pleasantly fat. She is a little unkempt, but erect, and self possessed. For many, she is the greatest poet in Russia.)*

Anna: Oh. *(She sits in the chair, devastated. Klarina moves to the other chair, sits by her.)*

Klarina: This is cruel.

Anna: Yes.

Klarina: I didn't send for you.

Anna: I believe you.

Klarina: I don't know where your son is, or what is happening to him. Have you heard anything?

Anna: Not in three years.

Klarina: You're looking very—

Anna: Thanks to you! *(Pause.)*

Klarina: Anna! *(Pause.)* You've known, all this time? *(Anna nods.)*

Klarina: It wasn't just me, you know! It was the obvious thing to do to you. Stalin had so much trouble with his own son, when it was suggested to him, he said it was the perfect solution.

Anna: He was right. You were right. It was. *(Pause.)*

Klarina: Well. What are you writing now?

Anna: Poetry in praise of Stalin.

Klarina: I mean, anything else?

Anna: Nothing else.

Klarina: *(Paces.)* Just tell me, please? It's what they have to know! What else can I do but ask you, my darling?

Anna: Nothing.

Klarina: So tell me!

Anna: Nothing. I've written nothing.

Klarina: They know about Requiem.

Anna: About what?

Klarina: The old woman standing in line at the prisons. You are writing a poem about her, and it is considered possibly dangerous.

Anna: An old woman in a prison line, dangerous?

Klarina: If the old woman is created by Anna Akhmatova, yes!

Anna: Interesting, as always, how your minds work.
Klarina: It is your mind and how it works, Anna Andreyevna, they are worrying about!
Anna: You are still beautiful.
Klarina: What's in the poem?
Anna: Men once wasted away for us.
Klarina: What overwhelming thing happens at the end of that poem?
Anna: We drove them crazy.
Klarina: I am very sorry to tell you that I am not the only one of your friends from the past to betray you! Others have too!
Anna: Most. The day Zhdanov attacked me, I hadn't read the papers. I slept in, went to market. I bought my fish, wrapped in a newspaper. I went home, unwrapped my fish. Newspaper, article, Zhdanov. Death to the poet. My son in prison again. I thought it was you.
Klarina: God, my head! *(Enter Marya.)*
Marya: Good afternoon.
Klarina: You, too?
Marya: Yes. You're getting nowhere. But stay. *(They sit in the chairs D., facing Anna.)*
Marya: How are you, Anna Andreyevna?
Anna: Well, thank you.
Marya: I wish I was.
Anna: So do I.
Marya: Has Klarina told you what I've done?
Klarina: No.
Marya: I told them what I knew about Requiem.
Anna: Oh.
Marya: You can imagine why.
Anna: Yes.
Marya: It was a boy.
Anna: So I heard.
Marya: They can do to my son what they did to yours. Or worse.
Anna: Yes.
Marya: So I told them my five words.
Anna: I see.
Marya: They think it's the old way of passing poetry on, but different, somehow, and worse.
Anna: I see.
Klarina: They think it is dangerous.
Marya: They're afraid you are writing about something to come after the death of Stalin.

Klarina: What happens at the end of Requiem, Anna? That's what they have to know!
Marya: They'll take it out of you, when they want to!
Klarina: They believe us when we say we don't know what happens!
Marya: But that can change!
Kiarina: You know we *don't* know!
Marya: We could die!
Klarina: If they don't find out!
Marya: It's only a poem!
Klarina: They can shoot us all!
Marya: Your son! Mine!
Klarina: You have to tell us, Anna!
Marya: You have to tell us something! *(Pause.)*
Anna: I will tell you this. If you love Russia, you can dig for her.
Marya: What?
Klarina: Dig? For something buried?
Klarina and Marya: Where?
Anna: In Petersburg. Where Mandelstam said it was.
Klarina: Mandelstam?
Marya: Petersburg?
Anna: I'm tired now. We had many good times, the three of us. When you were little, Marya, and Klarina loved the voice of God. No more.
Klarina: The voice of God?
Anna: That's what poetry is. You've forgotten. Goodbye. *(She closes her eyes.)*
Klarina: Anna.
Marya: Anna.
Klarina and Marya: Anna! *(Pause. Anna seems to be asleep. Enter Rudinsky.)*
Rudinsky: I'll wake her up. *(He slams a chair down directly in front of Anna, and sits in it.)* I have been living with your son. In the same cell. He isn't where you think he is. He is here. In Moscow. Maybe five blocks from here. Look at me! *(Anna keeps her eyes shut.)* I can get to him in an hour. I can tell him things. Imagine. *(Rudinsky gets up, speaks directly into her ear.)* He is going free. He will rot in a camp til he dies. His mother has used him to write a poem, for which he can be shot! *(Anna opens her eyes.)*
Anna: Five blocks?
Rudinsky: Five blocks. *(Satisfied, he sits down again.)* You've been playing games with your son's life.
Anna: Games? Do you think, after all these years, waiting to see him again,

I would refuse to tell you anything on earth? You silenced me as no other human being who ever lived. Tell me I can see him, and I will tell you anything you ask me.

Rudinsky: What happens to the old woman? What happens at the end of the poem? *That's* what you can tell us!

Anna: All right, but do I see my son?

Rudinsky: I can't promise, but yes, probably!

Marya: Anna, you gave me rain, a cow, boats and a statue. Is it the statue? Of someone—revolutionary?

Anna: If I tell you, will that set him free?

Rudinsky: It might!

Klarina: Tell us, Anna!

Marya: Please, Anna! *(Enter Pecdov. He carries a decanter of brandy and two glasses.)*

Pecdov: "We will meet in Petersburg, around the grave where we buried the sun." She'll tell me now. Out. *(Exeunt Marya, Klarina and Rudinsky. Pecdov takes the chair Rudinsky had set in front of Anna and puts it back in place. He pours a brandy and hands it to her.)* Brandy?

Anna: Thank you. *(Pecdov pours himself a brandy.)*

Pecdov: To a statue buried in the tomb of the sun. To your good health.

Anna: To yours. *(They sip the brandy.)*

Pecdov: So. Here we are.

Anna: You've done very well.

Pecdov: Yes, I have. The faithful disciple. Who sat at the feet of the master poets, with such humility. Such devotion to the great causes, until I discovered the great causes were the great egos of the great poets. Skillful parasites, just like Plato said, feeding on the State. So I became a Minister of the People, and slept well at night.

Anna: I am glad you sleep well at night.

Pecdov: Let us go back to Petersburg. To the grave of the sun.

Anna: All right.

Pecdov: I remember it, too. Better than you, perhaps. *(Pecdov closes his eyes and recites, broadly, in the Russian manner.)* "We will meet in Petersburg, around the grave where we buried the sun—" *(Anna closes her eyes, and recites.)*

Anna: "And then together we will say it for the first time, the wonderful word meaning nothing—" *(Both, eyes closed, recite.)*

Pecdov: *(Reciting.)* "In the new Russian night, soft and beautiful darkness, a black velvet nowhere, the beloved eyes of sacred women are still singing, flowers blossom that will live forever—

Anna: *(Reciting.)* "The city gathers itself like a lost cat, soldiers are stationed on the bridges, one automobile dashes blindly by, siren whooping like a screaming bird—

Pecdov: *(Reciting.)* "Tonight I will not carry my credentials, I have no fear of the soldiers. I will pray in the new Russian night, for the wonderful word meaning nothing—

Anna: *(Reciting.)* "For fun we will stand by a fire, maybe time will fall apart, and the beloved hands of sacred women will sweep the ashes back together—

Pecdov: *(Reciting.)* "Don't worry when the candles all snuff out, in the soft and beautiful darkness, the black nowhere. The bent shoulders of sacred women are still singing—

Pecdov and Anna: *(Reciting.)* "You will not see the sun, still burning in the night." *(Pause.)*

Pecdov: Mandelstam.

Anna: Mandelstam.

Pecdov: And poetry, the voice of God. Do you know how he died?

Anna: No.

Pecdov: Paranoid in a camp, certain his filthy grub was being poisoned. He tried to stay alive by stealing food from other prisoners. They beat him to death. Great poet of the Russian land.

Anna: I am not surprised.

Pecdov: I denounced him to Stalin.

Anna: I am not surprised.

Pecdov: He read ten of us a poem about Stalin, in which Stalin had cockroach eyebrows, and greasy fingers staining pages of books by men he would kill. It was the single denunciation of Stalin ever written down by anyone, and that one poem did it. Now it is your turn. But you are different. Not as a poet. As a mother.

Anna: How ingenious, the Devil. Killing a woman with her son. Mephistopheles, blush.

Pecdov: I always forget the Christian part of you. The nun within the whore. Never mind Mephistopheles. While Stalin lived, your son was safe. Kept in prison, used to torment you, but not to be killed. Now Stalin is gone, and others will make that decision. Who is the statue that makes people weep? *(Anna doesn't answer.)* I can let him go. You can be drinking champagne with him in half an hour. Or he can be shot. Not another second. Is there a statue?

Anna: Yes. *(Pecdov gets up.)*

Pecdov: Of someone revolutionary?

Anna: Yes.

Pecdov: Making Russia weep?

Anna: Yes.

Pecdov: Who?

Anna: I am the statue.

Pecdov: What?

Anna: I stand in front of that prison. My metal eyes weep tears. In my poem, I am the statue.

Pecdov: I don't understand.

Anna: Of course not.

Pecdov: You have built a statue to *yourself?*

Anna: Yes. *(Pause. Pecdov laughs, richly and loudly, sits.)*

Pecdov: Made yourself a monument? Made yourself *an icon?*

Anna: *(To him, explaining it.)* I have made a statue of an old woman, standing in a line outside a prison, waiting every day to see her son. In the line are many other women, with sons, daughters, husbands, sisters, mothers and fathers. All in prison. And to my country I say, if in some future year, you mark my life with a statue, I consent to that honor. But I will not stand in the gardens of my love affairs, or in the company of the splendid artists I have known, or before the applauding crowds who loved me, but there, in a line of women, by the riverboats and the doves, before an iron gate, which was never, not once, opened to me. Russia can remember me there, if she pleases.

Pecdov: My God! All this fuss! Anna Andreyevna, you are not a dangerous revolutionary. You are crazy old woman.

Anna: And you are an insect of a single day. *(A long pause.)*

Pecdov: It's not his fault your son has a madwoman for a mother. If I make an issue of this, I'll put myself up for ridicule. Keep your mouth shut and go in peace.

Anna: Will I ever see him again?

Pecdov: Soon, maybe. Stalin is dead, who knows what will happen. Never, maybe. Stalin is dead, who knows what will happen. Goodbye. *(Anna nods and starts to exit.* Certainly— *(Anna stops.)* Statues will be made. But not of you. Of Stalin, and in time, perhaps, of me. *(Anna goes to him. He looks at her.)*

Anna: Perhaps. *(Exit Anna. Pecdov stands thinking. He opens the window again. The bell tolls for Stalin. Light fades on Pecdov, thinking.)*

CAN CAN

for Mireille Bertrand

EX-G.I., a Southern country man, 30's.
FRENCH WOMAN, loving and very intelligent, 20's.
HOUSEWIFE, Southern, warm and sexual, 30's.
COUNTRY WOMAN, a worn, hard working waitress, 40's

Places: Nashville, Paris, Kitty Hawk, rural Kentucky.
Time: The present/the past

POPS was commissioned by the Rockefeller Foundation for the Whole Theatre Company, Olympia Dukakis, Artistic Director, and premiered there in October, 1986. It was directed by Romulus Linney, scenery by Michael Miller, costumes by Karen Gerson, lighting by Rachael Budin, music consultation by Elena Ruehr, production stage manager, Kathleen Cuneen, with the folowing cast:

EX-G.I................................Sam Tsousouvas
FRENCH WOMAN.................Adrienne Thompson
HOUSEWIFE.........................Robin Moseley
COUNTRY WOMAN..............Jane Cronin

CAN CAN

Four dark wooden stools, upstage and apart.

Music: the famous Offenbach "Can-Can."

Sudden light as the music ends discovers four people standing by their wooden stools.

Ex-G.I.: I won it in a Dusseldorf crapgame! Nine hundred American dollars. Me! Got my leave and took off!

Housewife: I went to the beach that day, threw baseballs at bottles, shot wooden ducks and won a Bunny Rabbit. With the rabbit came a meal ticket, at a country cafe, so I went there, too.

Young Woman: It was the year I entered the Sorbonne. I studied so hard I won a prize and my Grandmama tripled it so I had that summer deux mille francs, all my own!

Country Woman: The beach had chain swings, a loudspeaker playing Can Can music, and a shooting gallery with wooden ducks. I shot the ducks and won a prize. It was a Bunny Rabbit, and I took it with me to work at the cafe.

Ex-G.I.: I tried Copenhagen first and caught cold. I went to London and couldn't relax. Tried Paris, and all that brandy made me sick. I said, "Oh, hell, I want to go to the beach!" So I took the Mistral to the Riviera!

Young Woman: I always knew what I would do in my life. Never marry. Be a scientist. Swim every day for my heart, and have friends like Prokofiev for my soul. So I went to Avignon, to visit my Mama, swim, hear concerts and watch plays in the Palace of the Popes.

Housewife: Frenchy's Paris Fishfry this place was called. I had the catch of the day. The woman waiting on me saw my Bunny Rabbit and said, "Win that at the fair?" and I looked up, saying, "Yes," and felt, oh, I don't know, a little funny, she was so homely and countrified.

Country Woman: All by herself she was, sitting there like a doll in a shop, with that rabbit on her table. I took her order and said something and I saw she had a little line of sweat above her lips, like a moustache. Then she smiled at me and I smiled back.

Ex-G.I.: A buddy in K Company told me, go see Avignon if you can, the countryside looks like French painting, so I stopped off there, to sit in the town square, and have a sit-tron press-say!

Young Woman: I liked Americans. My friends did not, but I did. And that soldier, that day in the square at Avignon, I liked especially.

Housewife: I came back to Frenchy's Fishfry the next day, and I saw her again, all hard work and business and I said, "Hello. Remember me?"

Country Woman: "You won a rabbit," I said. "So did I. Yes, I remember you."

Ex-G.I.: She looked like a Massachusetts tomboy! Wearing a U.S. lumberjack shirt, flaps out over bluejeans, but she was French, all right, formal a little, and my God, intelligent!

Young Woman: He was very agreeable! He didn't talk very much, but when he did, he had good taste. He didn't know it, but he did.

Housewife: I went back every day and she waited on me, and I blushed, all the way up through the roots of my hair.

Country Woman: She was just a baby, thinking I was a game she wanted to play, but I saw different, and most near dropped the fried fish on the floor.

Ex-G.I.: She asked me would I come swimming with her friends, in a river under a Roman bridge. She was a student at the honest-to-God Sor-bone, studying Marine Biology. The sea, she said, the sea!

Young Woman: So we swam with the others in the river under the Roman bridge, and when he saw me in my bikini he was no longer interested in the others.

Housewife: And what I meant to say was, I want you to touch me, I just do. I don't know why. I was eighteen years old.

Country Woman: It's her momma, I said to myself. She don't have one, the pore child, but she said no, she had a momma, that's not what she wanted at all.

Ex-G.I.: We drank brandy that night under a bridge built by soldiers, centuries ago, and we talked, oh, soberly and sensibly.

Young Woman: When he took me home, I shook hands with him like a man and said it had been a pleasure and what was he doing tomorrow?

Housewife: All her teeth seemed broken. Lines cut everywhere into her face. There were scars on her arms, on the side of her throat, deep shadows made her eyes look hard. When I asked her why she looked like that—

Country Woman: I told her my life was like that, she was a child, was she coming back again tomorrow?

Young Woman: And the next day my soldier watched me say goodbye to my mama, getting on the train for Venice to visit my grandmama, and when it moved he was on it too and so then, zut! We ran through the cars like fools in a film, and then there I was with my soldier, never mind my grandmama.

Ex-G.I.: Pale she was! With splotches of crimson high on her cheeks! Like a woman in the kind of painting my K Company buddy said I ought to see. She told me she was the daughter of a French aristocrat, descended from a Fieldmarshal of Napoleon, and I said sure, that's why you like soldiers!

Country Woman: I never let her drive me home, or see where I lived. But we'd sit on the beach some when I got off work, and commence jabbering then, one with the other, and a body couldn't stop.

Housewife: I can talk to you! I can talk to you! Like to no one else, ever! Why is that? I'm not a little countryclub fool anymore, not with you. Why is that? *(The Young Woman moves her stool D.)*

Young Woman: It was my sister who was beautiful, not me. That is the way our mamma knew it would be. One with the beauty, one with the brains. But my soldier, he told me Mamma was wrong! I had both, and I did! For him, I did! *(The Ex-G.I. moves his stool D. next to hers.)*

Ex-G.I.: I got her off the train at Nice, where it was all fresh air and marble, and the sunlight dazzling! hectic! dancing! like the way that G.I. felt!

Young Woman: He took me to Nice, to the Bataille des Fleurs! He would beat me with flowers! I knew he had good taste!

Ex-G.I.: Big floats in the streets at night, covered with flowers and beautiful French-Italian girls, and I mean big strong men slapping each other with tulips!

Young Woman: People passing in the night, singing and throwing confetti in your face, if they liked what they saw. He got us the last hotel room in Nice!

Country Woman: There ain't nothing you can't say, not to me. *(The Housewife moves her stool D.)*

Housewife: I know that. It's like in church, in the choir, when I feel wonderful, when great feelings rise up inside me, can you understand that, the singing, all of us together, and she said— *(The Country Woman moves her stool D. They are all together now.)*

Country Woman: I sing like that too, honey, sometimes. But not in church.

Ex-G.I.: Hotel des Anglais, for God's sake! Room with blood-red wallpaper paintings of roses big as cabbages!

Young Woman: He tore roses off the floats and brought them to me piled high in his arms!

Ex-G.I.: I tore roses all to pieces! I scattered them over all that ugly room! Rug, bed and big old bathtub, which we jumped in together, and I said, "Why are you here, with me?"

Young Woman: You are my first man. I plan my life, and I picked you for *that. As long as I live, I will never forget you. Now give me some soap* and kiss me.

Housewife: Then on a Sunday, when I stood up to sing my solo, "Only A Rose Will Do," I saw somebody come in at the back of the church and oh God! There she was, in that congregation, like some old black sheep with her broken teeth, watching me.

Country Woman: In that spotless place, with the roses and the lillies smelling so sweet and all that perfume and fur pieces, well, I paid it no mind. You commenced to sing, and you were my flower then, my rose, my own.

Ex-G.I.: And I kissed her all right! And the next evening we sailed from Nice over the sea she studied in school on a night boat to Corsica! Where she'd never been, which I'd hardly heard of!

Young Woman: Where we lived ensemble for a month, in little hotels, on the beaches!

Ex-G.I.: Under the Corsican sun, among the palm trees!

Young Woman: And the flies, and the bad wine!

Ex-G.I.: And the beautiful cleansing sunsets and winds!

Housewife: And three months later, after my wedding, I stood there a bride, scatterbrained in taffeta and lace, thinking of nothing in the world but her, and God Almighty, there she came!

Country Woman: Scared, not meaning to trouble her, not mad or anything, just having to come, not able to help myself, not right then.

Housewife: In a cheap flower-print dress with a pink hat, preposterous, absurd, with dime store white gloves and all her scars and broken teeth.

Country Woman: The boy you'd married was fixing to dance with you, so I did it proper as I knowed how. I handed you a bottle of whiskey for your wedding night and a silver spoon for your baby. *(For the first time, they look at each other.)*

Housewife: Thank you.

Country Woman: You're welcome.

Housewife: Would you like some champagne?

Country Woman: No, I best go. You was just scared about getting married, that was why you done what you done to me, wasn't it. No need, honey. He looks like a fine young man.

Housewife: Can I get you some cake?

Country Woman: No. I just want to shake hands with your husband and kiss you and go—

Housewife: Some coffee, then? (The country women kisses the housewife on the cheek.)

Country Woman: And I did that and left her, and didn't know where I was, not for the longest time.

Ex-G.I.: Come on! Come on! You can do better than that! I'll race you back!

Young Woman: All right, all right. *(She chokes, gasps. She presses her hand to her chest. For the first time, they look at each other.)*

Ex-G.I.: Hey, now! What's the matter? You all right?

Young Woman: Just—a moment—please. *(She smiles, but painfully gets her breath.)* I'm all right now. I just can't go that fast.

Ex-G.I.: But you weren't running, or anything.

Young Woman: No.

Ex-G.I.: You got cramps, time of month, that it?

Young Woman: No.

Ex-G.I.: So what's the matter with you?

Young Woman: On dit maladie de coeur—tu comprends?

Ex-G.I.: Heart trouble?

Young Woman: Yes, heart trouble. In my family, very spectacular! We live passionate youths, perform miracles, and then our hearts turn to rubber. We say we wore them out, for the great Napo-leon! Flap-flop, flap-flop! Flap flop. I will have surgery soon. They tell me I am not so bad as my father was, at this age. So.

Ex-G.I.: He's dead, your father?

Young Woman: At forty-one. His father thirty-eight. So, you see, I will live a long long time. *(Pause.)*

Ex-G.I.: Really? This is the truth?

Young Woman: Oui, vraiment.

Housewife: "Who was THAT?" my groom said, laughing, and the hotel orchestra played and I was swept out onto the ballroom dance floor, away from my mother and my father and my life as a child, to my husband and my children and the day I had to see you again.

Country Woman: Honey, are you sure?

Housewife: we must!

Woman: Best not.

Housewife: I'll die!

Woman: It'll hurt. You think you know but you don't.

Housewife: I won't live! Please!

Country Woman: All right.

Ex-G.I.: What kind of surgery?

Young Woman: Open heart. Le dernier cri.

Ex-G.I.: It's dangerous?

Young Woman: Bien sur. You take a knife and go, whop— *(She slides a finger down her chest.)* —and pull it open and say, voila, Monsieur Le Coeur! A-ha-ha-ha! And then you do this and that to it, well, yes, dangerous. Are you sad for me?

Ex-G.I.: Aw shit, honey.
Young Woman: Oui, vraiment. Aw shit, honey.
Ex-G.I.: Well, but what they do now! I mean, doctors do almost anything now, right!
Young Woman: Almost.
Ex-G.I.: You got a good doctor?
Young Woman: The best.
EX-G.I: Hospital?
Young Woman: The biggest.
Ex-G.I.: Well, great.
Young Woman: So be my Budi.
Ex-G.I.: Your what?
Young Woman: You know, like soldiers have. I like that, what you call each other. "Hey, Boo-dee." Like that.
Soldier: Buddy.
Young Woman: Yes, Budi. Remember your old budi.
Soldier: I will.
Housewife: And that's what we did. On beach blankets, in the back seats of cars, through twelve years of motel bedrooms, married to Walter Richards and loving you.
Country Woman: We can stop.
Housewife: No, never. We can never stop.
Ex-G.I.: We said goodbye in the train station at Marseille, making jokes, flip and cheerful until we saw the train.
Housewife: You came in the motel room without knocking.
Young Woman: I was going to be a scientist and have friends like Prokofiev but when I saw that awful train, zut! Tears!
Country Woman: I couldn't come no sooner.
Ex-G.I.: My God, this is hard! I can't get my breath!
Housewife: You're going to leave me!
Young Woman: It's hard to breathe, yes. I'll never see you again!
Country Woman: I got to go. It's time.
Ex-G.I.: I was so happy with you! I'll never see you again.
Housewife: You can't! I won't let you!
Young Woman: It's not in the head, or the heart! It's in the stomach, like being beaten there!
Country Woman: Hush, now!
Ex-G.I.: Will we live?
Housewife: I will leave my husband! I will leave my children!
Young Woman: I think so! I'm not sure!
Country Woman: You know you can't. I wouldn't let you.

Ex-G.I.: You won't forget me?

Housewife: I will live on the floor at your feet! I can't love anybody else!

Young Woman: No, Budi. I won't forget you! I can't!

Country Woman: You got to accept it. For me.

Ex-G.I.: Goodbye. *(Pause. They turn from each other, and face out. Music: the beginning of the gentle waltz from Offenbach's "Orpheus in the Underworld.")*

Housewife: All right. For you. Goodbye.

Young Woman: My first man. Goodbye.

Country Woman: My little girl. Goodbye.

Ex-G.I.: It was wonderful. You were wonderful.

Housewife: For you, I accept. I don't care how it hurts.

Young Woman: I'd do it again!

Country Woman: I don't care neither! I'm glad, too! *(Lights fade, slowly.)*

Ex-G.I.: You're the best! Best thing ever happened to me!

Housewife: *(Simultaneous.)* Best thing ever happened to me!

Young Woman: *(Simultaneous.)* So are you! The best thing ever happened to me!

Country Woman: *(Simultaneous.)* Best thing! BEST thing! *(Facing out, they wave.)*

Soldier, Housewife, Young Woman and Country Woman: It was wonderful! Goodbye! Wonderful! God bless you! I'll never forget you! Goodbye! Goodbye! Goodbye! God bless you! I'll never forget you! Goodbye! Goodbye! *(The Offenbach waltz swells up, the light goes out on them waving, and takes them away from us.)*

CLAIR DE LUNE

for Lois Lanaette

ABEL, a retired midwestern farmer, 60's.
LICILLE, his thoughtful and troubled wife, 50's.

Place: A trailer park in Florida.
Time: The present

POPS was commissioned by the Rockefeller Foundation for the Whole Theatre Company, Olympia Dukakis, Artistic Director, and premiered there in October, 1986. It was directed by Romulus Linney, scenery by Michael Miller, costumes by Karen Gerson, lighting by Rachael Budin, music consultation by Elena Ruehr, production stage manager, Kathleen Cuneen, with the following cast:

LUCILLE......................Jane Cronin
ABEL...........................William Hardy

CLAIR DE LUNE

Moonlight.
Enter Abel, carrying two beers, a small wooden box and an aluminum-plastic beach chair.

Abel: Come on out, Mother! If I have to hear it again I want to listen to it out here! *(Enter Lucille, with a second chair and a small tape recorder with a cassette in it. She is looking at the cassette case.)*

Lucille: All right, Father. I'll play it in the moonlight! *(She puts down her chair, sits in it, places the tape recorder on the box.)*

Abel: Here's your beer, Mother. Let 'er rip! *(Lucille takes the beer, plays the cassette. On the little recorder, an orchestra plays "Clair de Lune." They listen. Lucille sighs.)*

Lucille: That's so pretty. Classics of the Night, it says here. That little piece means Moonlight, it says here. Who'd ever think a body could get so much pleasure out of one little tune. *(Abel takes a fishing reel out of his pocket.)*

Abel: Mother, I hope you do. You play it enough. *(It gets suddenly darker.)* Whup. There goes your moon, Mother. Right behind a cloud.

Lucille: Oh, fish. It was so pretty, a-shining on the lake. Like the music.

Abel: Thought we'd get a look at the camp swans. Beautiful critters, swans in the moonlight. Mean, though! All took up with theirselves. Hiss at ye! Peck ye! Can't tolerate nobody else but theirselves.

Lucille: Swans in the moonlight. The pleasures of Florida.

Abel: Yep. Beer! Trailer! Swans!

Lucille: Retirement, Father.

Abel: That's it, Mother! Retirement! *(He looks at his reel. "Clair de Lune" plays.)*

Lucille: Father?

Abel: Yes, Mother?

Lucille: We do right, coming here?

Abel: I think we did.

Lucille: We could have farmed another two years, maybe more.

Abel: But we didn't.

Lucille: I know we didn't, and I know I said yes, all right, let's go, but now, I just don't know.

Abel: Don't know what, Mother?

Lucille: If we should have come here. *(The segment of "Clair de Lune" ends, fading away suddenly, replaced by a Strauss Waltz. Lucille turns off* *the recorder, rewinds the cassette.)* I just don't know.

Abel: Yes, you do. You know what's wrong. Say it.

Lucille: I miss my children!

Abel: *(Quietly.)* Do you?

Lucille: Yes! *(Pause.)* I do!

Abel: Uh-huh.

Lucille: But it is peaceful here. I do like that.

Abel: So do I. No more phone calls in the middle of the night. Yelling and sobbing and screaming and crying. Weddings, divorces, other man's wife, other woman's man, whiskey, dope, and God knows what else. Pistols twice, shotgun once. Fists through windows, bloody shirts and dresses torn apart, abortions and carwrecks. Carwrecks! Eight of them, eight! Count 'em! Eight carwrecks! God Almighty!

Lucille: We got in trouble.

Abel: THEY got in trouble. Four trips to hell in a county courthouse. Half the crop going every other year to a god damned lawyer. All the world shaking its head at our children we done our best to bring up right! Mother! Let them untangle their own lives, and leave us to find a little peace in ours!

Lucille: But why? That's what I keep wondering about. Our children! Why!

Abel: We don't know why! Neither does nobody else, judges, police, doctors, nobody! Children go crazy. We done our best by 'em left 'em half the farm, now to hell with it! We have earned our rest!

Lucille: We gave them half the farm but was that enough? What I keep thinking about, Father, is what we didn't give them. Couldn't give them.

Abel: What's that?

Lucille: Joy! Some real pleasure in life! You know. What we had together. What we always had together!

Abel: Mother, I don't think anybody can give anybody that!

Lucille: But why not! They ought to! I tried to tell Sarah once, what it was like, seeing you for the first time, and not liking you at all, and then you just waiting for me, and waiting for me—

Abel: Well, I knew, Mother. I just knew!

Lucille: And from the first time, everything, I mean the first TIME together, like that, well now! Well now!

Abel: Mother—

Lucille: I mean!

Abel: Mother!

Lucille: I mean!

Abel: Mother, stop fretting about this!

Lucille: But it was good! It was always good! God help us, Father, after all these years, it's good now!

Abel: I know that!

Lucille: Then why not for them? Not one, not ONE of them! What is it we have, just took for granted, they can't never find, no matter how hard they try?

Abel: Now Mother, hush up!

Lucille: I WILL NOT! I never in my life wanted no man but you! And if what you're always telling me is the truth—

Abel: Truth, Mother! Only time I tried anybody else, I got sick, you know that!

Lucille: Then why? WHY? What did we have all them years, working and sweating and farming and making do, they couldn't have too? WHAT DID WE DO WRONG?

Abel: NOTHING! THEY did all that! Hush up!!

Lucille: WHAT DID GOD GIVE US HE KEPT FROM THEM?? *(it suddenly gets brighter.)*

Abel: Look, Mother. There's your moon again. Play that tune for yourself, and settle down. I don't want to hear this no more.

Lucille: All right. *(She plays "Clair de Lune" again. Pause.)*

Abel: There! Look, by God! *(They both point, staring at the lake.)*

Lucille: Swans, Father!

Abel: Swans! In the moonlight! *(Pause. Slowly.)* Strange looking critters. Jest gliding along.

Lucille: I don't think I like them so much.

Abel: Cause they're mean. Look good, but they're cold and mean inside. All took up with theirselves. Come between two swans, you get pecked to death!

Lucille: Who'd want to come between them?

Abel: I don't know. Somebody.

Lucille:

"The swan is a beauty easy to take,
Two are better, upon the lake."

Abel: You just make that up?

Lucille: No. Read it, yesterday.

Abel: Where?

Lucille: Reader's Digest.

Abel: Oh.

Lucille: It was in some article about zoos. *(Pause. Lucille turns off the music.)* I miss my children. *(Pause.)*

Abel: Yeah. *(He spins his reel. The moonlight fades.)*

GOLD AND SILVER WALTZ

for Martha Ann Miller

ROMULUS LINNEY, a playwright, 50's.

Place: A spotlight.
Time: 1986.

POPS was commissioned by the Rockefeller Foundation for the Whole Theatre Company, Olympia Dukakis, Artistic Director, and premiered there in October, 1986. It was directed by Romulus Linney, scenery by Michael Miller, costumes by Karen Gerson, lighting by Rachael Budin, music consultation by Elena Ruehr, production stage manager, Kathleen Cuneen, with the following cast;

ROMULUS LINNEY....................Romulus Linney

GOLD AND SILVER WALTZ

With a spotlight, the waltz plays its opening phrases. Enter Romulus Linney. Waltz ends.

Romulus Linney:

Thanksgiving Day 1972

Home bed fever 105 crashing down 103 climbing 105

crashing 103 etc waiting hospital bed telephone

rings say "Hello?" voice says "Rommy?"

(childhood nickname) say, "Yep" Voice says

"Rommy! This is E.C. Green!" Lucid 105 degree

fever plumblines me forty years My Peanut Days

that canny E.C. Green little kid always smarter

than all the rest of us always in these better

positions all the time acted Rumplestilskin in the

7th grade play me the dumb King all of

that so I say, "Why, hello E.C. How are you?"

He says, "Rommy, you really remember me?" I

say all lucid-fever-casual-wise, "Why of

course, E.C. How you been?" and we chat, me

burning up (18 days Lenox Hill Hospital it

turned out later) E.C. sent from Madison

Tennessee little town where we grew up to NYC-IBM-
Hilton-Hotel-Computer-School-Weekend E.C. still living
that little town, wife five children, still in
his good positions, and the sort of man who
likes to keep track So We go through some
of the names that we were Sort of thing like,
"Harold Barns? Rommy, he's working right now
at that crooked filling station where Lovely's
Drugstore used to be No I don't think I remember
any Hall girls what? Oh Army children! Yes of
course I do Sue Neatherly? She's living right
here and she's just fine Huh? What? Who?
Martha Miller? Rommy, I didn't know you knew
her." There is a silence other end of line.
"Of course I knew her E.C. she moved down from New
York State the year before my father died, so how
is she, and E.C. "Funny you asking, Rommy. We went
together after you left, later on in High School we
were sweethearts I tell you she meant a lot to me!"
And flash! Scorching fever-vision! Black tar
melting on the Gallatin Pike, and through the fire

strolling cool crisp pert New York Yankeechild

Martha Miller smiling, interested in me and I say

"Well, you know E.C. she meant something to me too

Martha Miller was the first girl I ever fell for smash!

slayed me dead she did but I was such a dumb little O

God Tennessee hick I couldn't act decent about it, say

something ugly was all I could do but I never forgot,

and you know E.C. now I think about it she really was

a remarkable open little person (in the 7th Grade for

God's sake!) I recall her trying more than once to

find out what I was really like—I think I threw a

a rock at her for that!" And flash! Fever-flash!

First invitation to love flash Martha Miller Flash! so

I say, "Well how is she, E.C.?" and E.C.—slowly—

"Well, Rommy. Martha Miller is dead. She died some

years ago aged forty she had married had two children

oh! isn't it a shame! Rommy, I tell you I took it

hard!"

And I say, "Gee, E.C."

And hazy, hot, fever curtains dissolve. On the day I

came back to the 7th grade, with my father buried

in cold ground far away from me, and Martha Miller

walked straight up to me and said she was so sorry

my father was dead! But that while we'd been gone

the grass in our front yard hadn't been cut and

she wanted me to see about that right away or it

would go wild get overgrown more tangled up

than it already was I told E.C. that and he said,

"Yes, that sounds like her she was always a sensible

girl, practical and encouraging." So We went

on through all the rest of them, the Murray Siddens

and Mary Jean Coles and everybody else and said

Goodbye. And two hours later it was Lenox Hill

Hospital left lobar pneumonia Doctors Nurses Wife

Daughter Friends but in my fever dreams that little

girl on the day my soul, bereft of its father, faced

this world of death and losses, there she was, pert

smiling interested Martha Miller plus of course

whatever her married name well whatever your married

name Martha Miller in my turn I am so sorry you're

dead! And I can't send you my books ask you to

plays in New York buy you a drink give you back

something for your childhood gifts of consolation and

courage So I will just get well, as you would

want me to And I will mow the lawn And I won't

let the weeds grow wild

("The Gold and Silver Waltz" is heard again, softly.)

But I will remember, here at least for just a moment,

a beautiful beautiful child, inviting me to live love

cut the grass and die, instructing me it is never the

ending that is important, it is always the beginning

(The waltz ends, the spotlight fades. Exit Romulus Linney.)

SONGS OF LOVE

for Martha Rucker Clabaugh

SUSAN LOGAN, a young, sensitive nurse, 20's.
LILLIAN BARBOW, a Southern matron, 50's.
BUDDY SLADE, her boorish brother, 40's.
FINLEY RUNNEY, a natty, careful young lawyer, 30's.
ELLIS RUNNEY, a very frail old man.
CORA SLADE, an equally frail old woman.

Place: Woodvale Nursing Home, Madison, Tennessee.
Time: 1986.

POPS was commissioned by the Rockefeller Foundation for the Whole Theatre Company, Olympia Dukakis, Artistic Director, and premiered there in October, 1986. It was directed by Romulus Linney, scenery by Michael Miller, costumes by Karen Gerson, lighting by Rachael Budin, music consultation by Elena Ruehr, production stage manager, Kathleen Cuneen, with the followin cast:

BUDDY SLADE...............Sam Tsousouvas
SUSAN LOGAN...............Adrienne Thompson
LILLIAN BARBOW...........Robin Moseley
CORA SLADE..................Jane Cronin
ELLIS RUNNEY...............William Hardy
FINLEY RUNNEY...........Peter Toran

SONGS OF LOVE

A part of a waiting room in a nursing home. Two chairs on one side of the stage, a chair and a table with a small radio on it on the other. A prominent entrance.

The radio is playing the pop version of the famous Tschaikowsky Piano Concerto.

The music fades under a voice with a very thick Southern accent.

Radio: A moment ago, you heard that gorgeous pop standard made from Rachmaninov's 2nd Piano Concerto. Continuing on our program this morning, "From Carnegie Hall to Tin Pan Alley and Back Again," we hear Tschaikowsky's 1st Piano Concerto in its golden oldie pop identity. Don't go away, classical purists, we will hear all these originals in their glory in one half an hour. But now, more Songs of Love! *(A soupy rendition of the Tschaikowsky keeps on playing. The door opens. Enter Susan Logan, a young nurse. She looks at the waiting room, thinks a minute, shrugs and goes to the door, to call some people in.)*

Susan: Please, come in! *(Enter Lillian Barbow, her brother Buddy Slade, both in middle age and Finley Runney, a young man. Susan wears her uniform with an attractive sweater over it. Lillian wears soft colors and flowing materials: a Southern lady's afternoon dress. Buddy wears a conservative, well cut suit, with cowboy boots and a hat not a cowboy hat but which he wears like one. Finley wears a very neat business suit. All three are well off.)*

Lillian: This isn't the Director's Office. Where's the Director?

Susan: He isn't in today. We can talk here.

Finley: Not at all?

Susan: I'm afraid not. I am Director of Nurses. I will be happy to do my best for you until he returns.

Finley: When is that?

Susan: Next month.

Finley: Next MONTH?

Susan: Director Wilson is a delegate to ANNHA. He's at the Convention.

Buddy: ANN—HA?

Lillian: What's that?

Buddy: Honey, could you turn off that radio? Loud music and wimmen talking give me the jim-jams.

Susan: Of course. I beg your pardon. *(She turns off the radio.)*
Buddy: Love song. Just what we wanted to hear.
Lillian: Buddy.
Buddy: Well, idn't it?
Susan: ANNHA stands for American National Nursing Homes Association. The yearly convention is being held this month in Omaha, Nebraska. As an elected delegate, Director Wilson has many important duties and won't be back for at least ten days.
Buddy: Swell.
Lillian: All right, we'll talk to you. *(She sits in one of the chairs. The others remain standing.)*
Susan: Fine.
Buddy: Put some some saltpeter in his food.
Lillian: Buddy.
Buddy: Get him a VCR and some Swedish Erotica.
Lillian: Hush!
Buddy: Or tie a damn knot in it, how's that? *(Lillian stands up.)*
Buddy: All right! Sorry! Don't mean to act up. *(She sits back down.)*
Lillian: We discussed this matter over the phone with Director Wilson and we both expected to see him here today.
Susan: Well, I'm sorry. He didn't tell me a thing. But I'll do everything I can for you.
Finley: Maybe you will and maybe you won't. Go ahead, Mrs. Barbow.
Lillian: Thank you, Mr. Runney. I apologize if my brother said anything offensive about your father.
Finley: Quite all right. Let's just go ahead.
Lillian: Very well. My mother, Cora Slade—
Buddy: My momma, too!
Lillian: Our mother, Cora Slade, has been in residence at Woodvale Nursing Home since January of this year. Beginning last month, she has been repeatedly molested here. After our phone conversation with Doctor Wilson three weeks ago, we believed the situation had been corrected.
Susan: Oh, I see.
Lillian: I thought you might.
Susan: Mrs. Slade and Mr. Runney.
Finley: Yes!
Susan: So what's happened now?
Lillian: You mean you don't know?
Susan: I saw them both this morning. They were getting along just fine.
Finley: Together?
Susan: Yes, in lounge chairs they like in the Day Room. They sit in them

side by side, with blankets, like passengers on ships in old movies.

Buddy: Two blankets or one?

Susan: One. Rather a joke here.

Lillian: Not to me, it isn't. Not to my brother. Nor, I trust, to Mr. Runney.

Finley: Absolutely not.

Susan: You feel they are doing something improper?

Buddy: He comes to her room, don't he?

Susan: During visiting hours, yes.

Lillian: And they shut the door?

Susan: If they wish.

Buddy: And they're in there together, all by theirselves?

Susan: Since Mrs. Slade is able to afford a single room, yes, again.

Lillian: Well?

Susan: Well?

Lillian: Director Wilson gave us his solemm promise this kind of behavior would not occur at Woodvale Nursing Home! *(Susan laughs.)*

Susan: Oh, did he?

Buddy: You diddledamn right he did, Lady, what's so funny about it?

Susan: I beg your pardon.

Lillian: You don't seem to understand, Miss—ah—I forget your name—

Susan: Logan, Susan. R.N.

Lillian: —Nurse Logan, how serious a matter this is. This is our eighty year old mother we're concerned about, in your care, your very expensive care, being sexually molested!

Finley: If you please. Molested is a strong word, used most often I believe, in connection with the abuse of children. My grandfather is not a sex criminal.

Susan: Mrs. Barbow, when was the last time your mother complained about Mr. Runney? *(Pause.)*

Lillian: Yes, I thought you'd ask me that.

Buddy: Momma don't say nothing.

Lillian: We think she's afraid to.

Buddy: Or worse. He's made her like it!

Lillian: Buddy, please!

Susan: Mrs. Barbow, has your mother complained to you about Mr. Runney's behavior?

Lillian: Not in so many words, no.

Finley: Then how do you know my grandfather has been "molesting" her?

Buddy: We got our sources.

Susan: Someone at Woodvale?

Lillian: Yes!

Finley: I've had calls, too! But not about a sex fiend! About a seductive old woman making a fool of a gentle old man!

Buddy: Oh, sure.

Finley: How she will not let him alone. How she hangs all over him when he should be getting his rest. How she drags him day and night in and out of her room!

Lillian: And what WE hear is how HE won't let HER alone! How SHE can't go anywhere without HIM! How HE'S in and out of HER room day and night any time HE feels like it!

Buddy: So what are you going to do about it?

Susan: *(Politely.)* What do you expect me to do about it?

Lillian: Separate them!

Susan: How?

Lillian: I don't care! Just do it!

Susan: Very well, but how?

Buddy: Saltpeter, VCR, Swedish Erotica, and a knot tied right there in his pecker!

Lillian: Buddy, hush up!

Buddy: Sorry!

Susan: You are asking me to use force?

Lillian: If necessary, yes! Lord knows what he may be doing to her! Our mother!

Susan: I will try to explain something to you. But first. *(To Finley.)* Mr. Runney, do you feel your grandfather and Mrs. Slade must be kept apart by force?

Finley: I may, yes. But what is it you have to explain?

Susan: It is a familiar story in nursing homes. A lady and a gentleman, of advanced age, both ambulatory and reasonably healthy, neither mentally impaired or senile in any way, form a final, strong attachment to each other. It is sometimes physical. There is a medical term for it: sexual recrudesence. Brought on by a new environment, new friends, freedom from past restrictions, like marriage and children and work at home. It happens. And it's a delicate matter.

Buddy: What's delicate about it for God's sake? If this horny old buzzard can get it up, then what's to keep him from going around here sticking it and place he wants to? He's in hog heaven, right?

Finley: Oh, really. Ugh.

Buddy: What's the matter with you, sonny? You unaquainted with the realities of life, or what?

Lillian: While I cannot approve of my brother's language, Mr. Runney, I can't say it is entirely beside the point.

Finley: Well, I can. My grandfather is not a buzzard or a hog, Mr. Slade. He is a Lieutenant Colonel, retired, United States Army, and this place to which he is confined is most certainly not heaven. Please let Nurse Logan finish what she has to say.

Buddy: Well, hoo-ee, get her.

Lillian: Buddy, you are my brother, and you are repulsive. Hush!

Finley: Just let her finish? PLEASE? *(Pause.)* Nurse Logan? *(Pause.)*

Susan: There's nothing else to say. Shall I tell them you're here?

Buddy: Do that. Just tell Momma we're here.

Finley: And my grandfather I am.

Susan: Certainly. It's 1:30. They should both be in the Day Room. I'll be right back. *(Exit Susan. Pause. They look about. Buddy sprawls in one of the chairs. Finley takes the chair next to Lillian. Pause.)*

Lillian: You say your grandfather was a Lieutenant Colonel?

Finley: He still is. Officers of the American Army, when they retire, keep their rank.

Lillian: When did he serve in the Army?

Finley: He won a battlefield commission in World War II. He became a Logistics Staff Officer for the Allied Expeditionary Forces, rising to the rank of Lieutenant Colonel.

Lillian: I see.

Finley: And your mother?

Buddy: Never you mind about our Momma!

Lillian: Hush up, Buddy. Our mother, Mr. Runney, is a plain Southern housewife, has been all her life. She never joined anything more exciting than her Garden Club. But for sixty years she served her husband and her six children with grace and dignity and honor. Now she is old, no doubt severely confused, and we will not allow her to be taken advantage of in her last years on earth! *(Enter Susan.)*

Susan: They're on their way.

Buddy: Wait a minute. Both of 'em?

Lillian: We want to talk to our mother, not to him.

Finley: And I want to talk to him and not your mother. Meet her here and I'll see my grandfather somewhere else.

Lillian: Thank you, sir. That's what we'll do!

Susan: Sorry. No.

Buddy: Whadda you mean no?

Susan: Mrs. Slade and Mr. Runney will only see you together. *(Pause.)*

Buddy: Huh?

Lillian: I beg your pardon?

Finley: My grandfather won't see me alone?
Susan: Together, or not at all.
Buddy: Mama?
Lillian: Is this their idea or yours?
Susan: That was a direct quote.
Buddy: From which one?
Susan: From Colonel Runney, with Mrs. Slade nodding her head.
Lillian: I don't agree to this!
Finley: I don't either!
Buddy: No way! *(The door opens. Colonel Runney and Mrs Slade stand in the doorway. They are very weak and vulnerable. They both show their hard age and frailty. Ellis Runney is a ragged gentleman with spindley and very weak legs, unkempt hair, clean but faded clothes, perhaps a ragged sweater too big for him and he has tremors in his hands. His skin is white and flaky, dotted with the blemishes of age. But he walks with upright pride, and a fierce, defiant eye. He holds in each hand a stick with a large white card attached to it. Cora Slade is a wisp of a woman, with snow white hair, skin like wrinkled parchment, an old woman's hesitations and uncertainties, and a ragdoll she clutches fearfully to herself. She is dressed in a Southern Granny dress, a very loose faded calico sack garment, and wears tennis shoes to keep from falling. She carries three letters. Neither is theatrically cute or adorable. They look as if any step outside the nursing home is absolutely impossible.)*
Susan: Well, here they are. *(Pause.)* Shall we sit down? *(Ellis holds up one of the cards on the sticks. It says in big shaky black letters: "NEGATIVE!")* You don't want to sit down, Colonel Runney? *(He holds up the other card. It says: "POSITIVE!")* Would you like US to sit down? *("POSITIVE!")*
Lillian: Oh, Mother.
Finley: Granpa Ellis?
Buddy: Momma, let go of that man and come on over here! Just do it RIGHT NOW! *(Cora and Ellis look at each other. As one, they turn and slowly start out the door.)*
Lillian: Now, Mother, please!
Buddy: Don't be like that!
Finley: We'll sit down, we'll sit down! *(He does. Ellis and Cora turn and look at them. Lillian and Buddy slowly sit. Ellis and Cora come back into the room and stand there together.)*
Susan: Do you want me to stay? *("POSITIVE!")* All right. *(She folds her hands, stands by. Pause.)*
Lillian: Mother, we want to know if you are all right here. *("POSITIVE!")*

Buddy: LET HER SPEAK FOR HERSELF! *("NEGATIVE")* MOMMA!

Finley: I told you my grandfather was a military man! Those cards mean what they say. Granpa Ellis. You still love me? *(Pause. "POSITIVE!")* You want to hurt me? *("NEGATIVE!")* You really do care about Mrs. Slade. *("POSITIVE!")* Have you—forced your attentions on her? *(Before Ellis can respond, Cora takes the "NEGATIVE!" sign and holds it up. Then she hands it back to Ellis.)* Granpa Ellis, are you in love with Mrs. Slade? *("POSITIVE!")* Mrs. Slade, are you in love with my grandfather? *(Cora takes the "POSITIVE!" sign and flashes it: "POSITIVE!" then gives it back.)* Then God bless you, Granpa Ellis. And you too, Mrs. Slade.

Susan: Well. That's honest and open and nice. Mrs. Barbow?

Lillian: Mother, why won't you talk to us? *(Cora smiles, looks at Ellis, who shakes his head.)*

Buddy: See that? Got her just where he wants her. Damn!

Lillian: Mother, all we are doing is making sure you are well and untroubled. But it is hard, when you won't even speak to us. *(Pause.)* Well, if you won't talk, you won't. Come on, Buddy. She's being impossible. Let her have him, and God help her. Let's go. *(She gets up. Cora hands Susan three letters. She reads the first one.)*

Susan: *(Reading aloud.)* "Cora Namwaite Slade and Lieutenant Colonel Ellis Marvin Runney announce their wedding very soon in a private ceremony in a private place."

Buddy: Married? Aye God, Momma!

Finley: *(Simultaneous.)* Oh, dear!

Lillian: Now we sit down! *(They sit quickly.)*

Susan: *(Reading.)* "Our bills here are paid. Security deposit plus three months rent at Bellevue Towers is paid. Our bags are packed. A taxi arrives here at fourteen hundred hours, to take us home."

Lillian: Home? Oh, Mother, really!

Finley: Since the taxi is coming at two, and it is now one forty-five, whatever is going to be done should I think be done quickly, don't you agree?

Buddy: Ain't no taxi taking nobody nowhere, I'll guarantee that!

Lillian: Mother, marriage is a serious step. *(Susan laughs. Finley laughs.)* Please!

Finley: Sorry.

Susan: I beg your pardon.

Lillian: Mother, you can't have known Mr. Runney—

Finley: Colonel Runney—

Lillian: LIEUTENANT Colonel Runney—for very long. You haven't been here six months yourself. You could make a dreadful mistake. *(Ellis* flashes: "NEGATIVE!" Cora puts her hand gently over his, and pushes the card down. The she smiles at Lillian and shrugs, conveying, "So what if I do?") Mother, it's very hard when you won't talk to me. I am your daughter, Lillian, who's done more for you than—and never mind that, just stop with these silly cards and speak to me! *(Cora raises the card in Ellis's hand: "NEGATIVE!")* It isn't just getting married. It's doing it without telling us, or consulting us. If we hadn't come here today, what would you have done? Just driven off with him? *(Cora and Ellis flash: "POSITIVE!")* You understand, Mother, marriage, even at your age, means sex? You would have to submit to this man's carnal desires? *(Cora waves: "POSITIVE!")* Mother, this is your daughter speaking. I know you better than this. You are not a promiscuous woman. You had your children and you moved into your own bedroom and slept by yourself in peace and dignity, and I admired you for it. I have done exactly the same. It is a great relief. But now you will have to accommodate a man again. This man, with real or imaginary sexual needs. *("POSITIVE!")* You put that down!! *(She smiles, speaks calmly.)* Mother, this is the point. You have been put in this home by your loving children because the plain fact is, you can't take care of yourself any more. Remember the lost check books? Yes. Remember the missed appointments you couldn't remember you made? Yes. Remember the forgotten house, which you lived in for sixty years and and one pretty day couldn't find? Yes. Remember the telephone calls to people dead thirty years and front doors left open and the burned food, the gas from the oven blowing up in your face, and the kitchen, pantry and dining room in flames? Yes. And now you want to get married, to upset the practical arrangements so carefully made for you. You are thinking about no one but yourself. What will you do? Take half your estate from your children and grandchildren, and give it to a man you hardly know? Next you'll want to make a new will, and give it all away! No. You are incompetent, Mother, and you are staying here. *(Cora nods to Susan. She reads the second letter.)*

Susan: *(Reading.)*

TO WHOM IT MAY CONCERN

I have examined Cora Namwaite Slade and Colonel Ellis Marvin Runney and I find them for their ages sound in mind and body. I approve their release from Woodvale Nursing Home.

Richard MacFarland, M.D.

Lillian: And who is he?

Susan: Their private physician. They are not in legal custody.

Buddy: But we signed her in here! We pay five thousand damn dollars a month for that room!

Lillian: And we control her estate, by Power of Attorney. There will be no moving anywhere without our permission. *(Cora nods to Susan. She reads the third letter.)*

Susan: *(Reading)*

TO WHOM IT MAY CONCERN

Cora Namwaite Slade, being sound in mind and body, hereby revokes Power of Attorney granted May 12, 1984, to her daughter, Lillian Slade Barbow.

Robert Costango
Attorney at Law
Senior Citizen's Legal Association

Buddy: You mean Momma can just walk out of here, and start writing checks?

Lillian: It can't be legal.

Susan: I think it is.

Buddy: Mamma's money! Paydirt, at last! *(To Susan.)* How much she pay you, Lady? Everybody knows you milk every tit you can get hold of in an old folks home.

Lillian: Buddy, really, just die, will you?

Buddy: She's earned her percentage! Lieutenant Colonel Runney, sir, he'll get half Mama's estate when she dies, tell me I'm wrong!

Finley: If she dies first, Mr. Slade. If my grandfather—

Buddy: Dies first, he'll leave her his swagger stick, right? How much is this Lieutenant Colonel in the damn Army worth, anyway?

Lillian: That is a vulgar question, in vulgarity put, does not deserve an answer, and at the moment, anyway, is beside the point.

Buddy: So what is the god damn point?

Lillian: *(Pointing.)* That doll.

Buddy: Say what?

Lillian: Our mother, Buddy, see, is clutching, if you haven't noticed, a rag doll. It is very important to her. She is obviously in a dependent, infantile state, therefore she is incompetent, therefore she can be proven so, doctor or no doctor. Would any responsible medical professional send an old woman out into the cold world with her dolly?

Susan: Dolls can be therapy for elderly women. Men, too, at times. She made that one herself. Colonel Runney helped her. We also bring in little animals twice a week. They are petted, handled, talked to. It calms everybody down, like that doll, and it brings old people toward reality, not away from it.

Buddy: She's got an answer for everything. Be quiet, Lillian, and let her answer this, if she will. What's in it for you? *(They all look at her.)*
Susan: *(Fed up.)* Have to know, do you? *(They look at Buddy.)*
Buddy: Hell yes I have to know. Let's have it!! *(They look back at Susan. Pause.)*
Susan: I like old people, Mr. Slade. They appeal to me. Not because of the fortune I extort from them or the salary I command as a nurse. Not because I enjoy seeing doctors give them drugs totally unnecessary, X-Rays they don't need, in some homes pack them in four and five to a room, order them liquor and make drunks out of them, neglect them, tie them down, beat them up, leave them fallen sometimes broken in their own waste, and frighten them in ways you and I will never understand until we face old age ourselves. It's in spite of all that, Mr. Slade, they still appeal to me. Why? Because at the edge of existence, with the ground crumbling away under their feet, with life tearing away everything it gave, with a few outbursts and tantrums, some whining and shouting, in this world they are still the most gallant people I know. And when a lady like Mrs. Slade and a gentleman like Colonel Runney meet and find each other, I watch them grow younger!
Lillian: Do what?
Buddy: *(Simultaneous.)* Aw, shoot!
Finley: *(Simultaneous.)* Now, really!
Susan: You can scoff at it, and deny it. Doctors can call it demeaning names like sexual recrudesence, but I think it's just fine, they're doing better right now with their love life than I am, and if they can get that together, I say let them keep it!
Lillian: Thank you, young woman, for what I will generously call a misguided professional opinion, and let me hear no more of it. *(She stands up, faces Cora.)* You are an old woman, Mother. Not a doll, not a girl. You are sick, you are senile, you need constant care, and that's what you are going to get. I will not let my own mother commit sexual suicide. *(Ellis steps forward, holding out, "NEGATIVE!")*
Lillian, Finley and Buddy: Not now! *(He backs away.)*
Lillian: Because it won't be a second honeymoon, Mother. It will be a nightmare of misery and pain and squalor which will kill you years ahead of your time. *(Ellis tries to hold out "NEGATIVE!" again.)* And you, sir! Can you, as an officer and a gentleman, do that to her? Take away her last years of peaceful existence? Not if you really love her! *(Finley gets up.)*
Finley: Granpa Ellis, I have had enough of these people. I will wait for you in the lobby, where we can talk to each other rationally. But you stay here. *(Ellis holds up "NEGATIVE!" while Cora takes and holds up, "POSITIVE!"*

They look at each other, in confusion, and lower the cards.) Listen to whatever they say. Think. Look. Then come out and talk to me alone, please. I do not think I will have much trouble in showing you how shallow and trivial these people are. After that, if you must live with HER, very well, but understand you will also have to live with THEM! I know you can't do it. I will be waiting. *(Exit Finley.)*

Lillian: And vice versa, Mother. How will you like that effete little snob looking down on YOU? *(Pause. Cora turns away.)* Come on, Buddy. She won't do it now. *(Exit Lillian. Buddy stands looking at his mother.)*

Buddy: Momma. I know I'm a fool. Put my foot in my mouth. But I dote on my Momma. Bettern anybody. I do. *(Buddy kneels in front of his mother.)* Don't marry nobody. Next Sunday, I'll pick you some blue gentians, just like I did when I was a boy, and you doted on me. I promise, Momma. All right? *(Buddy gets up.)* Good. I trust you, Momma. I'll see you next Sunday. Bye. *(He tiptoes out. Cora, shaken, moves away from Ellis. Susan sets a chair out for Cora, who sits in it, wearily. She looks at Ellis.)*

Ellis: I have to—go—talk to him. *(Exit Ellis. Cora, quietly, hugs her doll and sways back and forth, sadly.)*

Susan: He'll be right back. I'm sure he will. *(Cora shakes her head. Susan goes toward her, but Cora holds up her hand to keep her away. Susan nods. Softly.)* I'll wait here with you. *(Pause. She goes to her desk, sits. Pause. She tries to read a magizine, can't. She looks at Cora.)* Can I get you something? Some tea, some milk? *(Cora shakes her head. Pause. Susan tries to read again. Pause. Quietly, Cora begins to cry.)* Oh, Mrs. Slade.

Cora: He doesn't love me.

Susan: Oh, dear. *(Pause.)* We'll stay here as long as you want. I'll play you some music. *(She turns on the radio, tuned still to the program heard at the beginning of the play. Playing is the Tschaikovsky Concerto itself, one minute thirty seconds into the first movement, where the piano, between climaxes, plays trills and flourishes, music aimless and dull. Pause. Cora weeps, quietly, hugging her doll. She gets up and moves away from the music. A taxi horn is heard.)* The Taxi. *(The dull music plays. Cora moves slowly across the stage. Outside, the taxi blows its horn again. Cora sits in a chair on the other side of the stage. She sags, her doll almost falling from her hands, stricken with grief. The door flies open. In staggers Ellis. He holds up his "POSITIVE!" sign. The music bursts into a climax from speakers all over the theatre. Ellis goes to the chair where he last saw Cora. She isn't there! He is horrified. Susan points to Cora. He turns around. Cora rises. She and Ellis stare at each other. They stagger* *together. They embrace. They kiss. They drop the sign and the doll. Stumbling, limping, they stagger to the door and exit. Susan follows them to the door. Music. Light on Susan smiling.)*

JULIET

PHILIP FRENCH, 26, a melancholy director.
WILLY HARDT, 55, a bustling producer.
JANE ZANE, 50, a wealthy mother.

Place: The stage of an off-off Broadway Theater in SoHo, New York City.
Time: The present.

JULIET was first performed in the Ensemble Studio Theatre Marathon of One Act Plays, 1988, Curt Dempster, Artistic Director. It was produced by Laura Barnett, directed by Peter Maloney, setting by Ann Sheffield, costumes by David Sawaryn, lights by Greg MacPherson, stage manager, Tom Roberts. Cast as follows:

PHILIP FRENCH...........Thomas Gibson
WILLY HARDT............Sam Schact
JANE ZANE.................Robin Moseley
ESTHER FRENCH.........Lois Smith

JULIET

A small empty stage. One six-foot table, some chairs. A light bulb on a stand fades ups slowly, its light revealing a poster on a billboard. It displays borders of ice and snow, with an older woman's sad face at its center. Lettering reads:

HARDT PRODUCTIONS
IBSEN'S MASTERPIECE
GHOSTS

Enter Philip French. He blows on his hands, stamps his feet. He stares at the poster. He takes off his coat and sits, staring bleakly at nothing. He sighs.

He sighs again. He sits very still a long time, then sighs once more and sits there, motionless.

Enter Willy Hardt, with a big carton containing coffee and rolls. He goes to a switchboard, turns off the bulb on the stand, turns on some stage lights.

Philip: Hi.
Willy: AH!! *(Pause.)* Jeez, you scared me to death.
Philip: Sorry.
Willy: I just didn't see you.
Philip: I'm Philip French. Street door was open. I just walked in.
Willy: Well, I'm Willy Hardt, Philip. Glad to meet you. *(They shake hands.)* I got some coffee here, and danish. Want some?
Philip: Coffee, yeah. *(Willy takes out the coffee and rolls.)*
Willy: Just sitting in the dark, were you?
Philip: Thinking. Interesting theatre.
Willy: It's a great building. One of the oldest iron foundries in SoHo.
Philip: Great place for a theatre.
Willy: D'Agostino's.
Philip: What?
Willy: That's what's coming in. My lease is up end of the month, unless I'm in production, then I got it til the end of the show. That's why I got to get this play on now. I saw your Romeo? Wonderful what you did with Juliet.
Philip: Thanks.
Willy: Terrific tragedy. Fun production. You deserved those reviews.

Philip: I was happy with it.

Willy: Everybody says you are marvelous with actresses. "Good Woman of Setzuan," you did. "Barrets of Wimpole Street." "Streetcar" even. No matter what, you get women to do these great things onstage.

Philip: Yeah, well. Yeah.

Willy: So, yesterday "Romeo" Tomarrow "Ghosts" Your Agent said you were free. Right?

Philip: That's why I'm here.

Willy: OK. Off-Broadway contract, SSD and C minimum. Open here, and with luck, I want to move it.

Philip: All right.

Willy: You get approval on casting, so do I.

Philip: Fine.

Willy: And we start now. I mean, today.

Philip: OK.

Willy: You know the play?

Philip: Sure.

Willy: Any idea how you'd want to do it?

Philip: Straight.

Willy: Oh.

Philip: No concept, no gimmicks. No set in North Dakota with costumes made out of ice. A Norway living room, couch, window, fiord outside, and good actors. Straight.

Willy: I see what you mean. But, Philip, I tell you, maybe that word's a little over-reductive, for some people. Let's don't use it. How about "as written," instead. OK?

Philip: OK. As written.

Willy: Ideas about casting?

Philip: I know three actresses available right now who can do Mrs. Alving. All solid, none sensational, and I'd like it that way. I don't want anybody too big.

Willy: What about Jane Zane?

Philip: Jane Zane?

Willy: Yeah. What do you think?

Philip: Well. It's been awhile since that awful Lady Macbeth.

Willy: She needed a director, Philip.

Philip: And a voice. Not much happened to her in California, either, did it?

Willy: She's back now.

Philip: She *is* a good actress. Be happy to consider her.

Willy: Consider won't do. You gotta take her.

Philip: Oh.

Willy: One, she's signed, and two, we're living together.

Philip: Oh.

Willy: I'll tell you the truth, Philip. Benny Green was going to direct this play.

Philip: Oh, ho.

Willy: Benny and Jane didn't get along. I had to choose between them. It was Jane.

Philip: Why, said Ellery Queen, didn't the star and the director get along?

Willy: Jane has this uh, concept about Mrs. Alving. Benny didn't like it. Tell you the truth, I'm not nuts about it either, but she's the right actress, we're living together, what could I say?

Philip: Bye bye Benny.

Willy: Yeah.

Philip: And then you said, "Who's good handling tough women?" People said me, and you called my agent.

Willy: Well, no, not exactly, but sort of, yeah. So, we still in business?

Philip: What is this concept of hers?

Willy: I'll let her tell you that. She'll be here, eleven fifteen sharp.

Philip: She's young for the part.

Willy: Right, can't argue with that.

Philip: With a production concept that sent Benny Green over the hill.

Willy: Right again. That's the ball game. How about it, Philip, yes or no?

Philip: I want to do "Ghosts." She'd be good. OK.

Willy: Let's do it?

Philip: Let's do it. As long as I can level with her. Be absolutely frank with her.

Willy: Absolutely. We got a deal. *(He holds out his hand. They shake again.)* More coffee?

Philip: No, thanks.

Willy: I'll have some while we wait. She may be a minute or two late. You know.

Philip: Yep. *(Philip turns away, immediately sad again. He sits in a chair and stares. Willy watches him.)*

Willy: Do you mind if I ask you a personal question?

Philip: No.

Willy: You were just sitting here, in the dark, when I came in. You do that often?

Philip: Sometimes.

Willy: Hamlet. That's what people call you.

Philip: I know they do. And yes, I cut my wrists in a chapel while I was at Harvard, which you read about in the papers.

Willy: Yeah. Then you jumped out of a hospital window.

Philip: *(Smiling nodding)* You saw the photograph.

Willy: *(Nodding.)* That awning.

Philip: *(Nodding)* Saved me. Right.

Willy: Problems at Harvard?

Philip: Well—I was a freshman.

Willy: Come on.

Philip: I got shrunk, once a day for five years. I function.

Willy: Choate, Harvard, Austin Riggs, Yale Drama School. And now New York. But you look so sad all the time. Like right now, sitting in that chair. You do look like Hamlet. Or some guy whose best friend ran off with his dog. But you're hot stuff, and your shows are all happy. They crackle. They pop. Great energy, all that. You're wonderful with women, and everybody wonders what you're all about, Philip.

Philip: That's the way it is.

Willy: You're not in real trouble, are you? I mean, the mob or dope or bad S&M or anything like that?

Philip: Nothing like that. I'll do my job.

Willy: OK, that's enough for me. Get along with Jane, look like Hamlet, look like Lear. *(He starts out.)* I'm gonna check the stage door, and wait for her. *(He comes back.)* You decide about that poster. I just had somebody throw it together. *(Starts out, comes back.)* And oh yeah, when you're talking with Jane, say "as written" instead of "straight," OK? *(Exit Willy. Philip gets up, looks again at the poster. He sighs, sad again. He puts his hands to his head and utters a single sob. He sits, and stares at nothing. Pause. Enter Willy with Jane Zane, who is a beautiful and talented actress in her late thirties. She carries a huge tape recorder.)* Here she is. Just walked in the door. Janie, this is Philip French. Philip, Jane Zane.

Philip: Hello, Jane.

Jane: Philip French! I didn't see your superb "Romeo and Juliet." but I heard about it. You are a very talented young man. *(They shake and hold hands.)*

Philip: Your Lady Macbeth was wonderful.

Jane: Thank you.

Willy: Yeah, well, I thought we'd just, you know, kind of sort of meet, you know, and talk things over, sort of, easy easy, right?

Jane: Is that coffee, Willy?

Willy: And a big cheese and cherry Danish, just for you.

Jane: How nice. *(She puts her tape recorder down, sweeps off her coat, and smiles at Philip.)* Shall we put our cards on the table, Philip?

Philip: Sure.

Jane: Benny Green was going to direct this play.

Philip: That's what I heard.

Jane: We had a problem. I made a simple, constructive suggestion. Benny hated it. Did Willy tell you what it is?

Philip: He said I should hear it from you.

Willy: Coffee, Janie, and a danish.

Jane: Thank you, darling. *(To Philip.)* I hope you have an open mind.

Philip: Shoot.

Jane: Ibsen's *Ghosts*. Mrs. Alving. I know I'm young for the part. To play a mother with a grown son, I mean.

Philip: Willing to dye your hair? Makeup? Age?

Jane: She can be forty-five, married at eighteen. I can do that.

Philip: OK.

Jane: Mrs. Alving, then. Innocent, proper woman. She married a man who gave her syphilis. He died. She watched her only son, Oswald, grow up, knowing he could inherit the disease. Now she realizes all this happened because she was too bourgeois to leave a dissolute husband. She was bound, you see, Philip, by convention.

Philip: Yes, I see that.

Jane: But how do we pull that off today? Benny Green didn't want anything new. "It's a masterpiece," he says. "I want to do it straight," he says. "Straight?" I say. "Straight? We *can't* do it straight, syphilis is curable now, Benny, for God's sake, never mind the Women's Movement, all that. Something NEW, Benny, has got to emerge from this play, and I know what it is!" I tell him, and he says, "Over my dead body," and that was what happened to Benny Green.

Philip: Jane. What?

Jane: This. *(She holds up a cassette, pops it into the tape machine.)* Ibsen's *"Ghost"* ends with Mrs. Alving facing a dreadful choice. Her son Oswald has syphilis. Afraid he will go mad, become a vegetable, he gives his mother a vial of deadly poison, for HER to give to HIM, when his brain goes and he falls apart. "That day will never come!" says Mrs. Alving, and they settle down. Young man, mother. All is well. Peace. Until Oswald says to her, "Mother, give me the sun." The sun he wants, just like that, and she knows he's crazy, it's syphilis, paresis, he's gone. What is she going to do? She looks at the deadly poison, in the little vial. She looks at Oswald, her son. Back and forth. Back and forth. Curtain! *(Pause.)* Right?

Philip: That's what Ibsen indicates, yes.

Jane: Same old thing! But suppose we don't DO the same old thing!

Suppose she makes Oswald's life as a paralytic syphylitic blah-blah-blah-NOT worse than death! Instead of all that, Jesus, Scandanavian depression, Mrs. Alving not only does NOT give Oswald poison, she does NOT leave him jelly, asking for the sun. No, she will try, try something! Even if doomed, she is a mother!

Philip: All right, try what?

Jane: To SAVE HIS LIFE!

Philip: How?

Jane: Like this!! *(Jane punches on her tape reeorder. A contralto begins "My Heart, At Thy Sweet Voice," from the Saint-Saens opera "Sampson and Delilah.")*

Delilah: *(Singing.)*

Mon coeur s'ouvre a ta voix comme
s'ouvre les fleurs--
Aux baisers de l'aurore!

Jane: We hear THIS heavenly music! We see divine light! Mrs. Alving, the modern modern woman, throws away the deadly poison! Her mother's instinct erupts!

Delilah: *(Singing.)*

Mais, o bien-aime, pour mieux secher
mes pleurs,
Que ta voix parle encore!

Jane: She tears open her blouse, exposing her breast! Oswald! He sees it. Mother!

Delilah: *(Singing.)*

Dis-moi qu'a Dalila tu reviens pour
jamais!

Jane: Dimly, he stares at her. He moves toward her! She toward him! He holds out his arms!

Delilah: *(Singing.)*

Redis a ma tendress—

Jane: Son! Mother! Curtain!

Delilah: *(Singing.)*

Redis a ma tendress—

Jane: There. Tragedy, and grace. Dignity in her defeat!

Delilah: *(Singing.)*

Les serments d'autrefois—

Jane: Passion in her victory!

Delilah: *(Singing.)*

Ces serments que j'amais!

Jane: Today! *(Philip and Willy look at each other. Philip punches off the* *tape recorder.)*

Philip: Jane, Oswald wants light, not milk. *(Deadly pause.)*

Jane: Is that important?

Philip: Yes.

Jane: That kind of logic appeals to you?

Philip: Yes.

Jane: You don't like my idea?

Philip: It's dumb.

Jane: What?

Willy: Now, Janie—

Jane: WHAT did you say?

Philip: Dumb, I said. It's anti-female.

Jane: ANTI-FEMALE?

Philip: That means against women, right.

Jane: ME? AGAINST WOMEN???

Philip: You.

Willy: Now, Philip, wait a minute.

Jane: I'll kill him!

Willy: Janie, have some coffee. The danish.

Jane: I'll break his neck!

Willy: Janie, now listen. Philip let you talk. Now you let him talk. You eat, you drink. Philip, you talk.

Jane: Jesus! *(She grabs her danish and coffee.)* SO TALK!

Philip: One. Baring your breast onstage. Colette did it at the end of the 19th century. Zoe Caldwell did it in 1970 playing Colette. It just ain't modern. Two. Oswald has syphilis, not rickets, milk isn't going to help him. Three. Your divine music is Delilah singing "My Heart At Thy Sweet Voice" to Sampson in French, just before she cuts off his hair and his balls, while we are in Norway, speaking English, and that is all just too confusing. Four. You will look like you are playing Mrs. Alving to show off your boobs, which will be anti-female, any which way anybody can look at it and five, Henrik Ibsen wrote "*Ghosts,*" not Jane Zane.

Willy: Philip, please!

Jane and Philip: Shut up!

Jane: You blockhead. You pompous child. You can't talk to me like that. Mr. Hamlet Social Register, went to Harvard and cut his wrists, went to Yale and jumped out a window: weird, weird, weird, doesn't have girls, doesn't have boys, and Who the Hell Cares! WE are NOT going to get along! Willy, get somebody else!

Willy: Now, Janie—

Jane: WILLY!

Willy: I don' t think I CAN get anybody else, not now! So Philip was a little harsh about women, Janie. I got a show to get produced here, and Janie, honey, if you want to be in it you two GET ALONG! *(Pause.)*

Jane: You don't like my idea either.

Willy: Well—

Jane: Say it.

Willy: A grown man's mother wouldn't do that, Janie.

Jane: Both of you hate my contribution to death. Right?

Willy and Philip: A grown man's mother just wouldn't do that.

Willy: Janie. *(Pause. Jane nods. She stares at the wall. She shifts her weight, stares at the floor. She looks out into the house, staring thinking. Pause.)*

Jane: Willy. Someone's out there.

Willy: What?

Jane: In the house. *(All three peer into the darkness.)*

Philip: I see him.

Willy: Where?

Philip: In the back. There.

Willy: Bums. They get in the stage door and sleep here. *(Willy goes to the apron.)* Hey! You! We see you! *(No answer.)* Who are you? *(No answer.)* Nobody's allowed in the theatre. You can't stay here. *(A figure moves into one aisle.)* That's right, pal. Come on. We'll show you out. *(The figure hesitates.)* Come on. Buddy. You got to go now.

Jane: It's not a man. It's a woman. *(The figure comes to the edge of the stage.)*

Esther: Hello, Philip.

Philip: Hello, Mother. *(Esther French is a well-dressed, plain-faced woman. She carries a large piece of coarse paper, rolled up.)*

Willy: His mother?

Esther: I am sorry to bother you, Philip. I called this morning, but you were gone. Your agent said you'd be here.

Philip: It's all right, Mother. *(He helps Esther onto the stage.)* Willy Hardt, Jane Zane. My mother, Esther French.

Willy: Hi.

Jane: Hi.

Esther: Good morning. I really must speak to my son. It's very important.

Willy: Right now?

Jane: His mother? Really? *(Esther points to a chair.)*

Esther: Philip, please. *(Philip sits obediently. He and his mother face each other, while above them, Willy and Jane watch them. Esther takes from her purse a computer print-out sheet.)* I have sold everything. The house on

East 68th Street. The estate in Ammagansett. The Rock Garden Museum. All the bonds. Everything your stepfather left me. This is what I got for them. *(She hands the sheet to Willy.)* He won't believe me. Would you be a witness? *(Willy takes the sheet, looks at it.)*

Willy: God.

Esther: That is an appropriate response.

Willy: That's a lot of money. Here, Philip.

Philip: No. I believe her. *(Esther takes it back.)*

Esther: Do you know what it means? It means money is silly now. What was on paper, I could worry about, but not what's cold cash in banks. I can do anything I want. Fly to the moon. Interrupt a rehearsal. Do anything, and go anywhere.

Philip: That's fine, Mother.

Esther: But where do I want to go, Philip?

Philip: I don't know, Mother.

Esther: Philip, I want to go—to Hawaii.

Philip: Good, Mother. You'll enjoy it.

Esther: A cold winter in *Hawaii,* son!

Philip: I heard you, Mother.

Esther: No, you didn't. *(To Willy and Jane.)* He doesn't even remember.

Jane: Well, Hawaii's nice, Mrs. French.

Willy: Have a good trip.

Esther: But how can I get there?

Willy: I think, With that kind of money, you can get to Hawaii somehow.

Esther: So why don't I just go? Of course. What's the problem? Old lady out to lunch, lost all her marbles.

Philip: Mother, I'll take you home.

Esther: I've sold my home, my darling. I walked out of it with one suitcase. I'm at the Sherry Netherland now, for a week only. And where are you, my boy? In that sterile condominium I bought you, living like a monk? No girls, no boys, no one. Only your razor blades, to kill yourself with. *(To Willy and Jane.)* Twice, you know. Wrists once, ankles once. His throat will be next. Or another open window. *(Philip gets up.)*

Philip: Mother, this is too painful. We must go.

Esther: Sit down, please. *(Philip does.)* When you were that little boy, your father dead, and me not yet remarried, and we had to live together in that attic in Detroit, I strung a wire across it, and hung curtains there, for your privacy and mine. Over your bed, below a photograph of me in my wedding dress, you pasted picture after picture of the Hawaiian Islands. Sunsets and waterfalls, flowers and beaches, with my face smiling above them.

Philip: Mother, I was nine years old.

Esther: And you knew what you wanted. Do you know that much now? Do you remember this? *(Esther unrolls the coarse paper. It is a home-made poster. It says HAWAII. On it is pasted a childish collage of a Hawaiian sunset, the sea, palm trees and flowers, with the face of a Hawaiian woman smiling above it.)* You made this when you were nine. I kept it Philip, look at it! *(She holds it out, clumsily. Jane takes it from her.)*

Jane: Let me help you. Willy. *(Jane takes it to the billboard. She and Willy lay it smoothly over the "Ghost" poster and stick it there with pushpins. Esther sits at the opposite end of the table from Philip. Jane and Willy stand between them.)*

Esther: Whose face was that, Philip, really, above the island you dreamed about at night? It was mine. You know it was mine. *(Jane looks at Willy and smiles a wicked smile.)* You knew who you were when you made that poster. You don't now. You're lost. I waited in the dark, listening to you haggle over some old play no one cares about anymore. You are lost, in the theatre, this oh really, tawdry land of illusion and dirt, where second rate substitutes masquerade for everything that's real. Why pretend? What you want from life is me, and what I want is you! Let me give you what you really want!

Jane: *(To Willy.)* Grown man's mother wouldn't do that, eh? *(Jane looks at her tape machine.)*

Esther: When your father died and we lived together, we knew. Everything since has been chaos. Your step-father's money, our separations and quarrels, my agonies, your razor blades, dear God in heaven, you never got over what's on that poster; neither did I! We've tried to live apart and look! Come back to me, Philip, now! *(Jane looks at Willy, points to Esther, and punches on the tape. Music: the climax of "My Heart At Thy Sweet Voice" plays.)*

Delilah: *(Sings.)*

Ah! Reponds, reponds a ma tendresse!
Verse-moi, verse-moi l'ivresse!

Esther: Oahu, Maui, Kaui, Molokai, all the Hawaiian Islands and your picture of me, together up and down the wall of your childhood you pasted them, your mother in that Pacific Paradise, my face and my body against sea and sun and foam! *(Willy and Jane stare at them, aghast.)*

Delilah: *(Singing.)*

Reponds a ma tendresse! Reponds a ma tendresse!
Verse-moi, verse-moi l'ivresse!

Esther: I'm yours, my boy. Take the only thing you will ever in all your life really want! I am waiting for you, in a paradise of wind, sea, flowers, and your mother in the sun! I can give you the sun!!! *(Jane punches off the music. Silence.)*

Jane: Oh, dear. too much. I'm sorry, Philip.

Philip: It's all right. *(Philip speaks to his mother slowly but very firmly.)* It isn't, Mother, that I don't still dream of those islands rising out of the sea. I do. But the Hawaiian Islands have changed. On Oahu now, you can't find Diamond Head for the hotels and condos. Maui is choked with MacDonalds. Beautiful natives are tour guide clowns. And you are old and I am sad. My childhood? Millions can't buy it back, even if we dream of nothing else. What you must give, I must refuse.

Esther: But why?

Philip: To live.

Esther: With razor blades and windows?

Philip: I'll survive! In this tawdry land of illusion and dirt. In the theatre, Mother, where you live within me, as Mrs. Alving, as Lady Macbeth, and *as Juliet. (Philip gently detaches himself from Esther.)* Keep the money, go to Hawaii.

Esther: Alone?

Philip: Take your bankbook. You'll meet somebody. *(They stare at each other, facing the inevitable.)*

Esther: When will I come back to you?

Philip: We both know the answer to that.

Esther: Never?

Philip: Never.

Esther: But will you live?

Philip: I will.

Esther: Throw away the razor blades?

Philip: Yes.

Esther: *Promise?*

Philip: I promise.

Esther: Use something electric?

Philip: All right.

Esther: Stay away from open windows?

Philip: Always.

Esther: Do we say goodbye—now?

Philip: As good a time as any.

Esther: I won't come back.

Philip: I will dream of you in paradise. *(Pause.)*

Esther: *(To Willy and Jane.)* I am sorry I disturbed your rehearsal. *(She goes to the door.)* Goodbye, son.

Philip: Goodbye, Mother. *(Exit Esther.)*
Jane: Are you all right?
Philip: I think so.
Willy: She forgot the poster.
Jane: I'll take it to her!
Philip: No. *(Philip looks at his poster of Hawaii and the smiling face of the Hawaiian woman. Philip goes to the poster. He takes it down quickly, revealing behind it the bitter face of Mrs. Alving.)*
Philip: About Mrs. Alving.
Jane: Whatever you say.
Philip: No, let's talk.
Jane: Lunch?
Philip: Fine.
Willy: *OK! (Philip drops the poster into a waste can, and exits with Jane. Willy follows, turning off the stage lights and the light bulb on the stand back on. It illuminates, as before, harshly, the poster for Ghosts: ice, snow, and Mrs. Alving. Then the light bulb fades out slowly.)*

YANCEY

FRED, a New York actor at work, 30's.
YANCEY, a very countrified Southern, any age.
FLO, an emotional and very sexy actress, 20's.

Place: Outdoor location for a production of a Civil War drama.
Time: The present

Yancey was commissioned by the Actors Theatre of Louisville for its Apprentice Program and first performed there. It was first produced in New York in the Ensemble Studio Theatre's SHORTSTUFF in March, 1988. It was directed by David Shookhoff, with the following cast:

FRED.................Victor Slezak
YANCEY............Dan Patrick Brady
FLO..................Lisa Maurer

YANCEY

A bench. Enter Fred, an actor. He slaps a script down on the bench, sits, tucks his legs under him, and studies a part.

Enter Yancey.

Long pause.

Fred grabs up his script, muttering his lines, and turns in a stage movement, arm outspread. He sees Yancey.

Fred: Oh. Hi.
Yancey: Hey.
Fred: How you doing?
Yancey: Jes fine.
Fred: Good. *(Yancey smiles, nods, keeps looking at Fred.)* Anything I can do for you?
Yancey: Reckon not. *(Fred nods. Sits down to study his script again. Looks up at Yancey.)*
Fred: You sure?
Yancey: Reckon not. Leastways not now. You got to finish here first.
Fred: What?
Yancey: You'd make a good preacher.
Fred: Yeah, sure I would. You just get here?
Yancey: At's rite. I'm in the battle scenes. I get wounded in one of 'em, and killed in anothern, and lie in the hospital a-yelling in anothern. I walk on, is what I do.
Fred: Having fun?
Yancey: Until I heared you.
Fred: What?
Yancey: Heared you preaching. You ever do that?
Fred: Who, me?
Yancey: Yes, sir. You.
Fred: No, pal. Not my style.
Yancey: Ought to be.
Fred: You just like my acting.
Yancey: No, I reckon at's what I don't like.
Fred: Oh, yeah? What's wrong with it?
Yancey: Ain't real.

Fred: Now, wait a minute, buddy! Uh—what's your name?

Yancey: Yancey.

Fred: Yancey, eh? Shoulda known. Yancey what?

Yancey: Yancey Biggerload.

Fred: Yeah. Yancey Biggerload. Shoulda known. I'm Fred Stewart, and look, Mr. Biggerload—

Yancey: You jest call me Yancey.

Fred: You got it. Yancey, actors aren't perfect. Especially nasty New York professionals like me trying to play Robert E. Lee's chaplain in a Grade Z Outdoor Drama about the god damn Civil War.

Yancey: Ought not to swear.

Fred: Why not?

Yancey: Hit debases you.

Fred: Oh, hit does, does hit?

Yancey: Of a sartin.

Fred: Listen, Yancey, I got to study my lines, or that looney tune director we got, he's what's going to debase me. So go study yours now? We got a run through when this break's over, remember? Be prepared.

Yancey: Hit pleasures you to condescend to me, don't hit?

Fred: Do what?

Yancey: Condescend to me. Look down. I know I don't talk very good. My voice sticks in my throat. But I know what words mean. And I can't study my lines. I ain't got none. What I do is run, yell and fall over.

Fred: So run, yell and fall over. Really, Yancey. *(Pause.)* Yancey, I got to work.

Yancey: What you're a-doing is, you're dismissing me.

Fred: Bulls-eye!

Yancey: At's yore priviledge. *(Gravely, he turns and exits.)*

Fred: Brother. *(He starts to work on his script again. He mumbles a few lines, waves his arms, can't work. Pause.)* Yancey. *(Pause.)* Yancey! *(Re-enter Yancey. Stands waiting.)* Just what do you want with me?

Yancey: I want you to be a real preacher, not just act like one.

Fred: Oh, for Christ's—

Yancey: Ought not to—

Fred: All right! *(Pause. Softly.)* Why?

Yancey: Because few are chosen.

Fred: And YOU'RE choosing ME, is that it?

Yancey: God chose you. I can hear it in your voice. I can see it the way you stand and walk. You could do powerful things, for people who need you. You ast. I'm telling.

Fred: Yancey, why don't YOU go do those things, and let me just be an actor.

Yancey: Don't you reckon I would if I could? But listen to me a talking, look at me a-moving. I walk like sticks and talk like gravel. Onliest thang folks think laying eyes on me is, what boon docks is he from.

Fred: That doesn't stop preachers, Yancey. They love the boon docks. Just good old country preachers, doing a hell of a lot better than most actors. Go preach, Yancey. Enjoy!

Yancey: I can't do it. I know. I've tried.

Fred: What happens?

Yancey: I commence to sweat in my hands. Knees shake. All the words bunch up in my mouth and choke me there. I talk like I got the lockjaw. Can't move. Want to die. You wouldn't comprehend it.

Fred: OK. So what you're thinking about is finding some bigmouth bozo like me, and starting up a church?

Yancey: A ministry.

Fred: Where I do the preaching and you run the business. OK, I got it. Yancey, up until this minute, you've had a certain Applachian charm, a sort of sourdough refreshment, maybe even a kind of flower-like pleasantry. But it's wearing off fast.

Yancey: Why don't you say it the way you heard it first?

Fred: What?

Yancey: "You are as pleasant as the flowers are made." That's what folks say where I'm from. About children. Where you from?

Fred: I told you New York.

Yancey: Afore that.

Fred: *(Slight pause.)* Brooklyn.

Yancey: Don't mess with me. Tell me the truth.

Fred: All right. I'm from Wheeling West Bloody Virginia. *(Fred's accent now becomes Southern.)* And I didn't like it Yancey. I don't know how you saw it in me, but yep, my old man was a preacher. That's right. So, you got me there.

Yancey: *(Nodding.)* So I do.

Fred: And I didn't like him much more than Wheeling West Bloody Virginia, Yancey. A little bit maybe—he wasn't a monster, exactly.

Yancey: What was he then?

Fred: He was a preacher, that's what he was! You know what that means to me? A whole lot, that I'm NOT going to be! Get it?

Yancey: Of a sartin. You jest aiming to act like one.

Fred: Yancey, this is a PART I'm playing! I don't go around playing preachers everywhere! You know what I usually play? Heavies, Yancey, real mean s's of b's! Low down, Yancey! Drugs and drinking and kinky sex, Yancey! Something about me just comes over that way! And it gets me cast, it's fine with me!

Yancey: You go in for vice, and sin? *(Pause. Fred sighs.)*

Fred: No, as a matter of fact, I don't. I go in for ACTING, Yancey, that's what I do. It's what I like to do. As far as I'm concerned, one good honest play is worth five thousand sermons, and one good honest actor is worth a hundred thousand preachers. That's the way I feel. But for you, I can see it must be the same thing, only the other way around. I know how awful I'd feel, if all I wanted to do was get on a stage and act, and couldn't. About as bad as a guy who wanted to stand up and preach and couldn't. *(Long pause. Yancey stares at Fred. Enter, in a rush, Flo, who lives with Fred, wearing almost nothing and a pair of 19th century ladies boots.)*

Flo: I don't believe this, Fred! You know what that mangy mother wants me to do now? *(To Yancey.)* Hi.

Fred: Yancey, Flo. Flo, Yancey.

Yancey: Hidy.

Fred: We live together, Yancey. We're not married but we live together. OK?

Yancey: *(Softly.)* It's what you think you want.

Fred: *(To Flo.)* What is it, Baby?

Flo: He wants me to play the whole ballroom scene in that rosepink atrocity with the bustle that makes my butt stick out like a truckbed. I TOLD costumes about that! *(She flops herself down on the bench, starts pulling off a boot and stocking. Fred sits by her. Yancey stands watching.)* You put me in a bustle and I look exactly like I'm riding two pigs making it under a sheet. He says its period and it's his ass as well as mine getting seen in this production, so I wear the bustle. O God, my foot, this boot! Like I'm wearing a jaw! *(She hugs Fred.)* Tonight, we get a bottle of vodka and your good gold Columbian, and I mean we FORGET this, you make me FORGET it all GOODBYE, you just take Momma BYEBYE tonight, you promise?

Fred: I promise.

Flo: That's my honeypot. *(She gives him a kiss, hot and heavy. Fred kisses her back.)*

Yancey: *(Quietly.)* Stop it.

Fred: What?

Yancey: Leave each other alone.

Flo: WHAT did he say?

Fred: Cool it, Yancey.

Yancey: I won't neither cool nothing! Hit's only what you think you want! And at's all!

Flo: Where'd this come from?

Fred: He's in the show. What's wrong, Yancy? A man and a woman together?

Yancey: Y'ain't married.

Fred: No, we're not. You think we ought to be? Before we get drunk and smoke dope and take off each other's clothes and all that? *(Pause. Yancey breaks down. He holds his head, weeping.)*

Flo: *(Alarmed.)* Fred.

Fred: Let him cry. Come on, Yancey. What do you think? *(Yancey stares at Fred, in torment.)* Speak, Yancey.

Yancey: Hit's the waste. But you don't know what I'm saying.

Fred: No, I don't. Tell me.

Yancey: Hit's the powerful waste that hurts. You are going to stand up in front of all them people coming to see a play, and in you they will see all good things. A man honest and straight and tall and kindly faced and strong and loving the Word of God. They will worship with you, praying when you move to kneel, and singing when you turn yore face to heaven. But you are only an actor.

Flo: Fred, he's wacko.

Fred: He's trying to preach. Hush.

Flo: Oh! It's an improvisation.

Fred: Right. Improvise.

Yancey: What about you, actor? What do YOU want? I'm gonna tell you what you want. You want to leave yore awful self, to escape a-running from the miseries of a plank-plain life, into this other new way of walking, this other new way of talking, with a new voice and a new tongue, new legs and dancing hands, no longer yore old wretched self, but born again, in spotlights and laughing.

Fred: He's got me, all right, and about every actor I know.

Flo: Go, Yancey! Do it! Give us some sin! S—

Flo and Fred: —i—n. Sin! *(He doesn't have to be told. Yancey's stiff body becomes pliant and supple. His wooden voice melts into real eloquence. He is transported: a baby preacher in the rough.)*

Yancey: I will! I will! Sin you want! Sin you get! But not when you think you're happy, in your glory!

Flo and Fred: *(Clapping.)* GLORY!

Yancey: Not DANCING and SINGING!

Flo and Fred: *(Clapping.)* DANCING and SINGING!

Yancey: Not HOPPING and HOLDING!

Flo and Fred: HOPPING and HOLDING! Whoo!

Yancey: Not KISSING and FLOPPING!

Flo and Fred: KISSING and FLOPPING! Whoooooo!

Yancey: But alone! When the music is gone and the drugs! When the dancing was yesterday's and all the happy words of love! When you *know* you're far away from what you really want, far, FAR away—

Flo and Fred: Far FAR AWAY!!!!!

Yancey: From HIM, who loves you not for yore singing, or for yore dancing, or for your shining youth a-gleaming in the sun, but for yore lonely self, what you jest plain ARE, in that well-bottom creek-bed of yore soul! O lover! O dancer! O saint! O sinner! Yearning, thirsty, hungry, feeble, feverish and dying, far from God, who is yore home!! *(A pause. All three look at each other, astonished. Yancey blinks, comes to, as if he has been in a trance. Then Yancey smiles, a great huge joyous grin of relief and discovery.)*

Yancey: Was at me?

Flo: Yeah! I got goosebumps!

Fred: Way to go, Yancey!

Yancey: Hit was me! Hit was me!

(Blackout.)

THE DEATH OF KING PHILIP

MARY ROWLANDSON, a haunted pioneer woman, 60's.
MARY ROWLANDSON, herself when young and strong, 30's
REV. JOSEPH ROWLANDSON, her certain husband
KING PHILIP, an intelligent, embattled king.

Place: New England.
Time: 1675.

THE DEATH OF KING PHILIP was first produced by the Actors Theatre of Louisville, Jon Jory, Artistic Director, in November, 1983. It was directed by Ray Fry, set design by Paul Owen, costumes by Marcia Dixcy, lights by Karl Haas, sound by James M. Bray. Cast as follows:

MARY ROWLANDSON...............Anne Shropshire
MARY ROWLANDSON...............Deborah Hedwall
REV. JOSEPH ROWLANDSON.....Frederic Major
KING PHILIP...........................Michael Kevin

THE DEATH OF KING PHILIP

New England, 1675.
At Stage Left sits a colonial rocking chair. At Right a lectern. Left Center, the stump of a tree. At Center, before a cold wintery sky, a wooden structure suggesting the wall of a colonial house. Lights fade. When they come up, Mary 60 is sitting in her chair, holding her Bible.

Mary 60:
I can remember the time
when I used to sleep quietly
whole nights together
but now it is other ways with me.
When all are fast about me
and no eye open
but my own
then my thoughts
are on what is past.
(She reads her Bible.)
Hebrews twelve and six.
"For whom the Lord loveth
He chasteneth
and He scourgeth
every son
He receiveth."
(She closes her Bible.)
In the day I rest
but in the night season
I hunger again
I am unsatisfied
I must remember what my mouth has tasted
what my eyes have seen.
(Enter Mary Rowlandson aged 30, carrying a bundle of cloth representing a baby. She wears the same dress as Mary 60. She hums and sings to her baby.)
Mary 30: *(Singing.)*
HUSH LITTLE BABY PRETTY BOY
DO NOT CRY TONIGHT
DREAM OF BIRDS AND GOLDEN RINGS
AND RAINBOWS ALL ALIGHT

(Enter Reverend Rowlandson, carrying a Bible, but dressed for travel.)

Rowlandson:

You will be safe with our neighbors
Pray for us and mind our child
God sends me to War.

Mary 30:

I will.

Rowlandson:

We must each obey
and never doubt God's purpose
for His chosen people.
Now a Savage must be slain
a devil's rebellion crushed
until the future of our faith
ordained in this great land
by Almighty God
is secure.

Mary 30:

I accept. I do not question.

(Rowlandson kneels, holding out his Bible. Mary 30 kneels with him, touching it.)

Rowlandson: *(Praying.)*

Lord Jesus Christ defend us
that we may here inherit
for ages yet unborn
the glory of God's stern will
shining here
in darkness.
Amen.

Mary 30:

Amen.
Goodbye, husband.
God keep you.

Rowlandson:

Goodbye, wife.
God keep you.

(Exit Rowlandson. Mary 30 hums and tends her baby.)

Mary 60:

I have seen
the extreme vanity of the world.
One hour was I in safety
comfort and certain faith.
(She moves to Mary 30, standing behind her.)
Before I knew
what affliction was
I was sometimes ready
to wish for it.
I was jealous
I did not want to miss
my portion of sorrow
and I remembered that scripture—
Mary 30:
Hebrews twelve and six.
"For whom the Lord loveth
He chasteneth and He scourgeth
every son he receiveth."
Mary 60:
Well affliction I wanted
affliction I had.
(The sky turns red.)
On the tenth of February
came the Savages
in great numbers upon us.
(Far off sounds of gunfire and
people shouting.)
We heard shouting
and the firing of guns
and saw several houses burning
the smoke ascending to heaven.
(Shouting and gunfire becomes louder.
Mary 30 and Mary 60 stand together
before a blood red sky.)
Some believed the Word of God
would protect them.
They held their scriptures in their hands
in faith secure
but the Savages came upon them
scorned their groundless folly
ripped them open

and put their Bibles
in their bellies.
*(There is a loud sound of wood breaking,
a door being battered in. Mary 30
screams, and holding her baby, backs
away.)*
No use! No use!
(Darkness. Spotlight on Mary 60.)
I had often said
that before I would be taken
by Savages
I would die.
But their glittering weapons
and fierce aspect
so daunted my spirit
that rather than end my life
I chose to go with them
into captivity.
*(A drum begins to beat, slowly. Enter
Mary 30, her clothes now torn and
disheveled, carrying her baby.)*
The story of my captivity
began with a long remove
as a captive to be hostage
for ransom.
*(The sky is bleak and cold. As Mary 60
speaks, Mary 30 acts out what she is
saying.)*
When I begged for food
they gave me what they ate
a handfull of peas and time at night
to scrape the earth
for ground nuts and acorns.
I fell once from a horse
hurting my side and my baby's arm
but could not stop my march
nine days
as the milk dried up in my breast
and I slept on the ground outside
the camp of the Indian King.
(Mary 30 lies down.)

Now must I lie in the snow
and hug my baby
until it is no longer crying.
*(Mary 30 slowly lets the bundle of cloth
fall open, revealing nothing. She
stares at it. The drum stops beating.)*
On that night I thought I would die
but instead my sweet little boy
like a lamb departed this life
February 18 1675
he being then four months old.
*(Mary 30 slowly folds up the cloth again,
re-creating the baby.)*
And I could not but take notice
how at many another time
I would not bear the same room
where any dead person was
yet now the case is changed.
*(Mary 30 lies down again with her
dead baby.)*
Now I must
and now I can
lie down with my dead babe
and sleep side by side
all the cold night after.
*(Mary 30 sleeps. Suddenly, she wakes.
She opens the cloth again and finds
a Bible in it.)*
In the morning
there was a Bible in my arms
where the Indian King had it put.
They'd taken my baby
and they showed me the hill
where they had buried it.
There I stayed and read my Bible.
Mary 30: *(Reading.)*
Hebrews twelve and six.
"For whom the Lord loveth
He chasteneth
and He scourgeth
every son He receiveth."

(Pause. A change of light, warmer.
A few birds, singing.)
Mary 60:
King Philip.
(Pause.)
King Philip!
(The wooden wall at center turns,
revealing another wall of skins
and furs. Seated before them is
King Philip, smoking a clay pipe.
He is thirty seven years old. He
wears several layers of skins and
furs, over them draped a beautiful
and astounding robe. It is soft
doeskin, decorated with colorful dyes,
and overlaid with wampum, the shell-
money of the tribe.)
Philip:
Yes?
Mary 60:
I have things to tell you.
Philip:
Yes?
Mary 60:
King Sanochet is dead.
Philip:
And his tribe?
Mary 60:
Gone destroyed
They cannot help you.
Philip:
Then tell me how he died
my friend Sanochet.
Mary 60:
At bay
he spit upon his captors
and said loudly:
"Let them shoot me now
before I do anything here
to disgrace myself."
Philip:

And they shot him then
and he did not disgrace himself?

Mary 60:

Four Christian Indians
shot him then.

Philip:

Well yes.
Someone
had to be disgraced.

Mary 60:

When he was dead
they cut from his chest
slivers of his flesh
and ate them.

Philip:

Some Indians are very superstitious
otherwise they would not become Christians.
Goodbye, Sanochet
may I do as well as you
if disgrace overtakes me.
I may not
and of that I am afraid.
(He looks at Mary 30.)
Madame.

Mary 30:

Yes.

Philip:

I regret the death of your child.

Mary 30: *(Bitterly.)*

Do you.

Philip:

I do.
(Pause.)
Come. Sit you here.
(He points to the ground before him.)

Mary 60:

You must
you have no choice
sit with him.
*(Mary 30 sits on the ground before Philip.
He stands, suddenly, and sweeps the robe*

from his shoulders, holding it out.)

Philip:

Do you know what this is?

Mary 30:

A heathen garment
garish childish and hateful!

*(Philip drapes the robe over Mary 30
and holds her within it.)*

Philip:

That is my nation of children
lying now across your shoulders.
Beads made of shells polished
into beauty and so across you lie
thousands of beads each one a jewel
as precious here as any star
on the crown of your English King.
Together a fortune
the last I possess.
You could exchange that robe
for London silver
and be wealthy beyond all your dreams.
Is it not beautiful?

Mary 30:

No.
It is a heathen garment
garish childish and hateful!

Mary 60:

King Philip!

Philip:

Yes.

Mary 60:

Regiments of all the colonies
stand now beneath the command
of Captain Benjamin Church.

Philip:

Church?

Mary 60:

Six thousand soldiers
are marching now at his command.

(King Philip smiles.)

Philip:

Captain Church?
Mary 60:
To find you out
destroy your army
cut you into pieces
and end your war.
Philip:
It never stops
life never
stops playing with us.
Mary 60:
Your warrior chief Sagamore John
deserted betrayed you for Captain Church.
Your uncle, sister, and forty men
were shot swimming Taunton River
dead in the water
all but four.
Philip:
Four escaped?
Mary 60:
Four gave themselves up
to the mercy of Captain Church
and were beheaded at once
by Sagamore John.
Philip:
Four from forty
beheaded
is not a disgrace,
Captain Church!
And the other one just like that
Carver!
John Carver!
Do you, Mrs. Rowlandson, Madame,
know of him?
Mary 30:
I do not.
Philip:
He was exactly what his name
said he was.
A carver.
The bullets of the English

I may survive
but never the ironies
of their preposterous language.
Some years ago, Madame,
that same man, John Carver,
knelt at my father's feet
and kissed my father's hands.
"Save us!" he said. "Save us!"
From the land he was not yet strong enough
to steal.
John Carver. Benjamin Church.
And we are savages to name ourselves
Running Deer and Morning Sun.
For life never stops playing with us
it is the tiny kitten grown
to the yellow-eyed cat
who while eating the bird
must always keep it half alive.

Mary 30:
King Philip
you cannot sell something
and then want it back again.
You were paid
for all you gave us.
Then you resent it being taken.
And my baby is dead
my home destroyed
because you will not believe
that a bargain is a bargain!

Philip:
I can see, Mrs. Rowlandson,
that I will suffer as much from your tongue
as you from my captivity.

Mary 60:
King Philip!

Philip:
Yes?

Mary 60:
All the Poccaset nation is scattered.
Captain Church has blocked their march to you.
Your wife and child—

(Pause.)

Philip:

Yes?

Mary 60:

Gone, King Philip.

Philip:

Both?

Mary 60:

They were taken into captivity
by Captain Church.
They stand at this moment
before a Puritan court in Boston.
Their prosecutor
is my husband.

*(A light fails on the lectern and on
Reverend Rowlandson.)*

Rowlandson:

Here you see alone the intimates of the beast
the consort and spawn
of that satanic savage!

Philip:

My boy
My little man

Rowlandson:

Indians in their frivolity
are marvelous fond and affectionate
toward their heathen children.
Thus Almighty God brings our enemy to misery
before He quite destroys him.

(Light goes out on Rowlandson.)

Philip:

How are they going to do it?

Mary 60:

Many insist upon decapitation.
There is a great quoting of scripture
as certain justification for the axe.
But finally milder counsel prevails.

Philip:

What milder counsel?

Mary 60:

They are sold as slaves

bound unto the West Indies.
They fetch apiece
one English pound.

Philip:
Well, Mrs. Rowlandson?
Shall we speak again
of children?

Mary 30:
No.
I am avenged.

Philip:
One year!
One year, my little man,
and they would not have treated you so.
Did you know that, Mrs. Rowlandson?

Mary 30:
I know my husband said
you began your war too soon,
yes.

Philip:
One year more
I would have united
Narraganset
Nipmunk
Mohegan
and run you into the sea.
But while I play the diplomat
to bind together a proud angry people
while I lie and scheme toward my day of wrath
I sicken.
In the bickering and treachery
in the squalor of the spirit
in turning and twisting
my own divided nations
I myself revolt
sicken and for one instant turn
to seek release.
There was a young man John Sassamon
his name was who told me as Christians do
of a world of love.
I listen to that boy

telling me of Jesus Christ
turning in my tracks you see
toward any grace
that might deliver me
from plots of death all my own.
Oh I listen to him
earnest handsome boy
with shining confident eyes
lie smoking in my tent to dream of Christ Jesus
a beautiful young man with Sassamon's lips
John Sassamon's eyes John Sassamon's voice
I ponder his gentle Jesus
and sadly speak of my hateful life
and that boy betrays my schemes of war
to the English.
Life has its way with me.
I am a fool
and every path in the forest
leads now to death and to disgrace.
When they tell me
I scream
I jump up and down and scream you see
like the savage you suppose me to be.
Fools race away
to hunt him down the wretched boy
butcher him cut his throat stick the corpse
in lake ice
where
in the smile of the sun
he rose again like his Saviour
to lie gleaming upon the water
in public resurrection.
Now the English know it's true
King Philip is a liar
King Philip plots their death
King Philip has almost enough Indian nations
united to break open every English head
and the war begins
one year too soon.
Because for that one instant
I looked away

toward another and a better life
this one slays me
and my people all will die
where once my father
ruled the world.
I stopped to question
if I was bound forever
to plots of death
and schemes of war
and in that instant
I was found unworthy
a disgrace to my people
and so destroyed.
(He takes the robe from Mary 30 and spreads it on the ground.)
So I must give this now
to my warriors
and tell them if they can
cut it fairly
divide it among themselves
and prepare for the end.
(He takes a piece of rope from his belt.)
I will ransom you when I can
but you are the robe now
my only jewel.
You must come with me.
(She holds out her hands and he ties them.)
But be of good cheer.
You may see with those eyes
the disgrace I fear
and rejoice.

Mary 30:
And rejoice!
(The sky turns red. Philip, leading Mary 30 by the rope, travels before it.)

Mary 60:
King Philip
that night attacked Medford

riding so all have since declared
on a giant black horse with torches in both hands
and scarlet flames coming from his mouth.
Medford was indeed left in ashes
but not by a demon
by a man.
*(Wind. Flames are reflected on the sky,
with shadows of swirling smoke. Light falls
again on the lectern and Reverend
Rowlandson.)*
Rowlandson:
War rages
towns smoulder in ruins
but yet appears the hand of Heaven
amen and now amen
these battles turn
and we can soon extinguish
whole nations of these pestilent savages
at such a rate that soon
not one will be left alive
on the face of God's earth!
Mary 60:
With one hundred frightened men
all that is left of his great army
King Philip in the night destroys Hatfield
and plunges northward.
Rowlandson:
His power is broken
his forces are forlorn
his warriors sick their babies
dying on their mother's backs.
Bag and wretched baggage
remove and remove again.
Mary 60:
To his father's home
the lost capitol of his people
that was called Mount Hope.
Rowlandson:
Through the icy forests
across the frozen rivers
stung to death

writhing in his last agony
burning and slaughtering
with his stricken people
he wanders to judgement.

Mary 60:

Mount Hope.
Life never stops playing with us, he said.
He was right.
Now am I come upon his last remove.
King Philip has reached Mount Hope
with one hostage myself
twenty beaten men
their women and starving children
his heritage.

(Philip and Mary 30 arrive at Mount Hope. He drops the rope. She sinks to the ground. Philip pulls skins and furs from the wooden wall, hands her some to cover herself with and puts some over himself. Then he takes up a small clay jug and holds it out to her.)

Philip:

Here.

Mary 30:

No.

Philip:

You prefer to die sober?

Mary 30:

Yes.

(King Philip smiles.)

Philip:

You cannot bear the thought
of facing your Creator drunk?

Mary 30:

I will let you do that.

Philip:

Very well.
I will.

(He drinks. Pause.)

Mary 60:

You are home King Philip.

Philip:

Yes.

Mary 60:

It is gone
your father's home
your brother's camp when he was King
your dancing ground of childhood passage
to your manhood
your place of rule and command
when you feared no man.
Burning now.
There was no reason to destroy Mount Hope.
There were no Indians here.
Yet here they came split every stick
broke the earth of the council ground
where centuries of Kings have danced
then they burned the grass itself.
Will you remove again?

Philip:

No.

Mary 60:

Then King Philip
what will you do?

Philip:

All that is left to do
drink English rum
corrupt myself
and most perfectly prepare my spirit
for disgrace.

(He sits now with Mary 30 on the ground, holding his clay jug. A red glow appears before them, a meager fire. They clutch their skins and furs. Philip drinks. The sky behind them is icy cold. Wind.)

There!
See there!
Look where they stand!
The great King Massasoit
saviour of the English
and with him two small boys

straight by his side as arrows in the earth.
"Name them!" he says.
"Name my sons for the greatest of your heroes
for that is what they will be
in time to come
to befriend and protect your people
when I am gone
so much do I love you."
Life never stops playing with us.
My brother they named for Alexander the Great
and I for his father Philip of Macedon.
King Alexander! King Philip!
For the yellow-eyed cat who eats the bird
must always keep it half alive.

Mary 30:

How did he die your brother?

Philip:

A personal question from you?
What is happening to you, Mrs. Rowlandson?

Mary 30:

Life has played with me
as well as you.

Philip:

So it has.
Well, King Alexander one day
he went fishing.
With men and horses fine and sleek
all the joy of games and royal play
and while he played
then lay sleeping belly full of fish
a company of infantry
from the Governor of Massachusetts
hauled him to his feet
my brother the King
put a gunbarrel to his ear
and hopped him in the dust
behind his disgraced men
to prison
where he died of shame.
And I took his place.

Mary 30:

How can I be afraid of that?
It cannot happen to me.
Philip:
Do not be sure.
Mary 60:
King Philip.
Philip:
Yes.
Mary 60:
Your refuge is disclosed
by your own people.
Your warriors now spit on the ground
and betray you to Captain Church.
Philip:
Well my warriors
my good men
it is no fault of yours
goodbye!
(He drinks to them.)
Mary 60:
The English know you are here
alone at Mount Hope
They are very close
King Philip
upon you.
*(Philip puts away his clay jug.
He stands up.)*
Philip:
Then I must become
my own father
and my own son
and all my nation
so that every disgrace can be mine.
(He goes to Mary 30, takes the rope from her wrist.)
Goodbye, Mrs. Rowlandson.
They will find you here in safety.
I leave you the future
and the day when yours
are no longer the chosen people.
Mary 30:

King Philip!
Philip:
Yes.
(Slowly, Mary 30 reaches out to him. She touches him on the arm.)
Mary 30:
"For whom the Lord loveth
He chasteneth
and He scourgeth every son
He receiveth."
There is no shame.
There is no disgrace.
(Philip puts his hand over hers.)
Philip:
I will spare you my scorn
I will call you not only a fool
but a friend
and hope you will never know
what it means
not to survive.
(Wind. Thunder. Exit Philip. Enter Rowlandson, taking Mary 30 away.)
Mary 60:
In a storm
King Philip escaped the English
running into the forest
where Captain Church pursued him.
(Philip, on the ground, crawls through his forest. At the lectern, Rowlandson, appears again, with Mary 30, head bowed, standing facing him.
Philip sits up. He looks around him. He composes himself.)
Rowlandson:
Now is the Savage driven to his death
tracked down in his own forest.
(Pause. A few birds sing.)
Mary 60:
The death of King Philip.
My husband rejoiced in it
but I could not.

For I knew King Philip
as he did not.
While I cannot change
what was done to him
I will not believe
he was disgraced.
Rowlandson:
His hateful war
bringing to rubble twelve New England towns
is over.
Philip:
I had come naked
into the forest
to endure a winter alone
prove myself my father's son
and worthy of my nation.
Rowlandson:
In his own wilderness
this black beast must now live out
the final moment of his torment
and his damnation.
Philip:
This same clearing
Life never stops playing with us.
It has not changed.
It is just the same.
(Philip begins, slowly, to smile. He now sits as Mary 60 imagines him, musing, a man thinking something through.)
Rowlandson:
He was sitting on a log
when Captain Church and a Christian Indian
discharged two bullets
one passing through King Philip's heart
the other hitting his chest two inches higher.
He fell upon his face in the mud and water.
(Philip now truly smiles, remembering, like a man approaching a great peace.)
Philip:
I was sitting right here
when my brother Alexander came to me

knives bows arrows clothes food.
"Don't be a fool," he said. "Use these."

Rowlandson:

Captain Church nodded to the Christian Indian
who quartered the body.
The hands were sent to Boston
the legs to Springfield
and the torso quartered once again
hung down from four white birch trees.

Philip:

I sent my brother away.
I made my own bows and arrows
and knives of bone
howling in the teeth of winter
but never sorry.
I lived and lived and lived.

Rowlandson:

King Philip's head
was brought to Plymouth
on a solemn Thanksgiving Day
where to the glory of God
and the rejoicing of his enemies
that head was lifted on a pole
to stand in the middle of that Christian town
til flesh and skull and pole crumble into pieces.
(Light goes out on Rowlandson.)

Philip:

I survived that winter
as I was meant to survive it
I did not lie I did not scheme
I did not perish.
Life played with me honestly
I found my manhood
and returned to my people a King.
(Mary 60 and Mary 30 now turn to face Philip, who rises.)

Mary 60:

I can remember the time
when I used to sleep quietly

Mary 30:

Whole nights together

but now
Mary 60:
It is other ways with me.
In the night season I must remember
Mary 30:
The days of my youth
what my mouth has tasted
what my eyes have seen.
(Together they pick up the wampum robe King Philip wore when we first saw him. They take it to him and place it around his shoulders again. Mary 30 gets the headband with his three long feathers.)
Mary 60:
And in my dreams
I restore to him
his skins and furs
Mary 30:
I crown him again.
Mary 60:
I see him alone
in his forest his kingdom
called Mount Hope
Mary 30:
Over his shoulders
I drape the robe of shells
the riches of his nation.
Mary 60:
And there he stands
forever in my mind
by his home
and his grave
and his throne.

(They move away from him. A few birds sing, quietly. Philip holds out his arms as the fading light makes of him a statue of dignity and majesty.)

EL HERMANO

A MAN, a jaded, sallow, ugly lounge lizard, 60's.
A WOMAN, the same, 40's.
BARTENDER sturdy, cynical career Sergeant, 30's
BUDDY, a breezy, cynical career Sergeant, 30's
FRAZIER, a young draftee, fun loving but sensitive, 20's
TERESA, a spirited young Spanish woman , 20's
FELICIA, her aunt, quiet and subdued, late 30's
FRANCISCO, ESTEBAN, a young man trying to seem older, 20's

Place: A neighborhood bar in San Francisco.
Time: 1954.

EL HERMANO was first produced by the Ensemble Studio Theatre, Curt Dempster, Artistic Director, in February, 1981. It was directed by Pirie MacDonald, sets by Brian Martin, costumes by Rick Segal, production stage manager, Dede Miller. Cast as follows:

A MAN..........................Marc Platt
A WOMAN....................Eleanor Garth
BARTENDER.................Paul Geier
BUDDY........................Frank Girardeau
FRAZIER.......................Curtis Armstrong
TERESA........................Lisa Leguillou
FELICIA........................Christina Sanjuan
FRANCISCO ESTEBAN....Esai Morales

EL HERMANO

Part of a neighborhood bar in San Francisco on a slow night. Bar, tables. A jukebox is playing a vocal version of "Love Is a Many Splendored Thing" and the Man is dancing unhappily with the Woman. She is drunk, and he wishes he hadn't asked. She is approaching middle age and he is past it, a gray and sallow sixty. They are the only customers in the bar. The music stops. She runs her hand through his hair, eyes closed.

Woman: Now, that was nice. *(The man steps back and she almost falls.)*
Man: Yeah. Great.
Woman: What else can we play? Wait, just wait. *(She weaves toward the jukebox and studies it for a moment, her wan face lit by the garish lights. The man takes his chance and moves quickly back to his seat at the bar. The bartender comes to him and they talk, shaking their heads.)*
Woman: *(Brightly.)* How about *"Chances Are"?* Good recording here of *"Chances Are." (She turns, sees the man has deserted her, stands mournfully alone a moment, shrugs, and then climbs back on her stool at the other end of the bar. Buddy enters, looks around. The woman smiles at him with bleary friendliness. Buddy calls outside.)*
Buddy: Hey, Frazier! Come on! *(No answer.)* I'm through, pal! Come on! *(Frazier enters. He looks around.)*
Frazier: Great.
Buddy: You got other ideas? Other great bars in San Francisco you know about? *(Frazier sighs, shakes his head.)* Let's have a drink, and forget it. *(To bartender.)* Hey pal! *(They go to the bar. As he passes the woman, Buddy takes a look, makes a face and shudders. They sit. Buddy waves to the bartender.)* Two stiff drinks. Doubles. *(To Frazier.)* Brandy, okay?
Frazier: Sure.
Buddy: And no rotgut, pal. Hennessy, American Hennessy brandy, and I want to see you break a fresh bottle.
Bartender: Okay.
Buddy: Straight, water on the side.
Bartender: Okay.
Buddy: And leave the bottle up where we can see it.
Bartender: Okay! *(He goes behind the bar, muttering.)* Jerk.
Buddy: *(To man at bar.)* Hey, sport. *(The man nods back, wanly.)*
Frazier: How did we get into that place, anyhow?
Buddy: We saw the sign. You had to go in.
Frazier: Rhapsody Round-Up.

Buddy: Rhapsody Round-Up.

Frazier: Yeah.

Buddy: Yeah.

Frazier: You got around all right.

Buddy: You pay, you dance. That's life.

Frazier: Oh?

Buddy: Wasn't so bad. Wait until you see the Marshall Islands.

Frazier: I thought you hadn't been there.

Buddy: No, but I was on Guam for a week, and I heard. Sun. Sand. Gooney birds. And that's it. Tough duty. Rhapsody Round-Up, goodbye. Civilization, goodbye.

Frazier: This is civilization?

Buddy: Sure. This is what we protect, on the Marshall Islands. *(Buddy moves to the jukebox. Frazier follows.)*

Frazier: Yeah, I see.

Buddy: There's hope for you yet. *(Pause.)* You know why I got you an overnight pass out of that processing center?

Frazier: No, but thanks a lot. I appreciate it.

Buddy: I like you. Why do I like you? Because you're a dumbass college kid, and everything else that's stupid, and God knows you're the worst-looking soldier ever drafted, and as far as the Army is concerned, for a long time you ain't going to be able to find your butt with both hands, but you're a clean slate. I like that. Guys like you got so much to learn, only an old-time R.A. bastard like me can shape you up, before you sit on your bayonet. Now. Why didn't you go to O.C.S.? *(Buddy moves to a table. Frazier follows.)*

Frazier: I didn't want to be an officer.

Buddy: Afraid of responsibility. Okay. Get in, get out.

Frazier: Right.

Buddy: So you end up in the Marshall Islands.

Frazier: Well, so do you.

Buddy: Yeah, but I been other places first. *(Pause.)* A great war, when I was a young soldier. Riding to Berlin, with Patton. Smoked cigarette once, with Ike. Japan, two years. General MacArthur, Mount Fuji, lots of nookie. Iceland, well. All over the U.S. and this whole damn world, before I'm through. I'll see it all.

Frazier: And know the score.

Buddy: You bet your ass. You can't fool me, college boy. For instance, you got a big fancy vocabulary, even though you don't use it. You don't want to show up the dumb soldier with your choice and luminous array of verbal artillery.

Frazier: Hey.

Buddy: So I know a few fancy words myself. Little gift of gab. But listen to this. When I came into the American Army in 1944, there wasn't *any* word of *any* kind anywhere, for that force. That power. It took hold of me, and it shook the shit right out of me. And I said, God damn, this is it. This is real. This is where I belong. Where words are nothing. Where what happens, *happens,* and no two damn ways about it! The biggest, the best, the greatest game there is. So I play it. *(Pause.)* That make sense?

Frazier: I see it does to you.

Buddy: The soldier's game. Ain't no word for it. You just play it, and because it's so real, you love it. See? *(The bartender brings the bottle of brandy. He shows the Hennessy label to a still-skeptical Buddy.)* It *says* Hennessy. *(The bartender breaks the seal, opens the bottle.)* It *looks* like Hennessy. *(The bartender pours a tiny sip into Buddy's glass, like a French wine waiter. Buddy nods, picks it up, sniffs it.)* It is Hennessy. So run a tab. *(The bartender pours the drinks, moves away.)* And put it on top of the bar, where I can see that it *stays* Hennessy. *(Muttering, the bartender puts the bottle of brandy on the bar. Buddy warms the brandy with both hands, sniffing it with practiced pleasure. Frazier does the same.)* And I know what you're thinking. If I'm so smart and know-it-all, how come I couldn't get us laid tonight?

Frazier: I didn't say it.

Buddy: Rhapsody Round-Up was a bust. I got to have me something decent or nothing. So what the hell. Don't get doleful. That's a good word, right?

Frazier: *(Smiling.)* Right.

Buddy: Don't get morose. That's a good word, right?

Frazier: A very good word.

Buddy: Because if you do, you'll get putrescent. How about that?

Frazier: *(Laughing.)* Terrific.

Buddy: Win or lose. Here's to it.

Frazier: Skoal.

Buddy: Butts up. *(They clink glasses and drink. The woman passes by, on an erratic course to the ladies' room. She goes by close to them and brushes Frazier's shoulder. He looks after her with interest, starts to get up.)* No, no, Frazier. Jesus Christ.

Frazier: Why not? Marshall Islands tomorrow. Sun, sand, and gooney birds. It's going to be a long time.

Buddy: You want to spend it in the infirmary?

Frazier: Oh. *(He sits down.)*

Buddy: I see I gotta teach you everything.

Frazier: You've—uh—you've had venereal disease—uh—

Buddy: Once or twice.

Frazier: Playing the game.

Buddy: What you want, young soldier, is something decent. Okay?

Frazier: If you say so. Where do we get something decent?

Buddy: We don't. *(He sighs. Teresa and Felicia appear in the doorway. They stand there undecided.)* We blew it in that nothing dance hall. So we forget it tonight. We conserve energy. Skoal.

Frazier: *(Glumly.)* Butts up. *(They drink. Buddy yawns, stretches. The bartender moves to the end of the bar closest to the door.)*

Bartender: *(To Felicia and Teresa.)* Ladies welcome. Plenty of room tonight. *(Buddy sits up quickly.)*

Buddy: *(To Frazier.)* Well, wait a minute. Wait just a minute. *(He smiles and waves his hand merrily. Teresa smiles back and giggles. She tugs at Felicia's arm and they finally come into the bar, sitting at a table next to Buddy and Frazier. Teresa, young, voluptuous, wears a peasant blouse and a loud, patterned skirt. Felicia, older, is dressed modestly. At the bar, the man looks at Felicia with interest.)*

Frazier: Well, what do you think?

Buddy: I think something decent just checked in. Hold the fort. *(He moves quickly to the bar and whispers to the bartender who shakes then nods his head. No. He doesn't know who they are. Yes. Buddy can table-hop, dance. The man slides off his barstool with the same idea. The woman passes, coming back from the ladies' room. Buddy takes her by the arm and steers her between him and the man.)*

Buddy: *(To man.)* Hey, pal! *(To woman.)* Hey, honey! You know my fine friend here?

Woman: Sure. We was dancing a minute ago.

Man: Look, fellow, I'm busy.

Buddy: How about that? I figured you two'd hit it off. Hey, bartender, give my two friends a drink on me right away.

Man: Now wait a minute—

Woman: That's real sweet of you, thanks!

Man: Well, thanks.

Buddy: No, no, friend. It's my pleasure. Enjoy yourself. *(He pushes the man gently to the bar, a charming but well-muscled bully. Buddy turns to Teresa and Felicia, gives Frazier a wink, and moves in.)* Ladies, good evening. My pal and I would like nothing better this evening than the pleasure of buying you both a nice drink. Are you agreeable? Yes? No? Maybe? *(Teresa and Felicia smile.)*

Buddy: I know we're not formally acquainted, ladies, and that's the truth,

an: I just wanted to talk to her!
rtender: Here's one on the house. Come on. What are you getting
xcited about. Relax. Have a drink. What the hell. *(Grumbling, the man*
oes back to the bar. Frazier sits down stiffly. He composes himself, then
ees that Felicia is looking at him with tears in her eyes.)
an: Shit! *(He bangs the bar with his glass.)*
azier: *(To Felicia.)* Are you all right?
icia: Oh...gracias...I not...I not ready...that...yet.
azier: *(Smiling.)* Too old.
icia: *(Smiling.)* Too old.
zier: Well. Let's dance, then. Quieres bailar conmigo?
icia: Si. *(They get up and dance, slowly, awkwardly, gently. Buddy*
nces by with Teresa, bug-eyed.)
ldy: Ahoy, hotshot. *(He winks and rolls his eyes. Teresa has both arms*
rapped around him. She is breathing into his ear. She is melting against
m. Buddy must call time out. To Teresa.) Okay, okay, sweetheart, Jesus
rist, let's take a break. You're turning my belly to butter. I need a
nk. *(He picks his glass up from the table and takes a big gulp of brandy.*
resa leans against him and whispers something into his car. Buddy
okes and looks at her gleefully.) Yeah? Why *shouldn't* I drink so much
sa: Because...you...come home, yes?
dy: *(Beaming.)* You better believe it. I mean sure. Si si si. Now?
sa: Oh...ah...Si, ahora.
ly: What the hell. Now. Right now. *(Teresa nods her head happily.*
ldy puts down his drink, hops over to Felicia and Frazier, breaks them
pushes Felicia toward Teresa, takes Frazier aside.)
ier: Hey, what's the idea? I finally get to dance and you break it up?
ly: Baby, you'll dance later. Right now we're going home.
ier: Are you nuts? Oh. You mean to their house?
ly: That or a hotel, we'll see. A few bucks apiece and we can die
py. That Teresa is hot to trot So am I. Okay? *(Frazier turns and looks*
he girls. Teresa is whispering quickly to Felicia, who turns and looks
razier. She smiles a trifle sadly, and nods her head.)
er: Well...
y: Make up your mind. Think about the Marshall Islands. Gooney
s.
er: *(Briskly.)* Let's go.
y: F'ward, harch! All right, ladies, we're on our way. Frazier, leave
Bartender something. Rinky-tinky-tum! Off we go! How'm I doing,
hey! Bum-bum-bum-bum-bum! *(They make a conga line and start*
ng and dancing out of the bar. Teresa sees something outside. She

and as you plainly see, my pal and me, we're just soldiers, plain old dog-face G.I.'s, defenders of the United States. And that's it. So what'll you have? *(Pause. Then Teresa and Felicia burst into giggles.)* Got your funny bones, I see. Just a joker, that's all I am. But I can sure buy you both that drink, and even play us all some songs on that jukebox. So how about it? *(The same pause, the same burst of giggles. Buddy sighs.)* Oh, come on now. Yes or no, ladies? *(The same pause, the same burst of giggles.)* Well, fuck this. *(Disgusted, Buddy stalks back to the table, speaking to the man as he goes.)* Your turn, sport. *(But now Frazier is up. He moves to their table.)*
Frazier: *(Softly.)* Uh, buenas tardes. Habla usted espanol? *(Both girls smile.)*
Teresa: Si.
Felicia: Si. *(Frazier turns to Buddy.)*
Frazier: Got it?
Buddy: *(Beaming.)* Oh, ho! Bien, bien, muy-whooey bien! *(He moves back to the table.)* How much Spanish you know, Frazier?
Frazier: Not much. *(To the girls.)* Un poco? Un poco? *(Both girls smile and nod.)*
Teresa: Si.
Felicia: Si.
Buddy: Ask them about a drink. Come on, come on, soldier.
Frazier: Well, let's see now. Ah...
Buddy: Hell, I can do that. *(To the girls.)* Hey, el drinko, ne? Ah, musico? El drinko? Dancey-dancey? *(Both girls laugh. Felicia smiles at Frazier. Teresa's eyes are on Buddy.)*
Teresa: Si.
Felicia: Si.
Buddy: Well, you damn right! Now we're moving. Hey, bartender!
Bartender: *(Smiling.)* What'll it be, folks?
Buddy: Frazier, how you say Hennessy brandy in Spanish?
Frazier: Well...
Teresa: Beer.
Felicia: Beer.
Buddy: Yeah, well, there you go. Two beers, bartender, and two *double* Hennessy brandies.
Bartender: Drafts?
Buddy: Right.
Bartender: Sure thing. *(Buddy turns to the girls, beaming, very excited.)*
Buddy: Now, the drinks are on the way, let's see what we can do about a little musico, ne? *(He points, with enormous emphasis, at the jukebox.*

Teresa smiles demurely, gets up quickly. Buddy ushers her to the jukebox, singing as he follows her.) How'm I doing, hey! hey! Rinky-tinky-tum! Musica! Musico! Now let's see, ah...what's your name honey? What's your sweet fat little juicy old name. Hey, Frazier, how do you ask...

Teresa: *(Grins.)* Teresa.

Buddy: Well, Teresa, my name is Buddy. You Teresa, me Buddy. Okay.

Teresa: Okay.

Buddy: *(Puts his arm around her shoulders.)* Now, let's see what we got here. *(They look at the songs on the jukebox.)*

Frazier: *(To Felicia.)* Buenas tardes.

Felicia: Buenas tardes. Sientese, por favor.

Frazier: Gracias. *(He sits, somewhat formally. They look around a moment, then Felicia smiles and then they both smile.)*

Buddy: *(Dropping coins in the jukebox.)* Here we go. *(The jukebox blares out "Love Is a Many Splendored Thing." Grinning, Buddy takes Teresa in his arms and they dance, close.)*

Frazier: *(Fumbling for his Spanish.)* Well, let's see now. Ah...ah...

Felicia: *(Smiling.)* Si.

Frazier: Ah...me llamo Frazier...ah, senorita...?

Felicia: Senora. Me llamo Felicia. Mucho gusto en conocerie.

Frazier: Felicia. Ah, bonito. Bonito.

Felicia: Gracias. *(They smile, formally still, but with warmth. The bartender brings the drinks. Buddy dances Teresa over to the table.)*

Buddy: Ladies and gents, a toast to this fine evening. God bless you, my hot little pinto bean. God bless you, madam. God bless you, Frazier, you little devil. And God bless Buddy, who just might get his rocks off after all. Yes, sir! A toast to old Spain! Ole! *(Trying to make out what he says, the girls follow his motion and all clink glasses and laugh. They all drink. At the bar, the woman moves away from the man, insulted, dropping her purse and picking it up.)*

Woman: Well, I'm sorry. I'm *really* very sorry. *(Muttering, she goes to her stool at the end of the bar and sits.)*

Teresa: Nice beer. *(She slips her arm around Buddy's waist, and puts down her glass.)*

Buddy: My pinto bean. Dancey-dancey encore, ne? *(Teresa giggles and nods happily. Buddy grabs her and they dance out onto the floor again. We hear "Love Is a Many Splendored Thing" again, but softly now, played by an orchestra, gently.)*

Frazier: *(Slowly.)* Ah...Felicia, habla ingles? Habla ingles? *(Felicia holds up a finger and a thumb very close together.)*

Felicia: *(Smiling.)* Un pocito.

Frazier: Well, then...ah...Hagalo, pues. Hable un poco espanol. pocito ingles ahora.

Felicia: Oh, I try. Ah...I believe you very nice. Ah...ah...com "gracioso"?

Frazier: Gracisco? Ah...funny.

Felicia: Como se dice "cara"?

Frazier: Face.

Felicia: I think you—have—a—funny—face.

Frazier: Funnyface. Yeah, that's me, all right.

Felicia: *(Quickly.)* No, is nice.

Frazier: I look like a kid. I always have, always will.

Felicia: No. A boy. And-kind, and—ah—hombre nino. That young—and strong. Inside. I think.

Frazier: Okay. I'm a boy. What ever you say. And your E terrific. So are you.

Felicia: Gracias. *(The man gets off his barstool and comes ove Felicia.)*

Man: *(Indicating the dance floor.)* Hola, que tal, senora? Q conmigo?

Felicia: *(Politely.)* No, gracias. *(The man ignores Frazier an in a clumsy American accent.)*

Man: Me Ilamo Carson. Trabajo con mucho Histanos por placer cono certe. Como esta usted? *[My name's Carson. lot of Spanish people around here. Don't think I've met yo to know you.]*

Felicia: *(A little frightened.)* Buenas tardes.

Man: *(With a leer.)* Conozco mucho mejor el espanol que es vos a gustar mejor. *[I know a lot more Spanish than this You'll like mine better.]*

Felicia: Por favor.

Man: *(Indicating dance floor.)* Quieres bailar conmigo?

Felicia: No, gracias. No quiero bailar.

Man: *(Touching her arm.)* Oh si. Quieres. Puedo hacer *[Oh yes you do. I can do something for you around here.*

Felicia: *(Very upset.)* No, no, gracias, no... *(Frazier sta*

Frazier: *(To the man.)* That's it.

Man: What?

Frazier: I said that's it. Go back to the bar.

Man: Oh, go away, sonny. *(Frazier pushes back his cha (He lunges at Frazier. The bartender grabs him.)*

Bartender: Carson! Leave 'em alone!

grabs Buddy by the arm, pulling him away from the door, looking for a back way out.)

Teresa: No! No!

Buddy: What's this? What's the matter?

Teresa: Hermano! Broder!

Frazier: What's she saying?

Buddy: Got me. Honey, take it easy.

Teresa: *(To Felicia.)* No ils a venir esta nodre. *(To Buddy.)* He say he no come back, I no think he come here! Take me someplace! Ah, hermano!

Buddy: Wait a minute! Hermano who? Herman who?

Teresa: No, broder! Broder!

Buddy: Herman Broder? That it? Listen, honey, whatever his name, anybody give us trouble now, I'll take him apart.

Teresa: Eh! *(The confusion is suddenly stilled. In the door stands Francisco Esteban, a small, thin man, of indeterminate age. He is dressed in cheap clothes, immaculately cleaned and pressed, worn with a flair, and he stands ramrod straight. His long black hair is ornately combed. Teresa swears softly in Spanish. Felicia sighs and looks meekly at the floor.)*

Frazier: Buddy. Hermano means brother. *(Esteban walks slowly into the bar.)*

Esteban: Good evening.

Buddy: Oh, fuck.

Esteban: How do you do?

Buddy: *(To Teresa.)* Honey, this guy your brother?

Teresa: *(Hissing.)* Si! *(Esteban nods to her and to Felicia. He motions them back to the table again, seats them formally, and then turns to the two soldiers.)*

Esteban: Gentlemen, will you sit with us?

Buddy: Thanks. We were just on our way out.

Esteban: I cordially invite you.

Buddy: Some other time.

Esteban: *(Sternly.)* Please, sir!

Frazier: *(To Esteban.)* Thank you very much. *(To Buddy.)* Face it.

Buddy: Jeez-zus. *(He slumps down next to Teresa, who presses against him and clamps a hot hand on his knee. Frazier holds a chair for Felicia, and sits next to her. Esteban gestures to the bartender.)*

Esteban: *(Standing.)* Whatever the ladies and gentlemen were having, please bring again. What were you drinking, gentlemen?

Buddy: Brandy. *American* brandy.

Esteban: I will have that as well. And the bill is mine. Thank you. *(At the bar, the woman hears Esteban's voice.)*

Woman: Hey, Francisco! Yoo-hoo!

Esteban: *(Gravely.)* Good evening. *(She starts to get up and come over but he turns away from her brusquely. She sighs and goes back to her drink.)* My name is Francisco Esteban. What is yours, gentlemen?

Buddy: I'm Buck Jones.

Esteban: *(Shaking his hand.)* Mr. Jones, I am pleased to meet you. And you, sir?

Buddy: He's Flash Gordon.

Esteban: Mr. Gordon, I am pleased...

Frazier: No, not really. My name is Frazier Davenport.

Esteban: Oh. Mr. Davenport, I am pleased to meet you.

Frazier: *(Shaking his hand.)* And I am pleased to meet you, Mr. Esteban. *(Esteban smiles at him, politely. Buddy scowls. The bartender brings the drinks and sets them down.)*

Bartender: Draft beer for the ladies. American Hennessy brandy for the gents. Right? Right. *(Esteban watches him carefully, as if as the head of the table, he is personally responsible for each drink. He picks up his brandy.)*

Esteban: Gentlemen, I wish you good health and long life.

Buddy: Cheers.

Frazier: Thank you very much, Mr. Esteban. *(Frazier nods to Felicia, who smiles sadly at him. They all drink. Teresa presses Buddy's leg under the table, and drinks greedily. Esteban spills some of his brandy, betraying nervousness. His youth is now evident. He is under twenty. Buddy grins.)*

Buddy: That's a man's drink, sonny. Use both hands. *(He slips an arm around Teresa's shoulders. She presses against him, glaring at Esteban. Esteban drinks again, this time not spilling any of the brandy. He puts it down and faces them.)*

Esteban: *(Still standing.)* A good drink is a fine thing, gentlemen, no?

Buddy: Yes, But there *are* better things. Right, Teresa?

Teresa: Si!

Frazier: We appreciate your hospitality, Mr. Esteban.

Esteban: Thank you. I am pleased.

Buddy: You're pleased, we're pleased, hooray. *(He drinks, looks at Frazier, hoping to convey the fact that he isn't going to put up with this very long. Esteban lifts his brandy slowly as if daring his hand to shake, takes a deep drink. He sets it down equally deliberately, and clears his throat.)* Somebody give him a cough drop.

Frazier: Buddy.

Buddy: This'll take all night.

Esteban: Gentlemen, do you see that woman at the bar?

Buddy: Friend of yours?

Frazier: Yes, we see her.

Esteban: She is not a proper woman. Not always prostitute, you comprehend, but still not a proper woman. Nightly I slept with her last week, several times. Well, I was that way, you know. Once I paid her.

Buddy: And after that she paid you, right?

Frazier: Buddy.

Buddy: Look, what kind of a fuck-headed situation—

Frazier: Come on, Buddy!

Buddy: All right! So what about her?

Esteban: She is a good person. A good person, but you see, she will do that with anyone. *(He clears his throat again.)* She is not pleasant to contemplate and I do not speak of her lightly. And please do not be uneasy about the women. They do not speak English. I do not embarrass them. *(Pause.)* No, not a pleasant woman, but please, I do not speak of her in judgment. How could I? I went to her myself. Nevertheless, she is what she is. I do not respect her. It is sad, but that is the way you have it. You gentlemen understand me?

Frazier: I think so.

Buddy: That means keep talking, which you're gonna do.

Esteban: Now. *(He sits.)* I have been three years in your wonderful country. Since I have come, I have learn the language well and work very hard. Last month, I send for my sister, youngest of our family. Gentlemen, let me present my sister, Teresa Maria Consuelo Esteban. *(Teresa glares at him. She runs her hand up and down Buddy's leg.)*

Teresa: Hi, Budi!

Buddy: Hi, baby.

Esteban: Well, my sister is very young, you see. She is not yet used to your customs, here in your wonderful land. Our home, it was in Nicaragua and it was all much difference there. We were owners of land there and we had our peculiar ways. It is easy for her to forget them. Not for me. *(He drinks. He clears his throat.)*

Buddy: Big wheels in Nicaragua. I get it. What kind of land was it?

Esteban: Well, a great deal of land. Not exactly farm, you see. But a great deal of land.

Frazier: You were ranchers, maybe?

Esteban: Ah yes! Just so, ranchers. We were ranchers and in the evenings we would sit on the veranda and all our friends would come and drink with us. We would entertain them and there would be singing and fine dancing, upon occasion. But most often we would only sit and drink from silver glasses, and our friends would ride by in their wagons and wave to us, and the songs of the night— *(Long pause.)* Well, it was very beautiful, and we did that every night. *(Teresa presses herself against Buddy, clutching his leg.)*

Buddy: Ranchers, sure.

Esteban: But things went badly very suddenly. Many misfortunes and family troubles and losses. After a short time there were only three of us left. Three, where once had been a family of eight and of course many cousins.

Buddy: All riding up on black stallions in the moonlight.

Esteban: Now only myself and my sister. And, I beg your pardon, my aunt. Let me present to you, Senora Gonsalvez.

Buddy: Hi.

Frazier: *(Smiling.)* I am very pleased to make your acquaintance.

Felicia: *(Smiling.)* And I—yours.

Esteban: Life has been not easy for my aunt, gentlemen. She was once a very fine and beautiful young women, but she had a misfortune to marry a man who was not worthy of her and who treated her shamefully.

Buddy: Ain't life a bitch.

Frazier: I'm sorry to hear it.

Esteban: Yes, a hard life for her. When I sent for my sister, I of course insist that she come too, and send passage for both. I have hope that she would find a new life here, as I have, but as yet, no, she will not forget her man. We are stubborn people, even in gracious America. *(Teresa now is frantic, trying to get Buddy to get her away from Esteban.)*

Teresa: Vermanos! Vermanos!

Buddy: Okay, Teresa, take it easy. Well, Mr. Esteban, sir. You wring my heart. But since we are in gracious America, gracious San Francisco, to be exact— *(Esteban interrupts, like a little boy in spite of himself.)*

Esteban: Si! Si! My name, my name!

Buddy: What?

Esteban: Francisco, Esteban. San Francisco. *(Pause.)* Francisco—

Buddy: I get it! Swell. Fine. What I'm saying, San Francisco Francisco, is that here things are a little different than in the old country, if Nicaragua is an old country and I don't even know where the fuck it is, never mind its age. Follow me?

Esteban: Different, you say?

Buddy: Yessir. What you're doing—I think—is done one way in the old country but a little different in the new, in September 1954.

Frazier: Buddy what're you talking about?

Buddy: You'll see, dummy. *(To Esteban.)* I mean, Teresa here, she's old enough to take care of herself. Do it her own way.

Esteban: I do not comprehend.

Buddy: What do you do for a living, Mr. Esteban?

Esteban: *(Slowly.)* I take what jobs are at hand, sir. I have no choice.

Frazier: Jesus, Buddy.

Buddy: If you say so. But how long do you think it'll take for Teresa? She'll bust out on you one of these fine days, and move right along. Nothing you can do about it.

Esteban: I know that, sir. *(On her barstool, the woman coughs violently, spills her drink. Her eyes are glassy, her hair loose. She pulls herself up, waves a shaky hello to Esteban.)*

Woman: *(Weakly.)* Lo, Francisco. *(Esteban nods. She turns sadly to her drink and mutters to herself.)*

Buddy: Maybe marry a millionaire. Maybe end up like your pal there. That's the old U.S.

Esteban: I see.

Buddy: What do you do, keep her in the house all day? I think I know what you got in mind at night, but what does she do all day, sit home?

Esteban: *(Fiercely.)* No! No! The contrary! I start her to school soon! To learn English! To take opportunity!

Buddy: Soon.

Esteban: Yes! Learn to speak well and write well and take work in a fine concern with dignity. And meet a man—

Buddy: *(Slowly.)* Yeah?

Esteban: Of her own station in life, sir. I will see that it happens that way. *(Teresa runs her hand up and down Buddy's leg.)*

Frazier: *(Gently.)* I do think Teresa has other ideas.

Esteban: Of course! And were I not her brother, el hermano, I would have other ideas too. But sir, I am the unfortunate head of my family. Not the same as once it was but, gentlemen, it will be like that again. At the moment, it is I must take care for her, because she understands this no more than you. She wants to perform what she sees done around her. Let matters of no substance determine her future. It is true we are in difficult position here. It is true I have only money to pay for drinks, and that is all. It is true, I confess to you, we take the help we can get, and ask you to treat us—well.

Buddy: Yeah. I thought so.

Esteban: Nevertheless, I will not betray my sister! She is ignorant of herself, and what she truly is! *We must live!* But—we must—we must—also—

Frazier: Please, Mr. Esteban. We understand. It must be hard, coming here—

Esteban: *(Shaking.)* It is! That is her problem.

Buddy: And you think *we* got no problem? You ain't going to no gooney-bird islands! You're going to sit right here tomorrow night with your sister, and somebody else, and we go off to keep it safe for you! Why am *I* responsible for you? You ain't responsible for dick. I keep the peace, for you? *(Under his breath.)* Buncha spics?

Frazier: Buddy.

Teresa: Budi! Budi! Vermanos! *(She blows in his ear, rubs his leg.)*

Buddy: I understand her problem, all right. It's you, hermano.

Frazier: Buddy, lay off.

Buddy: Jesus, you don't get it, yet? I still have to wait for you, college boy? *(Buddy drums his fingers on the table, very angry. Esteban sits up, stiffly, silent. Pause. Buddy jumps up.)* Well, hell. Let's dance. Come on, honey. *(Teresa jumps up.)*

Esteban: No!

Buddy: What?

Esteban: I do not permit it!

Buddy: You don't *what? (Buddy is about to explode when the woman slides off her barstool and wobbles over to Esteban.)*

Woman: Hey, Francisco. I don't feel so hot tonight.Do something for me, can't you? I'm still good, you know that. Be a sport, Francisco, please. Please, Francisco, please. *(She leans against him, trying to look seductive. Buddy goes to the table, smiling a wicked smile.)*

Buddy: Does not permit it. Head of the family. *(He laughs.)* Well, listen, Mr. Hermano. Who permits this and doesn't permit that, with his beat-up whore hanging around his shoulders, and who's a whole lot younger than he makes out, with his big Spanish dance. Eighteen, maybe? Seventeen? In gracious America, it just don't work, this Big Brother shit. I mean, we just don't feature it here. *(Frazier starts up, but Buddy grabs him by the shoulder and shoves him back in his seat.)* In America, hermano, your sister don't do it for you. You let her go. She gets to find her own guy, and do it for him!

Frazier: Buddy, what the *hell* are you talking about?

Buddy: This is the first time you're trying it, kid, is that it? I bet you haven't even told *them* what you're up to. What did you think was going to happen, hermano? The understanding soldier would grasp your hand? Salute your gallant past? And like a grand gentleman, pass you the money under the table? That what you had in mind? Sure. Well, I ain't no grand gentleman and I ain't no bullshit soldier. I'm an honest man, and I like things *on* the table. *(He holds up a twenty-dollar bill.)* But here, good show and all that. I'll leave you twenty bucks for the fun of it. Okay, pal?

and as you plainly see, my pal and me, we're just soldiers, plain old dogface G.I.'s, defenders of the United States. And that's it. So what'll you have? *(Pause. Then Teresa and Felicia burst into giggles.)* Got your funny bones, I see. Just a joker, that's all I am. But I can sure buy you both that drink, and even play us all some songs on that jukebox. So how about it? *(The same pause, the same burst of giggles. Buddy sighs.)* Oh, come on now. Yes or no, ladies? *(The same pause, the same burst of giggles.)* Well, fuck this. *(Disgusted, Buddy stalks back to the table, speaking to the man as he goes.)* Your turn, sport. *(But now Frazier is up. He moves to their table.)*

Frazier: *(Softly.)* Uh, buenas tardes. Habla usted espanol? *(Both girls smile.)*

Teresa: Si.

Felicia: Si. *(Frazier turns to Buddy.)*

Frazier: Got it?

Buddy: *(Beaming.)* Oh, ho! Bien, bien, muy-whooey bien! *(He moves back to the table.)* How much Spanish you know, Frazier?

Frazier: Not much. *(To the girls.)* Un poco? Un poco? *(Both girls smile and nod.)*

Teresa: Si.

Felicia: Si.

Buddy: Ask them about a drink. Come on, come on, soldier.

Frazier: Well, let's see now. Ah...

Buddy: Hell, I can do that. *(To the girls.)* Hey, el drinko, ne? Ah, musico? El drinko? Dancey-dancey? *(Both girls laugh. Felicia smiles at Frazier. Teresa's eyes are on Buddy.)*

Teresa: Si.

Felicia: Si.

Buddy: Well, you damn right! Now we're moving. Hey, bartender!

Bartender: *(Smiling.)* What'll it be, folks?

Buddy: Frazier, how you say Hennessy brandy in Spanish?

Frazier: Well...

Teresa: Beer.

Felicia: Beer.

Buddy: Yeah, well, there you go. Two beers, bartender, and two *double* Hennessy brandies.

Bartender: Drafts?

Buddy: Right.

Bartender: Sure thing. *(Buddy turns to the girls, beaming, very excited.)*

Buddy: Now, the drinks are on the way, let's see what we can do about a little musico, ne? *(He points, with enormous emphasis, at the jukebox.*

Teresa smiles demurely, gets up quickly. Buddy ushers her to the jukebox, singing as he follows her.) How'm I doing, hey! hey! Rinky-tinky-tum! Musica! Musico! Now let's see, ah...what's your name honey? What's your sweet fat little juicy old name. Hey, Frazier, how do you ask...

Teresa: *(Grins.)* Teresa.

Buddy: Well, Teresa, my name is Buddy. You Teresa, me Buddy. Okay.

Teresa: Okay.

Buddy: *(Puts his arm around her shoulders.)* Now, let's see what we got here. *(They look at the songs on the jukebox.)*

Frazier: *(To Felicia.)* Buenas tardes.

Felicia: Buenas tardes. Sientese, por favor.

Frazier: Gracias. *(He sits, somewhat formally. They look around a moment, then Felicia smiles and then they both smile.)*

Buddy: *(Dropping coins in the jukebox.)* Here we go. *(The jukebox blares out "Love Is a Many Splendored Thing." Grinning, Buddy takes Teresa in his arms and they dance, close.)*

Frazier: *(Fumbling for his Spanish.)* Well, let's see now. Ah...ah...

Felicia: *(Smiling.)* Si.

Frazier: Ah...me llamo Frazier...ah, senorita...?

Felicia: Senora. Me llamo Felicia. Mucho gusto en conocerie.

Frazier: Felicia. Ah, bonito. Bonito.

Felicia: Gracias. *(They smile, formally still, but with warmth. The bartender brings the drinks. Buddy dances Teresa over to the table.)*

Buddy: Ladies and gents, a toast to this fine evening. God bless you, my hot little pinto bean. God bless you, madam. God bless you, Frazier, you little devil. And God bless Buddy, who just might get his rocks off after all. Yes, sir! A toast to old Spain! Ole! *(Trying to make out what he says, the girls follow his motion and all clink glasses and laugh. They all drink. At the bar, the woman moves away from the man, insulted, dropping her purse and picking it up.)*

Woman: Well, I'm sorry. I'm *really* very sorry. *(Muttering, she goes to her stool at the end of the bar and sits.)*

Teresa: Nice beer. *(She slips her arm around Buddy's waist, and puts down her glass.)*

Buddy: My pinto bean. Dancey-dancey encore, ne? *(Teresa giggles and nods happily. Buddy grabs her and they dance out onto the floor again. We hear "Love Is a Many Splendored Thing" again, but softly now, played by an orchestra, gently.)*

Frazier: *(Slowly.)* Ah...Felicia, habla ingles? Habla ingles? *(Felicia holds up a finger and a thumb very close together.)*

Felicia: *(Smiling.)* Un pocito.

Frazier: Well, then...ah...Hagalo, pues. Hable un poco espanol. Habla un pocito ingles ahora.
Felicia: Oh, I try. Ah...I believe you very nice. Ah...ah...como se dice "gracioso"?
Frazier: Gracisco? Ah...funny.
Felicia: Como se dice "cara"?
Frazier: Face.
Felicia: I think you—have—a—funny—face.
Frazier: Funnyface. Yeah, that's me, all right.
Felicia: *(Quickly.)* No, is nice.
Frazier: I look like a kid. I always have, always will.
Felicia: No. A boy. And-kind, and—ah—hombre nino. That means both young—and strong. Inside. I think.
Frazier: Okay. I'm a boy. What ever you say. And your English is terrific. So are you.
Felicia: Gracias. *(The man gets off his barstool and comes over speaking to Felicia.)*
Man: *(Indicating the dance floor.)* Hola, que tal, senora? Quieras bailar conmigo?
Felicia: *(Politely.)* No, gracias. *(The man ignores Frazier and speaks to her in a clumsy American accent.)*
Man: Me Ilamo Carson. Trabajo con mucho Histanos por aca. Es un placer cono certe. Como esta usted? *[My name's Carson. I work with a lot of Spanish people around here. Don't think I've met you before. Nice to know you.]*
Felicia: *(A little frightened.)* Buenas tardes.
Man: *(With a leer.)* Conozco mucho mejor el espanol que este pendejo. Me vos a gustar mejor. *[I know a lot more Spanish than this squirt here. You'll like mine better.]*
Felicia: Por favor.
Man: *(Indicating dance floor.)* Quieres bailar conmigo?
Felicia: No, gracias. No quiero bailar.
Man: *(Touching her arm.)* Oh si. Quieres. Puedo hacer mucho para ti. *[Oh yes you do. I can do something for you around here.]*
Felicia: *(Very upset.)* No, no, gracias, no... *(Frazier stands up quietly.)*
Frazier: *(To the man.)* That's it.
Man: What?
Frazier: I said that's it. Go back to the bar.
Man: Oh, go away, sonny. *(Frazier pushes back his chair.)* Why you— *(He lunges at Frazier. The bartender grabs him.)*
Bartender: Carson! Leave 'em alone!

Man: I just wanted to talk to her!

Bartender: Here's one on the house. Come on. What are you getting excited about. Relax. Have a drink. What the hell. *(Grumbling, the man goes back to the bar. Frazier sits down stiffly. He composes himself, then sees that Felicia is looking at him with tears in her eyes.)*

Man: Shit! *(He bangs the bar with his glass.)*

Frazier: *(To Felicia.)* Are you all right?

Felicia: Oh...gracias...I not...I not ready...that...yet.

Frazier: *(Smiling.)* Too old.

Felicia: *(Smiling.)* Too old.

Frazier: Well. Let's dance, then. Quieres bailar conmigo?

Felicia: Si. *(They get up and dance, slowly, awkwardly, gently. Buddy dances by with Teresa, bug-eyed.)*

Buddy: Ahoy, hotshot. *(He winks and rolls his eyes. Teresa has both arms wrapped around him. She is breathing into his ear. She is melting against him. Buddy must call time out. To Teresa.)* Okay, okay, sweetheart, Jesus Christ, let's take a break. You're turning my belly to butter. I need a drink. *(He picks his glass up from the table and takes a big gulp of brandy. Teresa leans against him and whispers something into his car. Buddy chokes and looks at her gleefully.)* Yeah? Why *shouldn't* I drink so much

Teresa: Because...you...come home, yes?

Buddy: *(Beaming.)* You better believe it. I mean sure. Si si si. Now?

Teresa: Oh...ah...Si, ahora.

Buddy: What the hell. Now. Right now. *(Teresa nods her head happily. Buddy puts down his drink, hops over to Felicia and Frazier, breaks them up, pushes Felicia toward Teresa, takes Frazier aside.)*

Frazier: Hey, what's the idea? I finally get to dance and you break it up?

Buddy: Baby, you'll dance later. Right now we're going home.

Frazier: Are you nuts? Oh. You mean to their house?

Buddy: That or a hotel, we'll see. A few bucks apiece and we can die happy. That Teresa is hot to trot So am I. Okay? *(Frazier turns and looks at the girls. Teresa is whispering quickly to Felicia, who turns and looks at Frazier. She smiles a trifle sadly, and nods her head.)*

Frazier: Well...

Buddy: Make up your mind. Think about the Marshall Islands. Gooney birds.

Frazier: *(Briskly.)* Let's go.

Buddy: F'ward, harch! All right, ladies, we're on our way. Frazier, leave Mr. Bartender something. Rinky-tinky-tum! Off we go! How'm I doing, hey, hey! Bum-bum-bum-bum-bum! *(They make a conga line and start singing and dancing out of the bar. Teresa sees something outside. She*

(He drops the bill on the table.) Okay, pimp? *(Esteban jumps up. The woman reels back against the wall. Chairs fall over. Everybody is up. Esteban stands shaking before them.)* You been pimping for your sister all night. You spic bastard. *(Esteban turns, pulling a knife. There is a click, and the blade gleams before them.)*

Felicia: No! Francisco!

Bartender: Hey! Hey, now! Francisco!

Buddy: All right, pimp! *(Buddy pulls a bigger knife, huge, and it opens with an even more deadly click.)* Come on. I'll fuck you, and *then* I'll fuck your sister. *(The women shrink back, scared. The man puts on his hat and gets out. The bartender pulls a baseball bat from behind the bar but stands back and waits.)* So? Come on? *(Pause. Slowly, Esteban lowers his knife. He sees plainly it would be unequal combat. He is flushed with humiliation.)* That's right. Close your knife. *(Esteban does.)* Now, come here. *(Slowly, Esteban does. Buddy holds the point of his knife out at him.)* Now close mine. You started this. Put your hand against it and push. *(Esteban swallows, puts his hand against the point of Buddy's knife, and pushes. As he gets the blade bent and almost in its socket, Buddy twists the knife a little, cutting Esteban's palm, just slightly.)* Something to remember me by. *(He puts his knife back into his pocket.)* You ready, Frazier?

Frazier: Yeah. I'm ready. *(Frazier takes the twenty-dollar bill and tucks it neatly into Buddy's shirt pocket. He turns to the bartender, and points at the bottle of brandy.)* Give me that. *(The bartender carefully tosses it to him. Frazier speaks to Esteban.)* May I see your hand, please?

Buddy: What the hell you doing?

Frazier: *(To Esteban.)* Sir, this is the best American brandy made. *(He pours it onto Esteban's palm, all of it, waiting for all the brandy in the bottle to wash the wound, shaking it to make sure there is none left. Then he tosses the empty bottle to the bartender. He takes a white handkerchief from his pocket, puts it on Esteban's cut, and holds him by the hand.)* You're doing good. If it was me, in your country, I don't think I could do any better. I hope things work out for you and your family. *(He ties the handkerchief around Esteban's hand.)* Keep that. Forgive the insult.

Esteban: Thank you.

Frazier: De nada. *(He steps back, motions with deference for Teresa and Felicia to go with Esteban.)*

Teresa: *(To Buddy.)* No! Give heem money! More money! I love you! *(Buddy shrugs and steps back. With scorn.)* Sheet. *(She stalks out of the bar. Esteban waits for Felicia, who stops by Frazier, looks at him a second, touches his face.)*

Felicia: A man. *(She leaves.)*

Buddy: Well, look, hermano. No hard feelings, what the hell. *(Esteban stares at him, leaves.)* So fuck you. *(Buddy and Frazier look at each other.)* You think that wasn't a pimp? *(Pause.)* You damn fool.

Frazier: You son of a bitch. *(A moment when neither moves. Then Frazier goes to the bar. Buddy goes back to the table. The bartender pours Frazier a drink. Buddy drinks the Hennessy, thinking. The bartender sets an overturned stool on its legs, takes a mop from behind the bar, and moves toward the brandy on the floor as the lights fade.)*

THE CAPTIVITY OF PIXIE SHEDMAN

for Texie Townsend Linney (1879-1956)

BERTRAM SHEDMAN, plain and troubled, 30's
PIXIE SHEDMAN, his spirited grandmother, of many ages.
COLONEL BERTRAM SHEDMAN, his colorful great grandfather, 60's.
DOCTOR BERTRAM SHEDMAN, his dutiful grandfather, 40's.
DOC BERTRAM SHEDMAN, JR., his youthful father, 30's.

Place: A studio in a New York City hotel.
Time: One afternoon and evening at the end of August, 1962.

THE CAPTIVITY OF PIXIE SHEDMAN was commissioned and first produced in its two act version by the Phoenix Theatre, T. Edward Hambleton, Managing Director, Steven Robmen, Artistic Director. It was directed by John Pasquin, set by Robert Blackman, lights by Jennifer Tipton, costumes by Linda Fisher, sound by David Rapkin, production stage manager, J. Thomas Vivian. Cast as follows:

BERTRAM SHEDMAN..........................William Carden
PIXIE SHEDMAN..................................Penelope Allen
COLONEL SHEDMAN............................Ron Randell
DOCTOR SHEDMAN..............................Jon DeVries
DOC BERTRAM SHEDMAN, JR..............Leon Russom

THE CAPTIVITY OF PIXIE SHEDMAN

(A studio on the top floor of an apartment hotel in New York. A Desk, on it a delicate French goblet, an old phonograph with some records, and a toy pistol. Beside it stands a clothestree, with a long scarf hanging from it. Shabby furniture, but a window overlooking the city in an afternoon that will change to night and stars. Bertram Shedman, a rather plain man in his thirties, is looking at the title page of a large, very old ledger book with handwriting in it.)

Bertram: *(Reading.)* THE CAPTIVITY OF PIXIE SHEDMAN. WRITTEN IN HER OWN HAND. A HARROWING TALE OF HER FATHER'S MURDER, HER OWN ABDUCTION, RAPE, AND LIFE UNDER THE YOKE OF BARBARISM— *(Pause.)*

Colonel Shedman: Oh, my God. *(Light brightens on three men and a woman sitting on a windowseat.)*

Bertram: *(Reading.)* —AS WELL AS HER FINAL ESCAPE FROM SAVAGERY.

Doctor Shedman: Pixie's terrible writing! *(The Shedman clan is in full light now. PIXIE SHEDMAN, who can seem to be different ages. COLONEL SHEDMAN, in his sixties, vigorous and handsome. DOCTOR SHEDMAN, his son, in his forties. DOC SHEDMAN, JR., in his twenties.)*

Bertram: *(Reading.)* "My Captivity was to a tribe I would willingly have served. Oh, that my name was written in a book."

Doc Shedman, Jr.: Awful!

Bertram: *(Reading.)* "I was making father's breakfast when, passing the open door of our cabin, I saw smoke ascending from our neighbor's roof. "Father!" I cried. He came to me quickly. "There!" I gasped. "Indians!" he said, and reached for his Bible.

Doc Shedman, Jr.: Just terrible!

Colonel Shedman: Where did she get that stuff?

Doctor Shedman: From bad books.

Bertram: *(Reading.)* "Secure in his faith, he went outside to preach the Word of God. But with bloody hatchets, they struck my father in the face, opened his stomach, and put his Bible in his belly."

Colonel Shedman: Nonsense!

Doctor Shedman: Noble white men, berserk Indians!

Doc Shedman, Jr.: Virtuous maidens!

Doctor Shedman: The truth was, Indians generally considered white women repulsive.

Colonel Shedman: It's all nonsense!

Bertram: *(Quietly.)* Well, wait a minute,

Colonel Shedman, Doctor Shedman and Doc Shedman, Jr.: Nonsense!!

Bertram: Be quiet.

Pixie: Thank you.

Bertram: Truth, Pixie, is what happened, and this didn't.

Pixie: Truth, Grandson, is what you know about what happened. You are holding it in your hand.

Bertram: I just want to see what happened.

Pixie: Then that's all you'll see. That's not the truth, that's just what happened.

Bertram: Your life has nothing to do with American Indians. Thay didn't murder your father. White men did. You did. On the day she was eighteen, and her father took her to that courthouse. June 1897. ***(Pixie stands.)***

Pixie: Poppa.

Bertram/Father: I swear to tell the truth, the whole truth, and nothing but the truth, so help me God. (COLONEL SHEDMAN ***walks back and forth before*** BERTRAM/FATHER.)

Colonel Shedman: You are a doctor of medicine and a pastor of a small Christian denomination, at one and the same time. Is that correct?

Bertram/Father: It is.

Colonel Shedman: How long have you practiced in this community?

Bertram/Father: I moved here one year ago.

Colonel Shedman: With your family?

Bertram/Father: My wife is dead. With my daughter.

Colonel Shedman: This charming young lady?

Bertram/Father: Yes.

Colonel Shedman: Now, Doctor, will you consider the defendant in this action, Mrs. Hattie Starns?

Bertram/Father: Gladly.

Colonel Shedman: She is a widow. Eighty-three years old. She calls me from the other end of the state to represent her. I take the case, come down here, and the first thing I discover is that you, Doctor, depose and assert that my client Hattie Starns is senile and incapable of administering her own estate. Is that a true statement?

Bertram/Father: The part about me is, yes.

Colonel Shedman: *(Smiling.)* That is why, using your deposition, the several children of Hattie Starns petition this court to grant them iron control over her and all she owns. *(Pause.)* Well, not unusual, is it? Aging children, ancient moneybags. The several children bring suit. Our attention falls immediately upon you, since you, under the laws of the great state of North Carolina, are the expert witness in the case. Deliver please your expert diagnosis.

Bertram/Father: Certainly. At eighty-three—

Colonel Shedman: Simply, please. In terms plain folks not doctors or preachers understand.

Bertram/Father: At eighty-three, Hattie Starns suffers from several diseases common to the elderly. None are dangerous at this time. Conjointly, however, they conspire to prevent a full flow of blood to the brain, causing senility. Her disease is old age, and I cannot cure it.

Colonel Shedman: How long have you practiced medicine?

Bertram/Father: Thirty-three years.

Colonel Shedman: Thirty-three years! What an achievement! But in those thirty-three years, you have practiced in the county only—

Bertram/Father: One year. I told you that.

Colonel Shedman: Quite so. And have you practiced here in the family of my old friend John Croy Alexander?

Bertram/Father: I did, yes.

Colonel Shedman: You did. That is the past tense. Has Alexander left town?

Bertram/Father: *(Smiling.)* He certainly has. He's dead.

Colonel Shedman: *(Not smiling.)* How tragic. Did you attend him in his last illness?

Bertram/Father: I did.

Colonel Shedman: And his noble wife, Deborah. How has she taken this dire calamity?

Bertram/Father: She's dead, too.

Colonel Shedman: And did you attend her in her last illness?

Bertram/Father: I did. She was seventy—

Colonel Shedman: Doctor, while I am not native to this county, I have many friends here. Like Reuben Hinkle, that vigorous man, whose father, I believe, lived to be a hundred and two. Is he—

Bertram/Father: Now, wait a minute—

Colonel Shedman: Latitude here is certainly for my client. Reuben Hinkle. Where is he?

Bertram/Father: He's dead.

Colonel Shedman: And you attended him in his last illness?

Bertram/Father: I did.

Colonel Shedman: Cromwell Pindall, nicknamed "Stag" Pindall, a man of legendary dimension and masculine energy—where might I find him?

Bertram/Father: You know damn well.

Colonel Shedman: Where is Cromwell Pindall!

Bertram/Father: Dead!

Colonel Shedman: Stag Pindall, dead?

Bertram/Father: He was eighty-five years old!

Colonel Shedman: And you attended him—

Bertram/Father: All my patients are old people!

Colonel Shedman: Are they, indeed? Next case, the amazing Harland Vickers. A strapping young man of eight and twenty years! A mountain-climbing, horse-racing, swashbuckling Hercules, and the best left-handed pitcher ever to play baseball in the state of North Carolina!

Bertram/Father: He collapsed near my home! He was brought to me!

Colonel Shedman: And was your patient for six months thereafter! Now where is he? Doctor?

Bertram/Father: Dead!

Colonel Shedman: And you—

Bertram/Father: *(Shouting.)* Yes! *(Pixie stands up.)*

Pixie: Poppa. *(Pause. She sits again.)*

Colonel Shedman: Well, I ask this distinguished community. *(He takes a large envelope from his coat pocket, fingers it, but does not open it.)* I have here, among other things, a list of fourteen men and women of this county. They were hale and hearty six months ago. They now sleep with their fathers. Every one of them attended by this expert witness.

Bertram/Father: That's slander!

Colonel Shedman: I can make a list. Anyone can make a list. What am I accusing you of? Mass murder? Of course not! *(Pause.)* No! Never! *(Pause.)* But I can't help wondering, doctor, along with everyone else, just what measure of success you have had treating afflicted humanity, since you tried to cure every person on this list, and they all died. D-I-E-D, DIED!!

Bertram/Father: God damn you, sir, and all your kind! *(Pause. Colonel Shedman shrugs his shoulders.)*

Colonel Shedman: Thank you, doctor. I call for my next witness the young lady sitting—there. *(He points at Pixie.)*

Pixie: Me?

Bertram/Father: My daughter?

Colonel Shedman: Young lady. *(To Bertram/Father.)* Step down, please. *(Bertram/Father and Pixie trade places.)*

Pixie: *(Frightened.)* I swear to tell the truth, the whole truth and nothing but the truth. So help me God.

Colonel Shedman: Did you receive, from the children of Hattie Starns, twenty-five acres of land and title to a building in this town?

Pixie: *(Shocked.)* I did not!

Colonel Shedman: You did not?

Pixie: No! *(He starts to open the envelope. Stops.)*

Colonel Shedman: Let me try again. Did you sign, quite recently, legal documents of any kind? Possibly without reading them?

Pixie: Why, no. Except, of course— *(Pause.)*

Colonel Shedman: Yes?

Pixie: My father— *(She looks at Bertram/Father.)*

Colonel Shedman: Speak to me, please.

Pixie: For my eighteenth birthday. My membership in the church. And a pledge.

Colonel Shedman: In ink, with a pen, and without, I will assume, examining them closely? *(Pixie stares at her father.)*

Pixie: Yes.

Colonel Shedman: May it please the court, in this envelope are the bills of transfer, with her signature upon them. *(He holds up the envelope.)* Hattie Starns understood that her children might find a doctor foolish enough to be bribed. Thank you, young lady.

Pixie: My curse upon you, too. God damn you, and all your kind! *(Colonel Shedman shrugs again. Pixie turns to see Bertram.)* You see? *(Pixie picks up the Captivity, and marks a place in it.)*

Pixie: Read.

Bertram: *(Reading.)* "Thus were we butchered by that merciless heathen, standing amazed, with the blood running down to our heels." *(Pause.)* But he really died of pneumonia. Three months later.

Pixie: Five. With complications.

Bertram: What?

Pixie: Criminal indictment. Terminal humiliation. He died with his scalp torn off, and his Bible in his belly.

Doctor Shedman: Ridiculous!

Doc Shedman, Jr.: Preposterous!

Colonel Shedman: All I did was win my case!

Bertram: You were harder on him than you had to be.

Colonel Shedman: He was dishonest!

Bertram: And fragile. *(He turns pages, looking for something.)* But here, Pixie.

Doctor Shedman: What does she say there?

Bertram: She says that she was raped. *(Indignation.)*

Colonel Shedman: Oh, really!

Doctor Shedman: Raped? Pixie? *(Simultaneous.)*

Doc Shedman, Jr.: Mother, Mother!

Bertram: That's what she says.

Colonel Shedman: Who rapes her?

Bertram: You do.

Colonel Shedman: This is grotesque.

Bertram: On a forced march through the wilderness.

Doc Shedman, Jr.: She stayed right there in town!

Doctor Shedman: Slinging hash at the Carolina Cafe. A waitress!

Colonel Shedman: Those are the facts!

Pixie: When men want to cover things up, all they talk about is facts. Just read what I wrote!

Bertram: *(Reads.)* "I was beaten, broken, starving, my life in ruins, but it must only be that I stand once more in the hateful presence of the savage chief." *(Pixie turns away. Colonel Shedman approaches her. She turns again and sees him. Bertram, always visible, holds the Captivity and watches.)*

Pixie: Oh.

Colonel Shedman: Good afternoon.

Pixie: Lunch?

Colonel Shedman: No. I have come to see you.

Pixie: What for?

Colonel Shedman: To tell you I truly did not know he was dead. Can you believe that?

Pixie: If you wish. Anything else?

Colonel Shedman: Was it really pneumonia?

Pixie: He didn't kill himself, thank you. Nobody can blame you for his death.

Colonel Shedman: You can. I can.

Pixie: What difference would that make? Go do yourself good somewhere else. You've wasted a trip. *(Colonel Shedman hands Pixie a large engraved card.)* What's this?

Colonel Shedman: Look at it, please.

Pixie: *(Reading.)* The Inauguration—Inaugural Ball—President William—Mrs. Ida—McKinley—January 14, 1897— *(Looks at him.)* That's today.

Colonel Shedman: I could be in Washington today, doing myself good. I am here with you.

Pixie: Do you want to order now?

Colonel Shedman: Three things, and I'll trouble you no more.

Pixie: One?

Colonel Shedman: I will not burden you with further sympathy.

Pixie: Two?

Colonel Shedman: Your father left you in considerable debt. With your permission, I will erase it.

Pixie: Three.

Colonel Shedman: I offer you a job.

Pixie: What?

Colonel Shedman: In Washington. With me.

Pixie: With you?

Colonel Shedman: As a staff secretary, you can be busy, free, and of service to your country.

Pixie: Work for you?

Colonel Shedman: The offer merits your careful consideration.

Pixie: Well, it does. *(She hands back the card.)* Is your family there?

Colonel Shedman: My son is in medical school. My wife won't leave North Carolina. Says I shouldn't either. *(Pause.)* She's much older than I am!

Pixie: Than you are?

Colonel Shedman: I married during the war.

Pixie: War?

Colonel Shedman: After the battle of Chancellorsville, where I was wounded.

Pixie: The Civil War?

Colonel Shedman: I recovered at her father's farm. An ignorant mountain boy, that's all I was. She taught me to read and write.

Pixie: In the days of Robert E. Lee.

Colonel Shedman: Can you imagine how old she must be now?

Pixie: No, and don't tell me.

Colonel Shedman: You can't be happy here.

Pixie: No.

Colonel Shedman: You are in a degrading position. I will change that. *(Pause.)*

Pixie: Your executive secretary?

Colonel Shedman: Whatever you say.

Pixie: My salary equal to any other?

Colonel Shedman: Agreed.

Pixie: When do you go back?

Colonel Shedman: I take the morning train.

Pixie: Then so do I.

Colonel Shedman: You will have no regrets.

Pixie: None. *(He holds out his hand. She takes it. He bows and leaves her. Pixie stares after him.)*

Colonel Shedman: That wasn't rape!

Doctor Shedman: That was opportunity!

Doc Shedman, Jr.: And she took it!

Pixie: No, that wasn't opportunity, that was rape, and I didn't take it, it took me.

Bertram: *(Reading.)* "Scenes From the Indian Camp."

Doc Shedman, Jr.: Can't you just tell us?

Doctor Shedman: Washington, as it was!

Pixie: Pow-wows. Tom-toms.

Colonel Shedman: Oh, my God.

Doctor Shedman: It's hopeless.

Doc Shedman, Jr.: What can you do?

Pixie: Warpaint and firewater. Washington as it was!

Bertram: Well, Pixie—

Pixie: And speeches! Boy, howdy! Speeches and speeches and speeches and speeches. His worst of all. I dare you!

Bertram: *(To Colonel Shedman.)* She dares me.

Colonel Shedman: I don't mind. *(He strikes a Daniel Webster orator's pose.)*

Pixie: Just you wait.

Bertram: Give him a chance.

Colonel Shedman: Sir, to your argument I will reply that this is the Senate of the United States, where great powers reside and clash. Here I witness the iron and the fire that forged the Republic. But here also, above all, I hear the gallant music of my Confederate past! Beautiful, imperishable, constant and doomed!

Pixie: Can you believe it?

Colonel Shedman: I hear again the words of my incomparable commander, the gentle lion of the South!

Bertram: *(Shaking his head.)* No, I can't.

Colonel Shedman: "Tell A.P. Hill to prepare for action! Let us pass over the river, and sit in the shade of the trees!"

Bertram: Wait a minute. Half that, Lee said. The other half, Jackson said.

Pixie: He didn't care. All he wanted was people cheering, and his bills passed.

Bertram: Didn't anybody laugh at him?

Pixie: That's what he was afraid of. *(Colonel Shedman rushes up to Pixie.)*

Colonel Shedman: I couldn't find you! Weren't you in the gallery?

Pixie: I was there.

Colonel Shedman: Did you hear that young scoundrel? He called me a geographical colonel and a celestial senator. What the hell did he mean by that?

Pixie: Never mind.

Colonel Shedman: I'm not an old man making speeches! I won my election just like he did!

Pixie: Hush. You made him look ridiculous.

Colonel Shedman: Did I?

Pixie: Of course you did.

Colonel Shedman: Really?

Pixie: Yes!

Colonel Shedman: What would I do without you. I—I have something for you. I saw it in an antique store, and thought of you. Here. *(Bertram hands Colonel Shedman a goblet. He gives it to Pixie.)*

Pixie: Oh.

Colonel Shedman: It's French. Used at court, they told me. Louis the Fifteenth.

Pixie: I will keep it always. Thank you.

Colonel Shedman: I have something else for you, Pixie. You must be aware of—though I didn't mean it to happen—or ever cross the—

Pixie: Line. Go ahead.

Colonel Shedman: I will deny it no longer! What I have for you!

Pixie: A speech, never mind that. What else?

Colonel Shedman: Energy, little girl! It is still mine, and we are young together! That is the law, and all the prophets! *(He takes her in his arms, clumsily, and kisses her. Pixie steps back, looks at him, then with slow sensuality, kisses him back.)* You understand me, then?

Pixie: It isn't difficult.

Colonel Shedman: Take this. *(He drops a key into the goblet.)*

Bertram: *(Turning pages.)* It says here a mountain cave, with wind, wolves, and a sunset. In reality—

Colonel Shedman: *(To Pixie.)* The Willard Hotel. Tonight, nine o'clock. We'll have supper in our room, and talk. There are so many things to say.

Pixie: And do.

Colonel Shedman: Yes! And do! Just so! *(He stares at her wildly, in love.)* Oh, you dear child? You beauty! Willard Hotel! Nine o'clock! Just so! *(He moves away. Pixie puts the French goblet back on Bertram's desk, and points to a place in the Captivity he is holding.)*

Pixie: Right there.

Bertram: *(Reading.)* "Thus was I slave to the rank embrace of this savage chief. Thus was I stripped of all my maidenly—"

Doc Shedman, Jr.: Oh, Mother!

Doctor Shedman: Some slavery!

Colonel Shedman: Some rape!

Bertram: *(Reading.)* "Maidenly innocence. For upon his blood-stained furs, beneath his shudder and convulsion, I received from my captor the bestial yoke."

Pixie: Night after night after night.

Bertram: *(Reading.)* "Yet within his embrace lay my deliverance. I did not see it at first, as I asked myself under the passing moons how I would survive this dreadful captivity, clasped as I was within the creaking passions of an ancient lover—"

Colonel Shedman: Pixie!

Doctor Shedman: *(To Doc Shedman Jr., smiling.)* What kind of passions?

Doc Shedman, Jr.: *(Smiling.)* Creaking. She said creaking passions.

Doctor Shedman: Of an ancient lover!

Doc Shedman, Jr.: *(Nodding.)* Ancient lover.

Colonel Shedman: Pixie!

Bertram: Hush! *(Reads.)* "But finally there it was, unmistakable: clear, plain, within the stammering and the weeping confidences of the bedroom—"

Doc Shedman, Jr.: Stammering.

Doctor Shedman: Weeping.

Bertram: "Among the clenched fists of difficult release—"

Colonel Shedman: Pixie!! God damn it!

Bertram: "It appeared. Survival. The key that fit the lock. And opened the door." *(Pixie moves away, with Colonel Shedman and Doc Shedman Jr. Doctor Shedman approaches Bertram.)*

Doctor Shedman: Clerk! *(Bertram, holding the Captivity at his side, becomes a desk clerk at the Willard Hotel.)*

Bertram/Clerk: Sir?

Doctor Shedman: Is Senator Shedman registered at the Willard?

Bertram/Clerk: Yes, sir.

Doctor Shedman: What's his room number?

Bertram/Clerk: I can't tell you, sir.

Doctor Shedman: Why not?

Bertram/Clerk: I can't tell you that, either.

Doctor Shedman: Ring his room.

Bertram/Clerk: He's not to be disturbed.

Doctor Shedman: I'm his son!

Bertram/Clerk: I'm sure you are.

Doctor Shedman: Now, listen—

Bertram/Clerk: There he is now. *(Colonel Shedman approaches them, Pixie on his arm.)*

Colonel Shedman: Well!

Doctor Shedman: Well. Father.

Colonel Shedman: My boy. Pixie, this is my son, who's just put a "doctor" in front of our name.

Pixie: *(Smiling.)* Doctor Shedman. How do you do? *(She holds out her hand.)*

Colonel Shedman: Son, may I present Miss—

Doctor Shedman: I know who she is. *(Pixie shrugs, drops her hand.)*

Colonel Shedman: We were just going to dinner. Join us?

Doctor Shedman: Mother's had a stroke. Evidently this afternoon. The telegram came to your office. You couldn't be reached. They contacted me. I tracked you down here.

Colonel Shedman: Is she alive?

Doctor Shedman: Read it for yourself. *(He hands Colonel Shedman a telegram. While Colonel Shedman reads, he and Pixie regard each other.)*

Pixie: I am sorry.

Doctor Shedman: So am I. *(Pause.)* I hope I wasn't rude to you.

Pixie: You were, but that's all right.

Colonel Shedman: This doesn't say how serious it really is.

Doctor Shedman: If you don't want to go, I'll go alone.

Colonel Shedman: Hush, son. We go together.

Doctor Shedman: The next train is six in the morning. I'll see you there, and not disturb you further. Good evening.

Colonel Shedman: Oh, stop acting like an idiot! I have appointments to cancel. Wait here. *(He goes to Bertram/Clerk. Backs turned, they confer. Doctor Shedman and Pixie regard each other again.)*

Pixie: He talks about her a lot. With love and respect. She likes gardens.

Doctor Shedman: Yes, she does.

Pixie: Roses and green beans? A long life in the sun? I envy her.

Doctor Shedman: A dull life, some would think. *(Pause.)* Do you enjoy your work? *(Quickly.)* I beg your pardon.

Pixie: Sometimes I do and sometimes I don't. Tell me more about your mother.

Doctor Shedman: Really, what do you care?

Pixie: I beg your pardon. Do you like being a doctor? Isn't this weather frightful? *(Pause.)*

Doctor Shedman: My mother is a time-worn Carolina country lady. She stays in bed now, most of the time, except for an hour in the summer, when she takes tea in her garden, and an hour in winter, when she makes preserves in her kitchen. Bed, kitchen, garden. I hardly remember her anywhere else.

Pixie: And now she may be dying, in North Carolina?

Doctor Shedman: Yes.

Pixie: While your father plays with me, in Washington.

Doctor Shedman: That is the case.

Colonel Shedman: *(To Bertram/Clerk.)* All right! I'll do it myself! *(To Doctor Shedman.)* Will you take her in to dinner? We might as well eat. I'll be right back. Son?

Doctor Shedman: If you wish.

Colonel Shedman: I do. You two be friends. *(He moves away. Pixie and Doctor Shedman stare at each other again, with interest.)*

Pixie: We don't have to be friends.

Doctor Shedman: Whatever you say.

Pixie: You hate to see you father—

Doctor Shedman: Old and foolish. Ah— *(He recites, quietly.)* "As the bird trims her to the gale, I trim myself to the storm of time, I man the rudder, reef the sail, Obey the voice at eve obeyed at prime." I'd prefer that, you see. *(He has now relaxed. He is young, hopeful, inexperienced.)*

Pixie: Who wrote it?

Doctor Shedman: Emerson.

Pixie: You read poetry?

Doctor Shedman: Some. And a father like mine, only verse can describe him.

Pixie: *(Smiling.)* That's the truth.

Doctor Shedman: *(Smiling.)* Certainly is.

Pixie: You can be very agreeable.

Doctor Shedman: I wasn't to you. I apologize.

Pixie: I accept that. *(Pause.)* Don't be too angry with him. Your father redeemed me from squalor in North Carolina. I pay him back in bed in Washington. A familiar political arrangement we both perform as well as we can. Let me beg you, give it no more thought than it deserves, and accept my heartfelt wishes for your mother's recovery. *(Pause.)*

Doctor Shedman: That is agreeable of you. Dinner?

Pixie: With pleasure. *(They move away together.)*

Bertram: Pixie? What did you do to him?

Pixie: *(Moving away with Doctor Shedman.)* Shut up and read!

Bertram: *(Reading.)* "Savages and their sons share secrets of burning devotion. The brutal father cherished his boy, while the boy, in his dreams, glowed with a fierce wonder: could he ever, in savage emulation, assume that father's place? And if so, how?" *(To Pixie.)* Like that?

Pixie: Keep reading. *(Colonel Shedman, as Bertram reads, appears before him, very nervous, very uncertain.)*

Bertram: *(Reading.)* "After the death of his Indian queen, my barbaric chieftain was obliged to mourn for many days. Free at last, he fled her melancholy tomb, back to my youth and bed. But the key had turned the lock. The door was open, and I was gone." *(Bertram closes the Captivity, and becomes the clerk again. Colonial Shedman approaches him, very upset.)*

Colonel Shedman: Clerk!

Bertram/Clerk: Sir?

Colonel Shedman: Is Doctor Shedman registered at the Willard?

Bertram/Clerk: Yes, sir.

Colonel Shedman: What's his room number?

Bertram/Clerk: I can't tell you, sir.

Colonel Shedman: Why not?

Bertram/Clerk: I can't tell you that, either

Colonel Shedman: Ring his room.

Bertram/Clerk: He is not to be disturbed.

Colonel Shedman: I'm his father.

Bertram/Clerk: I'm sure you are.

Colonel Shedman: Now, listen—

Bertram/Clerk: There he is. *(Colonel Shedman turns and sees Pixie and Doctor Shedman together.)*

Colonel Shedman: Lovers?

Doctor Shedman: Married.

Colonel Shedman: Married?

Doctor Shedman: Yes.

Colonel Shedman: Done?

Pixie: Done.

Colonel Shedman: Well, you fool.

Doctor Shedman: Now, father—

Colonel Shedman: Never mind! *(He bows.)* Congratulations. *(Rigidly, he holds out his hand. Doctor Shedman takes it. They shake. Colonel Shedman turns to Pixie, kisses her stiffly on the forehead.)* I shall, of course, give you a wedding present.

Doctor Shedman: That would be very good of you, father.

Colonel Shedman: You will need to make a living at once, for your wife, and children.

Doctor Shedman: Yes, I will.

Colonel Shedman: What do you say to three hundred and sixty acres of choice land? A three story house, with I believe, copper plumbing? And the opportunity to establish a first-rate practice?

Doctor Shedman: Do you mean it?

Colonel Shedman: Every word. You'll do very well there.

Pixie: Where?

Colonel Shedman: In Kansas. The southwest corner, bordering upon the great state of Oklahoma.

Doctor Shedman: Kansas?

Pixie: Oklahoma?

Colonel Shedman: A world of your own! Where no one will see what you will do to each other!

Pixie: I thought so.

Doctor Shedman: Father.

Colonel Shedman: Well, do you think I want to watch it?

Doctor Shedman: I married Pixie because—

Colonel Shedman: She married you!

Pixie: That's not true!

Colonel Shedman: Oh, please! *(Pause.)* Romeo and Juliet, is it? Well, we will see what happens when Juliet marries her Romeo not for love, and not for greed, but for revenge! God damn you, you bitch, and all your kind. *(Doctor Shedman strikes his father, knocking him down. Pixie restrains him. Then he tries to help Colonel Shedman get up.)* I will get up by myself. *(He does.)* My offer still stands. It merits your careful consideration.

Doctor Shedman: You can keep your property. Pixie?

Pixie: *(To Colonel Shedman.)* No, thank you. *(Colonel Shedman looks at them, nodding his head.)*

Colonel Shedman: Nevertheless, it still stands. And we'll see. *(Nodding, he moves away from them. They look after him. Standing behind Pixie, Doctor Shedman puts his arms around her.)*

Doctor Shedman: I love you, Pixie.

Pixie: I hope you do.

Doctor Shedman: You're mine now.

Pixie: Your mother's flower gardens. What did she grow in them? Lilies, tulips, roses? Beautiful things?

Doctor Shedman: Yes.

Pixie: All seeds looks the same. I am pregnant. Kiss me. *(A telephone rings.)*

Bertram: Hello......I've been waiting......You know I do......I thought we'd go to North Carolina together, for a weekend......I know you don't......Not at all?......Let me speak to your mother......Wait a minute! Don't! *(Pause. BERTRAM hangs up. He slams the Captivity down on his desk, takes a bottle of whiskey from a bookcase, pours a stiff shot into the goblet and drinks it. Then another.)*

Colonel Shedman: Talking to a child.

Doctor Shedman: There was a mother.

Doc Shedman, Jr.: It's a divorce!

Pixie: It's why we're here. Leave him alone. *(BERTRAM pours another. Between drinks:)*

Bertram: Standing amazed, with the blood running down to our heels. *(Pause.)* Cherished his boy, while the boy, in his dreams— *(Pause.)* But the key had turned the lock. The door was open. *(Pause.)* Marries her not for love or greed, but for revenge! *(Pause.)* All seeds look the same. Kiss me! *(Pause.)*

Pixie: *(Softly.)* Why the divorce?

Bertram: My wife says I'm a captive of the past. She says I can't tell the living and the dead apart.

Pixie: Not doing too well, are you?

Bertram: No, and neither did you, and neither did they, and I want to get back to your book. *(Reads.)* "Between the raging father and his barbaric son stood I, like a tender bud in springtime, caught between fire and ice."

Colonel Shedman: Oh, grotesque! Grotesque!

Doc Shedman, Jr.: Mother!

Doctor Shedman: Tender bud? Pixie?

Colonel Shedman: Ludicrous, I say!

Doc Shedman, Jr.: Tear it up!

Doctor Shedman: Throw it out!

Pixie: Read!

Bertram: *(Reading.)* "At first we made a brave show of our independence. My savage husband was virile, I was young, and so it seemed a while that my body was wiser than my mind."

Pixie: *(Declaims.)* "But time is implacable, horrors of the spirit are hidden, multitudinous and emergent, and the savage beast can only dream of escape from bloody antecedents. Mandates of fate and iron prevail, and I must watch the son to his father's will submit." *(Doctor Shedman nods. He goes to the desk, and positions the phonograph so it faces Pixie.)*

Doctor Shedman: All right. Keep your eyes closed. *(Pixie moves forward, eyes closed.)*

Pixie: But what is it?

Doctor Shedman: Just a minute. You'll see. *(He plays "Little Sweetheart of the Prairies.")* Open your eyes. *(Pixie does. She stares at the phonograph.)*

Pixie: My God.

Doctor Shedman: The latest Edison.

Pixie: Just look at it.

Doctor Shedman: With records. We can get more by mail. Dance music, all the best comedians, even grand opera!

Pixie: Fine, but what for? Why this now?

Doctor Shedman: To take with us.

Pixie: With us where? Turn it off! *(Doctor Shedman takes the needle off, and stops the phonograph.)*

Doctor Shedman: To Kansas, Pixie. We're going.

Pixie: You said we never would.

Doctor Shedman: Did I? I don't think I said never.

Pixie: We both did.

Doctor Shedman: Well, what do you want me to do? You're pregnant. I haven't had a patient in six weeks. It's all over town my wife was my father's mistress.

Pixie: I don't care what people think.

Doctor Shedman: I detest it. I want some peace and quiet.

Pixie: You're making a mistake.

Doctor Shedman: No, I'm not.

Pixie: You're giving in to him!

Doctor Shedman: How?

Pixie: He gets rid of us! Buys us out of here, with some farm in Kansas!

Doctor Shedman: Where I can live off the crop, make a home for the three of us, and build a real practice.

Pixie: You're making a mistake.

Doctor Shedman: No, I'm not.

Pixie: Yes, you are.

Doctor Shedman: Pixie!! Just pack the bags! We're going to Kansas!! *(He turns away. Pixie takes the record off the phonograph.)*

Pixie: God Almighty. *(She puts the record down, and turns away.)*

Bertram: *(To Colonel Shedman.)* You did do that.

Colonel Shedman: For their own good.

Pixie: Our good?

Doctor Shedman: Oh, please!

Colonel Shedman: All right, mine, too! But I did think they'd be better off in the wide open spaces. Which are deaf, dumb and blind.

Doc Shedman, Jr.: Kansas wasn't so bad, you know. I was born there.

Pixie: *(To Bertram.)* Read.

Bertram: *(Reading.)* "Thus did we remove, from a busy camp, with all its life and variety, to a barren and deserted world, a wilderness of flatland and sod and grass and nothing else." *(Bertram goes to the clothestree and takes down the scarf.)*

Pixie: *(Recites.)* "Oh how dreary, dank and dispiriting was that awful world. In spite of everything, I loved my young husband. All might have been well, but not in Kansas." *(Bertram winds the scarf around his neck, leaving one end dangling.)* "Where my savage husband's good intentions soon collapsed. After the birth of our son, the loneliness of the prairie turned him away from his quiet home to the common solace of drinking and dancing and self-indulgence. I was then most often alone, with only my child for company, and a few well-meaning, but primitive companions. And so, in a culture of savages I tried to live, searching for understanding with whatever friends I could find." *(Bertram takes some papers from his desk. Scarf dangling, he goes to Pixie as a Midwestern Poet. He stands with her, looking at a poem of his doubtfully.)*

Bertram/Poet: I'm not so sure about it.

Pixie: Confidence. That's what it takes.

Bertram/Poet: You'll help me?

Pixie: Of course I will. But you have to believe in yourself. That's first. Now, the title.

Bertram/Poet: "Selina Falls Railroad Crash."

Pixie: Nothing wrong with that. Let me hear the end again. *(Doctor Shedman, walking unsteadily, sees them, and stands watching.)*

Bertram/Poet: "Selina Falls Railroad Crash! How dread the sight, how clean Cut down in death the rash Of widows, mites, from Abilene!" *(To Pixie, anxiously.)*

Pixie: By mites you mean children?

Bertram/Poet: Of course.

Pixie: But doesn't mite also mean money?

Bertram/Poet: I'll just say children.

Pixie: That's better.

Bertram/Poet: Boy. This writing poetry.

Pixie: Confidence. That's what it takes. *(Doctor Shedman applauds loudly, surprising them.)*

Doctor Shedman: Wonderful! Magnificient!

Bertram/Poet: What? Oh. Doctor Shedman. Sir.

Doctor Shedman: Poets. The indomitable will. The triumph of the spirit.

Bertram/Poet: Well, thanks. I sure try. Of course, I can't beat Pixie. She's the best. The Kansas Lark, that's what we call her. Have you read her latest? *(He hands Doctor Shedman a poem of Pixie's.)*

Doctor Shedman: Not yet.

Bertram/Poet: It's deeply moving. Well, it's late. Good night.

Doctor Shedman: Farewell.

Pixie: Thank you for coming. *(Bertram/Poet turns away and stands by the desk, watching. Pause.)*

Doctor Shedman: Good evening, Kansas Lark.

Pixie: Good evening, Doctor Drunk.

Doc Shedman, Jr.: *(With his eyes closed.)* Ah, Ah!

Bertram: *(To Doc Shedman Jr.)* Do you remember? Do you?
Doc Shedman, Jr.: *(Eyes closed.)* Daddy.
Doctor Shedman: How is my happy home?
Pixie: As you left it.
Doctor Shedman: And my boy?
Pixie: Asleep.
Doc Shedman, Jr.: Mamma.
Doctor Shedman: I'll have a chat with him.
Pixie: I said he's asleep. You leave him alone. *(She blocks his way.)*
Doc Shedman, Jr.: *(In his sleep.)* Oh. Ah! Oh.
Doctor Shedman: Pixie Shedman. Poet of the Plains. She doesn't dance but she does sing.
Pixie: That's right. She does.
Doctor Shedman: A poem. *(He looks at her poem in his hand.)* "Hope." *(He laughs.)* What a title. Well, let's give it a try. Ahem. "Hope." *(He reads Pixie's poem.)* "And now is gone the happy days—No more." Is gone, are gone? Days, plural, are gone, surely. More than one, and all that. I don't mean to be pedantic, Kansas Lark, and I couldn't agree with the sentiment more, but really. "Now hushed the roundelays Of joyous voice, uplifted head: For bowed in grief, now faith is dead." Very well. But what is bowed in grief, now faith is dead? Uplifted head? This is sentimental hogwash, Pixie. I'll see my boy now.
Pixie: No, you won't
Doc Shedman, Jr.: *(In his sleep.)* Daddy.
Doctor Shedman: Yes, I will.
Pixie: He's asleep.
Doctor Shedman: That's right.
Pixie: You'll wake him up.
Doctor Shedman: You're right again.
Pixie: I won't have it.
Doctor Shedman: Pixie!
Pixie: You leave him alone! You're drunk!
Doctor Shedman: All right. *(Doctor Shedman looks at the poem again.)* We'll continue. *(Reading.)* "The heart that through the toilsome day Beat high with hope—" Oops! The title! Right there smack in the middle of the poem. Oh, very good. *(Reading.)* "The heart that through the toilsome day Beat high with hope—on rugged way. Above the strife of worldly gain With faith serene, is filled with pain." Oh, dear me. Pixie filled with pain. No, the heart filled with pain, sorry. After beating through the toilsome day, high with hope. You know, I think it has to be one or the other, but let it pass. It's strong and sensitive, and of course above the strife of

worldly gain, otherwise it wouldn't be poetic, would it?

Doc Shedman, Jr.: *(Asleep.)* Mamma!

Doctor Shedman: *(Reading.)* "High winds of stress and low'ring clouds. Obscuring mists—" Well, I think I know what you're talking about there— "Through darkness, maze, from crushing blow His hand will hold, give—" Wait a minute. His hand? Who's his? A mysterious intruder? Don Juan? Almighty God? The mailman? Well, we just have to guess, and that's poetic, too. All right. *(Reading.)* "His hand will hold, give faith to grow, Through pall of gloom, a joy again, Still sweeter after wind and rain." Rain, a-gain. The subtlety of it meets one at every turn. *(He stands looking at her, weaving a little, and smiling.)* Well, let me tell you this. I do sympathize with all this pain you're in, but we've been married four years now, and I'm in a little discomfort myself. Lacking the tongue of the poet, I just go dancing, like any clod, to kill my pain. And, like any clod, I have a drink, or two or three or four, with other clods. One such is a waitress at the Starlight Cafe in Hazleton. You wouldn't like her. She drinks, too. Not only that, she dances. Worst of all, the little girl's pregnant. And you know what, Pixie? Here's a couplet for you. "She won't be quiet, she'll cause a fuss, She's just going to try and blame it on us!" And you know something else? I don't care. Because my little waitress doesn't pretend to be something she isn't. She just likes to work, dance, drink and you-know-what. She doesn't mope around like Little Eva, and brood around like Lady Macbeth, and make me feel like a goddamned dog with a lot of goddamned doggerel!

Doc Shedman, Jr.: *(Groaning.)* Ah! Ah!

Doctor Shedman: Now. If my waitress really is pregnant, she will have my baby, with not one word from you. And if you don't like it, you can walk back to North Carolina, and write a poem about that! And now I will see my boy. Get out of my way!

Doc Shedman, Jr.: Ah!

Pixie: No.

Doctor Shedman: I've never raised my hand to you, Pixie.

Pixie: But you will now?

Doctor Shedman: Damn right. Move! *(They all move. Doc Shedman Jr. covers his face with his hands, groaning. Doctor Shedman goes after Pixie. She avoids him. He catches her by the shoulders, turns her around, and swings his fist at her. She ducks, steps back, and takes from Bertram a large toy pistol.)*

Doc Shedman, Jr.: *(Screaming.)* AHH!!!!

Bertram: BANG!!!! *(Pause.)*

Doctor Shedman: That's my gun.

Pixie: Right.

Doctor Shedman: You shot at me.

Pixie: Right.

Doctor Shedman: But you don't know how to shoot a gun.

Pixie: Right.

Doctor Shedman: You could have killed me.

Pixie: And the next time you step drunk into our house, I will. *(She tosses the pistol to him. He catches it.)* Keep it. But try to come between me and my son again, and I will find that gun again and next time put the bullet in your head.

Doctor Shedman: Your son?

Doc Shedman, Jr.: Ah!

Pixie: Right!

Doctor Shedman: He's my son, too!

Pixie: Is he? Critic? *(Pause.)*

Doctor Shedman: *(Pale.)* What?

Pixie: Silly little poet, am I? Well, you were pretty fancy yourself, when you married me. You didn't mind hearts full of pain and hope then. Because you were feeling it, it was all right! By all means have your waitress and your baby, because that baby may be the only baby that's yours!

Doc Shedman, Jr.: Ah! Ah!

Doctor Shedman: My boy, not mine?

Pixie: Maybe he is, and maybe he isn't! I don't know! I never will know, and neither will you! Because you weren't so terrifically exact when you pulled me out of your father's bed one day and threw me into yours the next! You didn't think about that, then? Well, think about it now!

Doctor Shedman: Pixie!

Doc Shedman, Jr.: Mother!

Colonel Shedman: She's lying! It can't be true!

Pixie: Oh, yes, it can! *(She points to them as she speaks.)* He *(Doc Shedman Jr.)* may be yours *(Doctor Shedman.)* and he may be yours *(Colonel Shedman.)* and none of us will ever know for sure, and how is that for sentimental hogwash, God damn you! *(To Bertram.)* Read. Read!!

Bertram: *(Reading.)* "For the scythe of time swings both ways—"

Pixie: Oh, with feeling! "Captives become wives, and wives become mothers. The lines of battle shift into bone and blood and their ancient weapons into the hands of women fall." *(The telephone rings.)* Your turn. *(Ring. Bertram answers the phone.)*

Bertram: Hello.... I'll take it.... I will.... I don't want anybody to represent.... No lawyers now!.... What?.... Wait a minute!

Pixie: Damn you, you bitch. And all your kind. *(Bertram slams down the phone.)* Congratulations. You handled that just right. *(Bertram glares at her. He starts to pour himself another drink, glares at her again, and puts the bottle away.)*

Bertram: Where were we?

Pixie: Trying to tell the living and the dead apart.

Bertram: Oh. *(He turns to see Doc Shedman Jr. staring at him.)*

Doc Shedman, Jr.: Son. *(Bertram turns away.)* Son. Look at me. *(With difficulty, Bertram does.)* Don't judge people too harshly.

Bertram: I try not to.

Doc Shedman, Jr.: I understand what you want to do, but you weren't there. Remember that.

Bertram: No. I wasn't. Not in Kansas.

Doc Shedman, Jr.: I never slept well when I was a baby. Nobody knew why. I just couldn't. All I remember is, I couldn't breathe! It was like something took up all the oxygen in the house, I don't know, and I just wanted to crawl. Out. As soon as I could, I did. Out the door! Onto the porch! Down the steps! To the earth outside!

Bertram: To Kansas.

Doc Shedman, Jr.: Yes, Kansas! Where—I could breathe! Oh, God. That sky. Enormous. Silent. Marvelous. And the land. Smooth, vast, clean. Nothing in my way. I loved it! *(He is filled, as he remembers his childhood, with a desperate energy.)* I loved it! At three, I had my first bird dog. At five, I made my own casting rods. At nine, on horseback, with a pistol, I hit a dove in flight. I was Southwest American Rifle Champion for six straight years. When I was thirteen, I killed a mountain lion. Nobody knew how he got to Kansas, or what he was doing there, but he came to me. My first shot broke his shoulder. My second shot broke his spine. He was still alive when I shot out his eyes. *(Pause.)* I hurt myself, of course, all the time. Ran into things, fell off horses. Broke both arms. This leg twice. Chopped my own hand almost off, with a hatchet once. Nearly got this eye put out.

Bertram: In a fight?

Doc Shedman, Jr.: *(Smiles.)* I didn't have many fights. My little playmates watched me shoot a deer, hang it up by its legs, cut its throat, skin it, cook it and eat it, and left me pretty much alone.

Bertram: You were free.

Doc Shedman, Jr.: Yes, free! In Kansas!

Bertram: With your mother and father.

Doc Shedman, Jr.: Yes. I overheard a man once call my mother a—a—

Bertram: *(Softly.)* A bitch?

Doc Shedman, Jr.: I broke his jaw. *(Pause.)* They were all right! They—disagreed sometimes—but it wasn't so—bad. They were good people, who lived in a fine and noble house. My father was handsome, and wise, and—against that blue sky—my mother was beautiful.

Bertram: *(Reading.)* "My boy was wild and headstrong. Between the savage father and his son was the barbaric custom, the unspoken promise: I will please you always. It then became my duty to my unfortunate child to steel myself to the spectacle of his fate, touching it, wherever I could, with a mother's hand." *(Bertram lowers the Captivity, thinks.)* When he was nine, he got a horse, from his father. *(Doctor Shedman, smiling, goes to Doc Shedman Jr.)*

Doctor Shedman: How do you like him?

Doc Shedman, Jr.: Fine!

Doctor Shedman: Fast enough for you?

Doc Shedman, Jr.: Oh yeah! He runs harder in the afternoon than he does in the morning.

Doctor Shedman: Be careful with him. Is he taking to you?

Doc Shedman, Jr.: *(Smiling.)* Bucks me a little. Tried to scrape me off a tree, but I had a talking to him.

Doctor Shedman: Made him see things your way?

Doc Shedman, Jr.: Yes, sir. We'll get along fine.

Doctor Shedman: Good. I want you to have— *(Pause, smile.)* —things I didn't. One of them was a good horse and an open road. You ride him wherever you want to go. Happy birthday.

Doc Shedman, Jr.: Thank you, sir. I will. *(Pixie approaches them. Doctor Shedman turns away. Bertram wraps a pitcher in a towel.)*

Bertram: And when he was twelve, he gave this, to his mother. *(He gives it to Doc Shedman Jr. who approaches Pixie.)*

Pixie: Your father tells me you want to go to military school.

Doc Shedman, Jr.: And West Point after that. That's for me, mother.

Pixie: Soldier boy.

Doc Shedman, Jr.: That's right.

Pixie: Ride your horses, shoot your guns, fight. What you've done in Kansas, forever.

Doc Shedman, Jr.: Mother, what better use can I make of my life than to defend my country with it? *(Pause.)*

Pixie: May I have my present now?

Doc Shedman, Jr.: Of course. *(He unwraps it, slowly and carefully. Pixie turns to Bertram.)*

Pixie: There. No, further in. There. Read.

Bertram: *(Reading.)* "My son's passion for war was a delusion, by which he only yearned to outstrip his father, as his father had tried to outstrip his, through me. But my child was still a boy, foolish enough to believe, as they no longer could, that his mother would allow him the freedom he assumed had always been theirs." *(Doc Shedman Jr. hands Pixie the pitcher.)*

Doc Shedman, Jr.: There.

Pixie: Did you pick this out?

Doc Shedman, Jr.: From a catalogue.

Pixie: It's beautiful. Delicate. Not the choice of a soldier.

Doc Shedman, Jr.: Mother, that's what I have to be. I live outdoors! I ride and shoot and hunt the way I breathe! I was born for the army.

Pixie: Never.

Doc Shedman, Jr.: It is the most honorable of all professions. What can you possibly have against it?

Pixie: You are descended from senators, doctors of medicine and men of God. Your version of all that will be the parade ground, the battlefield and the whorehouse? Never!

Doc Shedman, Jr.: Then what will I do? College? Divinity school? I have to move! Go! Be a man!

Pixie: A man too careless of right and wrong to make law, too heedless of human suffering to treat the sick, and too lacking in spirit to serve God. All you want is to play with your horses and your pistols and be a little boy forever.

Doc Shedman, Jr.: I will be what I am!

Pixie: You will be, you poor fool, what life and your mother make of you. Do you think I stood up all these years to your father and your grandfather to be buffaloed by you, Wild Bill? Robert E. Lee? Ulysses S. Grant? Napoleon? You?

Doc Shedman, Jr.: Mother, stop it.

Pixie: My darling, how are you going to cut down your enemies on a field of battle, when you can't cut the first string of your mother's apron?

Doc Shedman, Jr.: I will! I will!

Pixie: Then why do you have to say it twice? Move! Go! Fight!

Doc Shedman, Jr.: You—you—

Pixie: Bitch? God damn me, and all my kind? Say that, to your mother.

Doc Shedman, Jr.: Ah! *(He raises his hand, to hit her.)*

Pixie: Well? *(He can't.)* Go ahead, soldier. Strike. *(Doc Shedman Jr. turns away.)* You are a gentle boy, not a savage. You will be a better man than your father, and his. There is more to you than that. Are you crying?

Doc Shedman, Jr.: Yes.

Pixie: There, you see? *(She turns to Bertram.)* You or me?

Bertram: *(Staring at Doc Shedman Jr.)* You. *(Doc Shedman Jr. sits, heavily. He is older and very ill.)*

Pixie: *(Reciting.)* "But a savage my son was born, and a savage he remained, through all his youth and manhood. For his mother, he grew up becalmed, tractable, noble and civil, considerate in time of his own family, yet the beast was still wild. It was folly to tame him. For a captive himself, trapped in peace, he burned within, consuming himself in fires he could not spread."

Bertram: Stand aside. *(As a doctor, Bertram approaches Doc Shedman Jr.)*

Bertram/Doctor: *(Softly.)* Good morning.

Doc Shedman, Jr.: *(Looking up.)* Good morning. *(He must speak now in a hoarse whisper, with difficulty.)* I didn't see you, Doctor.

Bertram/Doctor: I bring you bad news.

Doc Shedman, Jr.: Let's have it.

Bertram/Doctor: It's in the windpipe. Below the larynx. Here. *(He points to his own throat.)*

Doc Shedman, Jr.: That deep?

Bertram/Doctor: Yes. You know what it means?

Doc Shedman, Jr.: Yes.

Bertram/Doctor: We'll do a tracheotomy, when we have to, and put in a metal pipe, to keep you breathing.

Doc Shedman, Jr.: All right.

Bertram/Doctor: In the meantime, radium. We know it's painful.

Doc Shedman, Jr.: I burn.

Bertram/Doctor: It's all we have, Doctor.

Doc Shedman, Jr.: I understand, Doctor. *(Smiles.)* Forward, march.

Bertram/Doctor: You're a good soldier. *(Pause.)*

Doc Shedman, Jr.: What did you say?

Bertram/Doctor: I said, you're a good soldier. *(With a soundless grin, Doc Shedman Jr. laughs.)*

Doc Shedman, Jr.: Tell me something. Did you really want to be a doctor?

Bertram/Doctor: No.

Doc Shedman, Jr.: What did you want to be?

Bertram/Doctor: You'd never believe me. Did you want to be a doctor?

Doc Shedman, Jr.: No.

Bertram/Doctor: What did you want to be?

Doc Shedman, Jr.: A good soldier. Oh, this life. I might have been one, too.

Bertram/Doctor: Aren't you a good doctor?

Doc Shedman, Jr.: I spend all my time reading hunting magazines instead of medical journals. Ever go to a field trial?

Bertram/Doctor: You mean bird dogs?

Doc Shedman, Jr.: Yes.

Bertram/Doctor: When I was a boy.

Doc Shedman, Jr.: Remember who you saw run?

Bertram/Doctor: Manitoba Rap.

Doc Shedman, Jr.: Good dog.

Bertram/Doctor: Becky Broom Hill.

Doc Shedman, Jr.: Saw her, did you?

Bertram/Doctor: Mary Montrose.

Doc Shedman, Jr.: Oh, the best! I saw her, too, on the plains of Kansas! The best!

Bertram/Doctor: But one.

Doc Shedman, Jr.: Whose dog was any better?

Bertram/Doctor: Yours. *(Pause.)* Shedman's Captain Bob.

Doc Shedman, Jr.: You saw Bob run?

Bertram/Doctor: Many times.

Doc Shedman, Jr.: What do you know? Yes, he was wonderful! My champion. Bob. I bred him, raised him from a pup. What a superb animal. He could run all day. Afraid of nothing. Intelligent, bold, loving. My God. How can you tell a man what it was like, to be in love with a dog. Wonderful creature. *(He is overtaken by a coughing fit. He puts his hand to his mouth, breathes with difficulty. He wipes his mouth with a handkerchief, and gets his breath back. Pause. Bertram speaks to the father who cannot hear him.)*

Bertram: I was your boy, not your dog. What I wanted, more than anything else, you gave to Captain Bob. Oh, this life.

Doc Shedman, Jr.: Excuse me, Doctor. What were we saying?

Bertram/Doctor: That we will do our best.

Doc Shedman, Jr.: Thank you.

Bertram/Doctor: Sleep now. Rest.

Doc Shedman, Jr.: I will. *(Doc Shedman Jr. closed his eyes. He sleeps.)*

Bertram: Woof, woof. Bow wow. *(Pause. Bertram rises, his face ashen. He faces Pixie.)*

Pixie: So?

Bertram: So that was my father who just died.

Pixie: Right in front of you. I saw it. How many times does he have to do that?

Bertram: What?

Pixie: Die for you. How many times must you haul him to life, out of the grave, then bury him all over again? Come on.

Bertram: Where?

Pixie: Where they left it to me to put them.

Bertram: Oh.

Pixie: How old were you the first time we went there together? Eleven, twelve?

Bertram: Twelve. Give me your hand. *(Pixie holds out her hand. Bertram takes it. They travel, slowly.)* I remember all the flowers we saw on the way. No red roses for us. *(Points.)* There.

Pixie: Bloodroot Poppy. It was used to make warpaint, and dye. It can still change the color of a man's eye.

Bertram: There.

Pixie: Allegheny Goatsbeard. The blossoms are always infested with insects.

Bertram: And there.

Pixie: White Baneberry. Whose stalks redden with age. Whose white fruit is poison, and gleams in the shade. *(They arrive at the cemetery in Pixie's North Carolina town. Colonel Shedman steps forward and speaks to Bertram.)*

Colonel Shedman: I was ninety-seven years of age. We had all come back to North Carolina. I'd been asked to speak at the dedication of a bridge in the Smoky Mountains. I felt a buzzing at the back of my head. I saw darkness. I reached into the air, and fell. When I regained consciousness, there was a woman's shawl under my head. I saw a woman's face peering into mine. I could not speak. *(He holds out his hand. Pixie holds out hers.)* Pixie.

Pixie: Goodbye. *(Colonel Shedman goes to the window seat, and sits there, against night and stars.)*

Doctor Shedman: I was sixty-two years old. I was drinking in my room, playing the radio, and dancing a jig. I felt a tug at my arm, then a slight pinch in my chest, and then a crushing fist closed over my heart. I knocked over my night table, which brought my wife from her room. She called for help, and sat close by me, staring at me. I could not speak. *(He holds out his hand. Pixie holds out hers.)* Pixie.

Pixie: Goodbye. *(Doctor Shedman joins Colonel Shedman.)*

Doc Shedman, Jr.: I was forty-one years old. After the operation, which sank a steel tube into my neck, the clouds started coming into my oxygen tent, and I knew I would never speak again, or live any longer. It was in my will to be buried with them. I would go to my grave with her face the last thing above me on the earth. *(He holds out his hand. Pixie holds out hers.)* Pixie.

Pixie: Goodbye. *(Doc Shedman Jr. joins Doctor Shedman and Colonel Shedman on the window seat, where they sit together against the night and the stars, staring straight ahead. Recites.)* "Thus did life itself, more savage than any of its creatures, bring them low within a year, in a fashion after their own wild hearts: striking one from a bridge, ambushing another in his dance, and driving into the throat of the third an arrow of steel. And I said to myself, God help me. I am free." Read the end.

Bertram: *(Reading.)* "Therefore for my grandson and his issue have I conceived this work, as indeed the American captivities of old were always written, looking back from safety. I survived. May my grandson, in his day, do as well. The End." *(Pause. Bertram closes the Captivity. Pause. Bertram, on his knees, bends over, head in his hands.)*

Pixie: You'd been to that cemetery, dry-eyed, through all three funerals, but when you came there with me, you fell down on your knees, and cried. *(Bertram weeps. Pixie turns, walks a few steps away, looks back, returns.)* Get up. *(No response.)* You hear me? Twelve years old is old enough to understand. They are dead. You are alive. Keep it that way. *(No response.)* Don't kneel to the dead! Get up! *(Bertram does, swiftly. He holds his hand up over Pixie, as if to strike her.)*

Bertram: And that's when I hit you.

Pixie: You thought I put them there.

Bertram: You did. I'm not twelve years old now. *(He tosses the Captivity onto his desk.)* You destroyed all three.

Pixie: I survived all three!

Bertram: Revenge!

Pixie: Survival! What did you expect me to do? Crawl up on a funeral pyre and die with them, like some woman in India?

Bertram: Pixie! One man breaks your father. You sleep with him. His son, you marry. His son, and yours, you fucking mother to death, and then, after you've buried them all, you dig them up again and call them savages in your Captivity! You wasted them every way you could!

Pixie: You can't be this stupid! People struggle! With each other! If you don't understand that, what do you understand?

Bertram: I understand, you cruel and vindictive woman, what you call struggle is the underhanded murder of your own family, and the gall to compare it to the struggle of American Indians. I want no part of it or you.

Pixie: Rather be dead yourself?

Bertram: Yes!

Pixie: Then you will be, and soon. Because only the dead speak to you. *(Pause.)* The way you were as a boy. The way you are now. *(Pause.)* You're right about the Indians.

Bertram: Then how dare you—

Pixie: Because that's how it felt!

Doc Shedman, Jr.: Come along, Mother.

Colonel Shedman: He has to figure it out by himself.
Doctor Shedman: You belong with us.
Pixie: Well, you did read it.
Bertram: Yes, I did.
Pixie: You did call me back.
Bertram: Yes.
Pixie: Goodbye, Grandson.
Bertram: Goodbye, Grandmother. *(Pixie and her three men sit on the windowseat against the night, city and stars, and the light goes out on them. BERTRAM closes his grandmother's book slowly. Lights fade on BERTRAM.)*

GOODBYE, HOWARD

CHARLES, a broadly Southern high school boy.
NURSE, an efficient R.N., 30's.
EDNA, a tart-tongued old lady, 70's.
ALICE, a worried old lady, 70's.
SARAH, a sweet old lady, 70's.
DOCTOR BAILEY, a confident doctor, 60's.

Place: A waiting room, Duke University Medical Center, Durham, North Carolina.
Time: 1960.

GOODBYE, HOWARD was first produced at the H.B. Studios in 1968. As one of the three one act plays in LAUGHING STOCK, it was produced by the Manhattan McGuire, Producing Directors, in April, 1984. The plays were directed by Ed Howard, sets by Paul Bryan Eads, costumes by Sally Lesser, lights by Judy Rasmuson, sound by Gary Harris, production stage manager, Pamela Singer. Cast as follows:

CHARLES................Timothy Wilson
NURSE....................Peggity Price
EDNA.....................Helen Harrelson
ALICE.....................Jane Connell
SARAH....................Frances Sternhagen
DOCTOR BAILEY.....Harold Guskin

GOODBYE, HOWARD

A waiting room at Duke University Medical Center, Durham, North Carolina in the fall of 1964. It is late on a Sunday night. Benches, a telephone booth, a closed concession stand, and an arrow pointing offstage under a sign saying: ELEVATORS. Charles, a high school boy, is alone in the waiting room, struggling with a textbook.

Charles: *(Reading slowly, strong accent.)* When the day—that he must go hence—was come— many—a-com-pan-ied him to the river-side—into which as he went, he said—"Death, where is thy sting?—And—And as he went on deeper he said—"Grave, where is thy victory?"—So he passed over—and all the t-rumpets—trumpets trumpets—sounded for him—on the other side. *(Enter Nurse, in a hurry, looking for someone.)*

Nurse: Excuse me, sonny. Did three ladies just come through here?

Charles: Huh?

Nurse: Three ladies. Three elderly old ladies. All dressed up.

Charles: Well, I haven't been here very long, and I been studying my lessons, but I don't think so. There was a big fat lady, with a little boy, but she wasn't very old. There was a man with four daughters, all sick, but he was a man. Anyway, they all went home.

Nurse: No, three old ladies. Very—ah—well, three old ladies.

Charles: They might have been here. Then again they might not.

Nurse: Thanks a lot. *(Exit Nurse, quickly.)*

Charles: *(To himself.)* I wonder what's the matter with her? For a nurse, she sure was nervous. A nurse is supposed to keep calm. Be confident. *(He reads his book. Enter Alice, Sarah and Edna, three elderly Southern ladies. They are carefully and meticulously dressed: white gloves, snowy coiffures, expensive rings, necklaces, and furs, elegant handbags and silky print dresses. They sit together in the waiting room.)*

Alice: Edna's right, Sarah. You're not doing Howard any good suspecting every soul in this hospital.

Sarah: I am not either suspecting every soul in this hospital. I just want to be kept informed. Somebody ought to be back up there now, finding out.

Alice: Edna, make her hush. I'm so tired.

Edna: Hush, Sarah.

Sarah: I am only thinking of our sworn duty to Howard.

Edna: We know that. Now be quiet. *(Pause. They wait, uncomfortably. Charles smiles at them.)*

Charles: Good evening.

Sarah: How do you do?

Alice: How do you do?

Edna: For Christ's sake.

Charles: There was a nurse here looking for you.

Alice: For us?

Charles: She said three old ladies. I reckon that's you all right. *(Sarah jumps up.)*

Sarah: You see?

Edna: Sit down, Sarah. *(To Charles.)* What kind of a nurse?

Alice: How old was she?

Charles: Not very old. He wore a white jacket.

Alice: That's not Howard's nurse.

Edna: Not Doctor Bailey's nurse.

Alice: If it's important, Doctor Bailey will tell us. I'm so tired.

Sarah: Sit here, if you want to! I'm going back up there! *(Exit Sarah.)*

Alice: She can't sit still one minute.

Edna: Let her go. Buy a magazine, and let her go.

Alice: You know I can't buy a magazine. I don't have any change. Do you?

Edna: No.

Alice: Besides, the whole concession stand is closed. We found that out when we found we didn't have any change.

Edna: Right. Right.

Alice: Sunday night. Everything's closed. And I'm so tired.

Charles: Me, too. This waiting around really gets to you, don't it? *(They stare at him.)*

Alice: I beg your pardon?

Charles: This waiting around. It's something else. I'll tell you. *(Gets up to come over and chat.)* When my buddy Willy Kram picked a fight with Buddy Flats, he didn't see old Buddy was wearing football cleats. Willy got himself stomped in the left kidney. Had to be brought here. I come around and play cards with him.

Edna: This is very interesting.

Alice: Edna. Be polite. Cards?

Charles: Blackjack. Willy'll clean you out if you don't watch it. Give him a seventeen, even an eighteen, and he'll say, "Hit me," and I'll be darned if it won't be a three or a four nine times out of ten.

Edna: Why aren't you up there playing cards with him now?

Alice: Edna.

Edna: Well, why isn't he?

Charles: Willy's folks keep coming to see him. He's got a lot of relatives.

I slip out and wait here. Or wander around. One time I followed a bunch of nurses into a room with a glass wall, and watched a man get his leg cut off. Never saw anything like it.

Edna: And you're going to tell us about it.

Charles: If you want me to. There wasn't that much to it. Cut, saw, fold back a big flap, and sew again. It was more like making up the corner of a bed, than anything else. Made me think, what goes on in hospitals can be a lot more simple than we'd like it to be.

Edna: You're a very bright young man.

Charles: Thank you.

Edna: I mean, you have such a logical mind.

Alice: Now, Edna.

Charles: Thanks again. I do try to think straight. For instance, I bet you ladies are rich.

Edna: How did you figure that out?

Charles: All those bracelets, and big rings. And those fancy furpieces sure ain't rabbit or fox. I know. I hunt.

Edna: So many talents. So many sides to this fascinating personality.

Charles: Well, *are* you rich?

Edna: Persistent, too.

Charles: Thanks again double. Are you?

Alice: Young man, what we are now more than anything is tired. Why don't we all sit down and practise repose. Just—repose.

Charles: Oh. Yes, ma'm. *(He smiles and sits. They all wait. Enter Sarah, dramatically. She looks at Alice and Edna, tears in her eyes.)*

Sarah: Yes! He's gone! *(She goes to them and looks at them mournfully for a moment. They all bow their heads. Then Edna straightens up.)* Now! You know what we have to do.

Alice: Yes, we know.

Edna: Yes, yes! God damn it.

Sarah: Then let's about it! There's the telephone! *(They go to the telephone booth, opening their purses, fumbling within.)*

Edna: Wait a minute. No change.

Alice: Sarah has some. Sarah?

Sarah: What?

Edna: Change. You got change?

Sarah: No, I don't. I thought I did but I don't.

Edna: Swell. How are we going to use the phone?

Alice: Young man! You hoo, young man!

Charles: Yes'm?

Alice: Do you have any change?

Edna: Pocket change.

Alice: Change. You know. Change?

Charles: Not much. I told you about Willy Kram. He'll clean you out. *(Charles digs into his pocket.)* Here's twenty-seven cents.

Edna: Oh, my god.

Alice: It costs eighty-five cents just the first three minutes.

Sarah: We have to call all the way to Pine Valley.

Charles: Pine Valley? You all from Pine Valley?

Edna: Yes, we're from Pine Valley. Now where the hell are we going to get change?

Charles: You might try the nurse at the main desk.

Edna: Right. *(Exit Edna.)*

Charles: Pine Valley, eh? Didn't I say you had to be rich?

Alice: Yes, you did. You certainly did.

Sarah: When?

Alice: When you were gone.

Sarah: Oh.

Charles: I went to Pine Valley once. With my uncle in the seed business. Nothing there but old people, golf courses, and bookstores. Everybody rich, except me and my uncle. *(Thinks.)* Why don't you call collect?

Sarah: Oh, that would never do. The party we are calling would never accept the call.

Alice: Never.

Sarah: That is just the way she simply is.

Alice: Always.

Charles: Well, this is all the change I got. Sorry. *(Enter Edna.)*

Edna: The damn woman won't give me any change. She says she doesn't have any. She says go downtown.

Alice: But where's that?

Sarah: This is so very distressing.

Charles: What happened?

Sarah: Our brother just died. He was such a fine man.

Charles: I'm sorry to hear it.

Sarah: We'll miss him so.

Edna: Oh, for God's sakes, never mind that now. We have got to get on this telephone, and call home.

Alice: How can we, without any change? Tell me that!

Edna: I don't know, God damn it!

Sarah: Please don't wrangle like this. You have no right to wrangle and snap, when this young man is being so nice. He can't help it he only has twenty-seven cents in change. Can you, young man?

Charles: No'm. I'm lucky to have that, after playing blackjack with Willy. Certainly am sorry I don't have more.

Sarah: Just so you know we appreciate your concern.

Edna: He knows. He certainly knows.

Alice: Wait a minute! Young man, could you run downtown and get us some change? Please?

Charles: Downtown's two miles off. I only got a bicycle.

Alice: Here's five dollars. Please, sir!

Charles: Well, maybe. I guess I can try.

Edna: *(Whispering.)* He won't come back. You give him five whole dollars, and he won't come back.

Sarah: Edna! What a thing to whisper, right out loud! She didn't mean that, young man.

Edna: Yeah, I'm sorry. Just get the change for us. If you do, you can have a dollar.

Sarah: Now you've insulted him.

Edna: No, I haven't, for God's sakes. You aren't insulted, are you?

Charles: I don't think so. I'll see what I can do for you.

Edna: Thanks ever so god damn much. *(Exit Charles.)* He won't come back. Wait and see.

Alice: Just think. You wait and wait all your life for great important moments like this. When they finally come, you're so tired, you don't know what to do.

Edna: I know what to do. Make these phone calls, and go home.

Sarah: Yes, Edna. You make everything sound so easy. Bum bum bum. Just like that. Leave it to Edna.

Edna: What's wrong with you?

Sarah: I was listening to my younger sister. She was, I think, attempting to make a philosophical point, and I was doing her the courtesy to simply listen.

Edna: Hell, I'm her sister, too.

Alice: Tired, I tell you. Worn out.

Sarah: I'm just going to say it. It's just your rude, crude attitude, Edna. It is simply excruciating at a time like this, and it is boring as well! That's what I said. Boring!

Alice: On the floor. I could just lie right down on the floor.

Edna: I heard you. And I can't bore you any more than you bore me, baby sister, and have every last year of our blessed lives.

Sarah: Well, I know that.

Alice: And die. And just simply die. *(Enter Charles.)*

Charles: I'm back! Got change from the hospital taxi driver. He was asleep, and didn't like me waking him up. Didn't want to give me change, neither. But when I said desperate rich old ladies, he gave it to me. Here.

Sarah: See. What did I tell you?

Edna: I don't believe it.

Alice: Give it here! Give it here! *(Alice grabs the change from Charles. She rushes into the telephone booth.)*

Sarah: Give him a dollar, Edna.

Edna: What?

Sarah: You said you'd give this young man a dollar. Don't just go off forgetting what you said.

Edna: Oh, yeah. Alice!

Alice: What?

Edna: Give me a dollar.

Alice: What for?

Edna: Never mind. Just give it to me. *(She takes the dollar. She holds it out to Charles.)* Here. We certainly do appreciate your help. Now *call,* Alice!

Sarah: We certainly do.

Alice: We certainly do. *(She fumbles a dime into the coin slot.)* Operator! Operator!

Charles: No, thanks.

Edna: What?

Charles: I don't need a dollar. It's my pleasure to help you ladies out. *(To Alice.)* Ma'm.

Alice: Operator! Operator!

Charles: Ma'm!

Alice: What?

Charles: You have to dial the operator first before she'll answer. *(Alice peers out from the phone booth.)*

Alice: What? *(Charles makes a circle with one finger.)*

Charles: Dial. You know? Dial.

Edna: Dial! *Dial,* Alice!

Alice: Oh, yes! *(She dials.)*

Charles: Thanks for the dollar all the same.

Edna: All right if you don't want it, all right.

Sarah: You're such a nice young man. Isn't he a nice young man, though?

Edna: We already told him that.

Alice: Hello, Operator. I want to call Pine Valley, please. The number I wish is M O 4-3296.

Edna: 3 6 9 2! God help us, Alice!

Alice: I always do that. Just a moment, please, Operator. That number is

M O 4-3692. What? No, Pine Valley is right. Yes. M O 4-3692 in Pine Valley. That is correct. Thank you so much.

Sarah: Wrong number. Just think. We would have gotten somebody up late at night. Some strangers. *(Thinks sadly.)* They wouldn't care a bit Howard died, would they?

Edna: Why should they?

Sarah: Sad. It's sad, I tell you. *(She takes a handkerchief from her pocketbook, and wipes tears from her eyes.)*

Alice: Ringing! It's ringing!

Sarah: *(Sniffling.)* Do excuse me, young man. I don't mean to make a spectacle of myself. But he was such a fine man. He was our only brother. I loved him so. *(She begins to cry.)*

Charles: That's all right. I understand. When my pet squirrel Charley died, I cried all night.

Edna: Jesus.

Charles: Not to mention our bulldog, Bozo. I'm still not over that.

Sarah: It's so sad! Just so sad!

Edna: Sarah, for Christ's sake! Alice is trying to hear.

Sarah: Oh, I'm sorry. I'm so sorry.

Alice: It's ringing! It's ringing!

Edna: What did you expect it to do, sing?

Alice: Hello? Here she is! *(The three ladies gather quickly around the phone.)*

Sarah: She won't be upset, will she?

Edna: Of course she'll be upset.

Alice: Hello? Hello?

Sarah: I don't mean about Howard. I mean about calling so late.

Alice: Hello? Hello, Mother?

Charles: Mother? *Mother?*

Alice: Hello, Mother? Is that you? This is Alice. Alice. No, *Alice.* Yes, dear. Yes, I'm just fine, thank you. Now Mother, are you feeling all right? Feeling all right. You're not too tired to talk?

Edna: Oh, go ahead and tell her.

Sarah: Oh, so brutal. My dear Edna. So brutal.

Edna: Hush.

Alice: Mother, it's Howard. *Howard.* No, this is Alice speaking to you, but it's about Howard. I'm afraid he's gone. Gone. No, dear, *gone.* He has left us forever. Yes, that's right. Yes, he is dead, Mother. No, dead. Howard's dead. D-e-a-d, *dead! (She puts one hand over the receiver. Wearily:)* I don't know whether she understands or not.

Edna: Keep at it.

Sarah: Oh, Howard. Howard.

Alice: Yes, Mother. Yes. You still feel all right? Good. What? No, it wasn't a bad trip. What? Yes, the dogwood is out here, too.

Edna: Barncastle. Get Barncastle on the line.

Alice: What?

Edna: Barncastle! Barncastle!

Alice: Oh, yes. Mother, is Mr. Barncastle there? He is? Well, Mother, may I speak with him, please? Thank you. It's been nice talking to you, too, Mother. What? No, have some coffee. It might not keep you up. Go ahead. Just let me talk to Mr. Barncastle now, please. That's right. Thank you, Mother. They send their best, too. And their love, yes, of course. *(She takes a deep breath, holds the phone, waits.)* Mr. Barncastle? Is that you, Mr. Barncastle?

Sarah: *(To Charles.)* Edmund Barncastle is our personal family attorney. He has been for years and years. He is staying with Mother during this crisis.

Alice: Is mother all right? Good. Now, Mr. Barncastle, the list, please.

Edna: Giving away our secrets again, Sarah.

Sarah: Oh, I am not. You know as well as I do how complicated this will be. *(To Charles.)* Howard was an internationally prominent man, you see.

Edna: Can't keep her eyes closed, can't keep her mouth shut—

Sarah: Well, he was! God bless him!

Alice: No, I don't have the list. We thought you had it. What? We certainly did leave it with you. Well, where is it then? Ask Edna? Just a moment. *(She leans out of the phone booth.)* No list.

Edna: He's lost the god damned list?

Sarah: How can you talk like that? How can you express yourself like that at a time like this?

Alice: He says he hasn't lost it. He never had it. He says you have it.

Edna: He's bloody senile! Give me that phone!

Sarah: Oh, Edna! That is not necessary! That is simply not necessary! *(Edna grabs the phone, pulling the receiver as far out of the booth as she can.)*

Alice: I am just so tired.

Edna: All right, Barncastle. What is this bullshit about the list?

Sarah: Oh! Young man, put your two hands right over your two ears. When our sister gets like this, we don't know what she'll say. We beg your pardon.

Charles: Shucks. You ought to hear Willy Kram.

Edna: Yes, sure I remember. I went over the list with you. I left it on your desk, right by your tacky plastic globe of the world. So we were in a hurry. I remember plain as day leaving it there, and it is you who have the list. What? Don't take that fucking tone with me!

Sarah: Edna!

Alice: Tired. Tired.

Edna: All right, *all right!* I'll look. Then will you be satisfied, and find the list, wherever you put it? OK! *(She props the receiver under her chin, opens her purse, rummages.)* If brains were dynamite, he wouldn't have enough to blow his nose. *(She pulls out a piece of paper with names on it. Stares.)* The list. What the hell?

Sarah: See! See! You had it all the time! Imagine talking to dear Edmund Barncastle like that, when you had the list all the time. *He* didn't do anything wrong! You did!

Alice: I could sleep forever. *(She takes the phone from Edna.)* Hello, Mr. Barncastle. Alice again. We have located the list. Never mind how. I know we were supposed to leave it with you, but we didn't.

Sarah: You mean Edna didn't.

Edna: All right, rub it in. Rub it in. *(Glares at Charles. Sharply.)* Haste makes waste!

Charles: Yes m'am.

Alice: All right, then. I will have to read them to you over the phone. Are you ready? Pencil and paper? Good. Telegrams first. What? All right, I'll wait.

Sarah: So many to notify at once. Telegrams must go out instantly. People of the very highest station are involved.

Charles: He must have been a very important man.

Sarah: Oh, Howard. You were. You were. Wasn't he, Edna?

Edna: Sure he was. Right by that globe. That tacky plastic globe.

Sarah: Howard was Under Secretary of the Navy in 1924. Of course, he was lots of other things before that. State Senator from Grainger County. Congressman for two whole terms.

Edna: I can see it now. Lying right there.

Sarah: But in 1924, he was named Under Secretary of the Navy. By President Coolidge. A personal friend, you know. I remember the President very well. Don't you, Edna?

Edna: Sure. And I left it there. I know I left it there.

Alice: Oh, you do have the telegrams, after all? You have that on another list?

Edna: Another list?

Alice: Oh, she made two?

Edna: No, I didn't.

Alice: One for telegrams, which you have, and the other for the cards which we have. I see.

Edna: It isn't possible.

Sarah: Of course it is. Now who's senile?

Alice: All right, then, you'll send out the telegrams. Now for the cards. Are you ready. Yes, from this list. Ready? I'll wait.

Charles: Cards?

Sarah: Oh, yes. A great many. There would be a great many more, but Time With His Sickle, you know. Those who are left must know right away, even though they will make no public statement. Howard was very particular. It is all terribly important.

Alice: Oh. Yes. *(Reading.)* Judge Horace A. Kegly, Morris, Mississippi.

Sarah: And you can't send telegrams to everyone. Think of the sheer expense.

Charles: But doesn't a newspaper do this? I'm only in high school, but isn't that what an obituary page is for?

Sarah: Oh, heavens, no! To learn about Howard from the daily press?

Alice: Doctor E. Baxley Reed, 1404 Trout Boulevard, Swineburne, Georgia.

Edna: Two of them? *Two* of them?

Sarah: So many have been so concerned for so long, you see.

Charles: I just hate to see you put to all this trouble.

Sarah: It's our duty to Howard. Howard will be eighty-six next January 4th. We've had plenty of time to get the cards printed and ready.

Edna: Howard will not be eighty-six next January 4th, either. He won't ever be eighty-six at all. He just died.

Alice: Miss Tilly Stillman Bates, Box 3, Stand Around, North Carolina.

Sarah: You see? That's so brutal, Edna. Just so crude, coarse, and brutal. Oh, Howard.

Edna: Don't blame me. It isn't my fault he never made eighty-six.

Sarah: You didn't feel the way I did. None of you loved Howard the way I did. He always received from me the most honest tender affection and steadfast regard. Oh, Howard.

Edna: If you are going to boo hoo, then boo hoo, but don't talk a lot of nonsense. Especially in front of a strange child nobody knows.

Alice: Please! I am trying to get all this through to Mr. Barncastle. Colonel and Mrs. Morton Tombs, Wainright, Idaho. No street address.

Charles: I'm sorry if I butted in. I didn't mean to.

Edna: Now, I didn't say that. Did I say that, Sarah?

Sarah: You suggested it. You always do.

Edna: Do what?

Sarah: Suggest unpleasant things in an unpleasant manner. It's the story of your life.

Alice: Congressman Billy Joe Butterworth, Junior, Dudley, Arizona.

Edna: If I hurt anybody's feelings tonight, do forgive me. Give me sackcloth. Give me ashes. But it's been a hard night.

Sarah: Not just for you, Edna. Other people exist, too, you know. Other people exist, too.

Edna: They sure do.

Alice: Professor Ernest H. Mill, Ph.D. Broken Stone State Teachers College, Momeyer, Florida.

Sarah: Young man, you're not offended, are you? I hope not. You've been so nice.

Charles: Why no, ma'm. I just hope you don't put yourselves out too much.

Sarah: That's sweet. But we all have our duty, don't we?

Charles: Yes, ma'm. Mine seems to be taking care of rich old ladies. Ha ha.

Alice: Mrs. Maedell Odell, Laughing Brook Nursing Home, Green Bush, Kansas.

Sarah: What a fine young man. We certainly do appreciate your kindness.

Edna: And his wit. His wit.

Alice: Hush! Hush! Hush! *(Pause.)* T. Melwin Fones, Author. Dogstar Press, Wancheese, North Carolina.

Sarah: Oh. Someone's coming. *(Enter Nurse.)*

Nurse: Well, well, ladies. How are you?

Sarah: Why just fine, thank you.

Nurse: Good. Well, he's resting comfortably now. You can all get a good night's sleep.

Edna: What? What's that?

Alice: Commissioner of Highways Harvey Grover Turner, Retired, State Capitol, Columbia, South Carolina.

Sarah: Resting? Did you say resting?

Nurse: Why, yes. Of course, he'll stay in intensive care for awhile, but you should all go back to your hotel and get some sleep.

Edna: You mean he's not dead? You mean he's not dead?

Alice: Reverend Oscar Dobbs DeMille, Saint Mary's Episcopal Church, Ordinance, Kentucky.

Nurse: My goodness. No, he's not dead. How did you ever—

Edna: You mean he's still up there? Alive?

Nurse: Yes, yes! Of course he's alive. I'm dreadfully—

Edna: Sarah! For Christ's sake!

Alice: Edwin Mulchman Pohlman, Senior Editor, Southern Ladies Gazette, Tampa, Florida.

Sarah: Oh, dear.

Edna: I'm going to wring your neck! I'm going to break it first, and then I'm going to wring your neck!

Sarah: *(Flustered.)* But it was you who told me he was gone, yourself. When I went up there just a little while ago. I swear you did.

Nurse: I didn't even know where you were.

Sarah: Well, *somebody* in that white jacket told me Howard was dead and gone. I know they did!

Alice: Mrs. Avery Williams Tallentyre, Owl Creek Mountain Lodge, Sunshine, Wyoming.

Nurse: What room did you go to?

Sarah: Why, Howard's room, of course. But I didn't even get in the door. You—or somebody just like you—came rushing out in that blinding white jacket, saying, "Jesus Christ, he's dead," and you ran off down the hall.

Nurse: What was the number of that room, please?

Sarah: *(Promptly.)* Eighty-two. Howard's room number. Eighty-two.

Nurse: Full number?

Sarah: Ten. Ten eighty-two.

Edna: Wrong floor?

Nurse: Wrong floor. My goodness.

Alice: And one each to all living Congressmen from the two terms Howard was in office. You will find *that* list in the top drawer of his desk in his study. All right, then, Mr. Barncastle. Thank you so much.

Edna: Alice! Wait a minute, Alice!

Alice: Goodbye. *(She hangs up the phone.)* What?

Sarah: He's still alive!

Alice: Who's still alive?

Edna: Howard! Howard!

Alice: That's not possible.

Edna: Sarah made a mistake. Didn't she, Nurse?

Nurse: There has been a mistake. I'm dreadfully—

Alice: *(Terror.)* That can't be! *(She grabs the phone off the hook again.)* I hung up! *(She opens her bag.)* I don't have any more change!

Sarah: Well, I thought I was on the right floor. I know I was. This is going to be very ludicrous and painful and embarassing.

Nurse: Well, don't worry about that now. Everything is quite all right, after all. Your brother is sleeping peacefully. You get yourselves some rest.

Alice: All right? Don't worry? What about all our telegrams and cards?

Sarah: It couldn't happen. A thing like this to a person like me. I don't understand it.

Charles: Ladies, Nurse is right. Let me get that taxi and take you all home.

Alice: Leave? Now? Don't be ridiculous! You go get me more change! I have got to have more change!

Charles: But—

Alice: Doesn't anybody understand? The telegrams and the cards will be on their way! We have got to stop them! Now go get me more change!

Charles: *More* change?

Sarah: Oh, dear Lord in heaven, yes! This is terrible. This is awful. It will kill mother.

Nurse: Mother?

Sarah: And Howard is so particular. He will be furious. I have made a dreadful mess. This spells total and perpetual disgrace.

Alice: Change! Get me change!!

Charles: Maybe I can and maybe I can't. That taxi driver was mad enough when I woke him up the first time. I don't think he'll give me any more.

Alice & Sarah & Edna: Young man!!!

Charles: I'll try! I'll try! *(He starts to dash off. The nurse grabs him.)*

Nurse: Hold it! How much change do you need? *(Counting. Confusion.)*

Alice: *(Finally.)* Two more quarters. I have one left, and it takes three and a dime, and I have the dime!

Nurse: Here! Two quarters! Here! *(Alice snatches both quarters and goes back into the phone booth.)*

Sarah: Oh, thank you! Thank you! This is really so kind of you!

Nurse: Not at all. My goodness. *(She watches them with apprehension. The three ladies are now a hectic sight: they hop about in nervous confusion, gripping their bags and furs, almost clawing at the phone booth, as they wait for the call to go through. They listen. Alice turns to them with a gaze of terror.)*

Alice: The line is busy.

Sarah: Oh, no. No, no, no.

Edna: That god damned Barncastle is sending everything out! Stop him! We have got to stop him!

Alice: Yes, but how? *(Listens.)* Bleep bleep bleep! Busy busy busy! It's hopeless!

Edna: Western Union! Call Western Union!

Sarah: Yes! Yes! Stop all telegrams!

Edna: Oh, no, Sarah, for Christ's sake! Send that fool Barncastle a telegram. Let *him* call Western Union at home and tell them stop, cancel, desist! That's it! Hurry, Alice!

Alice: Yes! Yes! *(Yells into the phone.)* Western Union! Western Union!

Edna: Hang up first, you idiot! Get your money back!

Alice: Oh, yes. *(She hangs it back on the hook. Nothing happens.)*

Nothing's happening. Nothing's coming back. *(She slaps the telephone.)* Where's my change? *(To all.)* I need some more change!

Nurse: I don't have any more.

Edna: Let me at that thing! *(She gets into the phone booth with Alice.All three start beating the telephone. Enter Doctor Bailey.)*

Doctor Bailey: Quiet, please! Please! Quiet! *(They turn to him. The nurse runs over for a brief conference.)*

Sarah: Doctor Bailey! Oh, heaven help us, it's Doctor Bailey. He's here at last!

Edna: Fine. Swell. What can he do now? Barncastle is sending everything out. What good is a god damned doctor? *(Doctor Bailey takes charge.)*

Doctor Bailey: Now then, ladies. Compose yourselves. I want each of you to take a slow deep breath. Ready? *(He breathes in. They do, too.)* All right. Are you listening to me? *(They nod, staring at him, each arrested in a frantic pose.)*

Edna: Yes?

Alice: Yes?

Sarah: Yes?

Doctor Bailey: After the operation, your brother's condition seemed satisfactory. He slept quietly for awhile. Then severe respiratory complications occurred. I am deeply sorry to tell you he died just a few moments ago.

Alice: *(Hanging up.)* Whew!

Edna: Oh, thank God! *(They all look at each other.)*

Alice, Edna and Sarah: Goodbye, Howard!